Margott Schuerings

From King of Pop to Mahatma

Journey of a Great soul

1st English Edition, 2014
(translated from German Edition 2010)

👁 ADWAITA

Cover Art: "Michael Jackson" courtesy of Petra Schwabe
The German Library - CIP-unit recording
A track record for this publication is available at the German library.

Schuerings, Margott:
From King of Pop to Mahatma
- Journey of a Great Soul /
Margott Schürings
1st English Edition
Hohenpeissenberg: Adwaita-Verlag, 2014

Copyright: 2014 ADWAITA-Verlag
www.adwaita-verlag.de

EAN 97839342810365
E-Book 9783934281047
Cover: BoD
Translation: Margott Schuerings
Reader: Alex Knight

Contents

		page
	Foreword	
1.	July 1st 2009 – Stepping in the Flow	8
2.	Michael's Angel	10
3.	The Last Curtain	13
4.	Man in the Mirror	15
5.	Two Birds	18
6.	The Dance Lives on	19
7.	Tanner and Shoemaker	26
8.	From Caterpillar to Butterfly	31
9.	The Search	39
10.	The New Children	46
11.	Human Rights of Children	50
12.	Judgment	59
13.	The Searcher	64
14.	Magic	72
15.	Birthright	77
16.	Armband	80
17.	Below the Belt	83
18.	The True Story	85
19.	Cry for Help	88
20.	Pack of Lies	92
21.	We Had Him	101
22.	The World in You	103
23.	Planet Joy	106
24.	Ability of Distinction	107
25.	Joy	109
26.	Power	112
27.	Spiritual Teacher	115
28.	Black Soul	117
29.	Addiction Reigns the World	120
30.	Michael Jackson and Sathya Sai Baba	123
31.	Humanness	125
32.	Dangerous	130
33.	King of Hearts	134
34.	Cutting the Ties	137
35.	Innocent	145
36.	Touring	152

		page
37.	Conditioning	157
38.	Selected	161
39.	Trapper	166
40.	Fall of the Wall	171
41.	Love is Spreading Out	176
42.	The Sin Fall of Measuring	182
43.	Memorial	184
44.	Eternal Moonwalk	189
45.	Philanthropy	193
46.	HSU – Heart-Soul-Union	204
47.	Soulguard	209
48.	Genius	214
49.	The Place Where God is Visible	220
50.	Michael in Private	224
51.	Michael's First Christmas	226
52.	Michael as Dad	232
53.	I am the Light of the World	236
54.	This is my dream	242
55.	One Year Later	249
56.	To be Continued	252

Appendix   254
- Touring
- Songs, films, books
- More books, films and CDs

Foreword

A great soul has left the earthly stage on Jun 25th of 2009. Suddenly ... Silently ... Gone ...
Since my youth I have been fascinated and enthusiastic about Michael Jackson's music. But that's not all – since the year 1992 he has been my "Great Love." At that time I happened to discover the poem "Consciousness" in the booklet of the newly published album, "Dangerous," and at that time there an invisible bond was created between us. A long time before, I had started on an inner journey searching for my self. I read everything published on this subject and studied religions, teachings of wisdom and ancient traditions – starting with the time- and ageless Veda to Islamic Sufism and Jewish Kabbalah to Christian esoteric teachings. And now I was finding the deepest Truth of the highest Wisdom and nondualism – advaita in Sanscrit – in the words of a pop star who knocked my socks off.
"Dancers come and go in the twinkling of an eye but the dance lives on....I keep on dancing and then, it's the eternal dance of creation. The creator and creation merge into one wholeness of joy. I keep on dancing and dancing.......and dancing, until there is only...... the dance."
(Michael Jackson, Dancing the Dream)

The dancer is gone .... the dance lives on.

Thank you Michael, I love you more.
Margott Schuerings, 29 August 2010

1. First of July 2009 – Stepping in the Flow

Five days after the disappearance of the dancer from the earthly stage, I lay in bed reading Michael's last interview, where he talks about how his music and words came about:

"The key to being a wonderful writer is not to write. You just get out of the way. Leave room for God to walk in the room." (Ebony, 2007)

The mystery of this "getting out of the way" had revealed itself to me some years before, and since that time now and then I have had the experience that only in this way the wisdom of a higher source is able to get in the lead. This "getting out of the way" inspires our doing, so that it can emerge from Spirit instead of personal ideas and thoughts. Thomas Hübl from Austria is living true to that principle: "The greatest artist is nature itself. Without filter and personal toning she brings its master works on the screen of life. The great masters of art have imitated her by simply getting out of the way, when life was painting, composing and writing through them." (Hübl, 2009, p. 53)

This "getting out of the way" ends the dominance and dominion of mind and narrow thinking over life. That does not deny that the mind is a valuable instrument for many goals and purposes. On the contrary. Without mind, intellect and thinking we would be stranded in daily life. But the mind is only a limited instrument that was created for certain purposes like any other instrument. The calamity of humanity loomed in ancient times when the human mind with its thinking usurped knowing how life is functioning, when it set itself up as controller of nature and being, and made itself the ruler over life and death. Exactly at this point, when thinking has turned into the almighty ever-present and all-seeing tyrant, it's no longer fun. Like a dictator it assumes the right to intervene in all issues of men, nature and life. Through studies of spirituality and my own deep-going experiences, I came to understand step by step that life is following its own rules and laws, which are completely unknown to the mind and also will be unknown to it, because they are located in a region and on a level where the mind and the thinking don't have access, in a room which is beyond thinking and which may only be set foot in by something beyond mind, regardless of which name we give to this higher power.

Michael Jackson often uses the name God for this power. However, the name is not essential because this higher power was given innumerable names during history of humanity, depending on religion, time, culture and society. This "getting out of the way" Michael talks about is mind getting out of the way, whereby man is enabled to perceive, free from filters and conditioning, and a door to new rooms is opened with solutions, creations and answers to which usual thinking has no access. In the biographies, works and words of the great ones in this world, of the artists of the century, the pioneers, and the world's transformers, we find the assertion for this mystery. Transformation, innovation and creation happen without there being somebody who does something, without there being a doer who creates something. There is nobody's intellect which is the origin of the product, and thus there is no intellectual property. The proprietor and creator is IT or THAT or God – who would never hit on the idea to call the creation his intellectual property, because in the moment it was created and manifested, it belonged to everybody.

Man therefore is not the maker, not the origin of the product, but the instrument through which the product is produced which brings to form that which "God" lets into the room. Michael Jackson himself says that his lyrics and music do not originate from him, but that they write themselves and then Michael only picks them up from somewhere at some time. He brings the sounds and tones from the invisible realms to the earth. The earthly author is the pen which brings to paper what is freestanding. A pen does not reason if it should write down what the led to and where the way continues, instead of thinking about it and hatching a plan of how to get to a place.

When a creeper is climbing up a wall and meets a projection, where it cannot continue straight, it will straightforwardly creep around the projection, overcome the obstacle and continue to climb up. An intellectual would register the obstacle and make a plan immediately for how to sweep the obstacle out of the way. While the plant has long since overcome the one in charge is dictating, it does not reflect, it does not discuss, but serves selflessly. An instrument has no opinion and no will of its own, but is willing to be led. It follows the flow of life, integrates itself and feels in the bones where it is obstacle, man is still in the phase of planning to find a solution for his problem. The plant follows the higher lead; man creates a problem. As already said, which name we give to the leader - God, Source, Higher Wisdom, Atman, Allah, Jehovah or whatever else, or if it stays nameless and is called THAT or IT, is totally irrelevant and a matter of individual inclination or individual or collective conditioning. Masters, artists and geniuses of all times have thus brought into the world, into manifestation, the True, Good and Beautiful, by getting the "I" out of the way. The "I" with all its imaginations, insubstantial concepts and narrow reflections.

"People ask me how I make music. I tell them I just step into it. It's like stepping into a river and joining the flow. Every moment in the river has its song. So I stay in the moment and listen." (How I Make Music, Dancing the Dream)

Michael has said in interviews, that for example the songs "Billie Jean" and "Beat It" have come to him "from somewhere."

2. Michael's Angel

On awakening on the morning of 1st of July 2009, the idea emerged from the flow to write a second book about Michael Jackson. That was the last thing I ever could have imagined the day before. At that time I was sure that after the publication of my book, "Das Mysterium von Michael Jackson und Sathya Sai Baba" in 1999 the chapter, "Michael Jackson," was closed for me. That does not mean that I was no longer interested in his music and films, for I was observing Michael's plans and was alert to a new album being released or if Michael somewhere sometime would perform again. I knew since 1997 that he had no more plans to tour again and Michael Jackson had confirmed this again after the last two concerts, "Adventure Humanity - Michael Jackson and Friends," in 1999 in Seoul and Munich. But I myself had no intention to do more research and write again about Michael.

What I had discovered from 1992 to 1999 with increasing enthusiasm about Michael Jackson, and tried to share with the world, the world didn't want to know. The media, which used to pounce on everything in relation to Michael Jackson, ignored my book completely. Only one journal published a critique; the "Frankfurter Allgemeine Zeitung" (FAZ) wrote on 13th of June 2000 about "Two odd birds - J. is great, and Margott Schürings his prophet." At that time the word prophet seemed to me ironic, but at least the book was worth a critique to one journal and in this case a serious one. But prophet? Couldn't it be held more simple? My book in my opinion was riddled with new and exciting insights and revealed relations which nobody had noticed before – not even most of the fans at that time knew Michael's book with poems and short stories, "Dancing the Dream," from 1992, and as of today I have found not one biography which mentions this work, which Michael himself has called his most autobiographic work.

Some years later I noticed that my book was soaked by a sort of mentality that resembled a head teacher, so that the fun while reading was missing. With my own "head teacher" I was again confronted very intensely in March 2007 in the Sahara desert in Tunisia. At that time I was on a two-week tour, which had been announced as a retreat of stillness. I wanted to know how I would feel in a place without any forms to hold on, in a place where the eye had nothing to register. Unfortunately I could only enjoy the longed-for stillness for three days, when everyone in our small group withdrew in the sand desert with only a tent and water as our supplies. On the other ten days our tour guide was acting as "head teacher" and commented on each of our remarks and always had to butt in. At that time I realized how lousy a "head teacher" can be and therefore I took my "own" stay in the Sahara.

"I'm starting with the man in the mirror." And slowly it dawned on me, how great the healing force and power of a "love that never interferes" can be, as

Michael Jackson describes it in his poem, "Two Birds." After the publication of my first book some readers gave me the feedback that they were not able to master this balancing act from Michael Jackson to Sathya Sai Baba. Okay, perhaps I did not succeed in transmitting the essentials. Only a few people recognized my original intention and had access to the spirit of the work. Most readers were not able to read with the heart and saw only the letters, but not the spirit of the letters.

Who really has focused on the picture of Michael Jackson's angel, which is circling about Sathya Sai Baba, and pondered on this? This cover also came to me from somewhere. "Michael's Angel" is a painting by the Bavaria-born painter and shaman Petra Schwabe which some time before came to her "occasionally" while she was "getting out of the way." (www.petraschwabe.net) She paints images of the soul – that means one's angel – according to customer order. The order for Michael's angel she had received in a dream at night. Searching for the design of my book cover in autumn 1999, "accidentally" I was zapping to the talk show "Fliege" on TV, where Petra Schwabe was a guest and presented some of her angel paintings. When amongst others I caught sight of the beautiful painting of Michael Jackson's angel, I was somehow electrified. Incidentally – as she later told me - her place of residence was mentioned, so I could seek her out directly. When I called her some days later, she invited me spontaneously to her home at the Chiemsee. There I actually received the right to use Michael's angel for the cover. I was even allowed to take the original painting to my home to take photos from it.

The huge crown of Michael's angel is open above to express the opening to some higher force or an awakened crown chakra. In the region of the heart we see a little girl, symbol of the inner child and sign for the coming of Paris. Michael's hands in the region of the heart indicate mudras, that are traditional spiritual signs of blessing. In the background are sun and moon and two pulling dolphins, symbol of the unity of Yin and Yang. The painting is loaded with symbols and is self-explanatory. May everyone who is interested in the message which it holds decipher it oneself. Thanks to Petra for your trust.

I was as a single mother always low on funds, which was partly due to my family conditioning, where was created a consciousness of lack. When in the past I told my mother about my plans and ideas hoping to find someone to share my enthusiasm I heard a disappointing "Isn't that very expensive?" Since then I don't tell her anything which in the broadest sense has to do with money. Instead of these inherited stones in my way, I managed somehow, due to my enthusiasm for the newly found insights, to finance the costs for the first edition of 10,000 copies of the book "Mysterium".

I was a greenhorn in the publishing business. How did it come about that I printed 10,000 copies? "Accidentally" at that time, the book of Jochen Ebmeier "Das Phänomen Michael Jackson" came my way. Wow I thought, someone else from the scientific sector who makes the work of Michael – and not his person

– a theme of discussion and appreciates it. In the year 1999 Michael was in Munich to give his last big concert "Adventure humanity - Michael Jackson and Friends" on 27th of June 1999 in the Olympic stadium, an event of ten hours, where numerous stars from all genres performed - from Andrea Bocelli to Ringo Starr and Status Quo, The Scorpions, All Saints, Luther Vandross, Vanessa Mae, to Boyzone and many more. Like always Michael resided in the „Bayerischer Hof" at the Promenadenplatz in Munich and of course Margott must – how could it be otherwise – go there to mix with the fans and get a glimpse of Michael.

When I stood in the noisy crowd in front of the hotel and was awaiting things to come, suddenly beside me I saw Jochen Ebmeier from Berlin. I did not know him personally, but I recognized him from the photo on his book cover. Right away I approached him and told him about my book project – which he was not so much interested in - and asked him about his own. When the number of copies published came up, I was informed that the 7,000 copies of the first edition of his were sold out in a few weeks. Thus Margott concluded right away: then you print 10,000, thus there will be enough at first. A word and a blow. But things happened differently.

Six years later I had sold about 1000 copies and given away another 1000. Eight thousand copies of my heart blood work had already made a house moving and were now gathering dust in the cellar. I would not store the flop forever and thus step by step all the "residual copies" landed in the shredder, until in summer 2009 there were left 30 copies. And I thought that the mission Michael Jackson was finished. Not a bit of it! As has been said before, thinking is a function of the mind.

On first of July 2009 the title of a second book emerged out of the depth of the ocean: **From King of Pop to Mahatma.** When getting out of the way, you only observe how the void of the room is filled and then decide if you are ready as an instrument or not. Perhaps the world is ready now to look closer and to listen more intently, when Baba is discarded from the book, I thought. But Mahatma, doesn't that go too far? The term Mahatma is Sanscrit and is composed of the words "Maha" and "Atman," which means "Great Soul" and describes what man is by nature. In India it is an honorary title for the greatest spiritual masters, whereby in the West we got to know specifically Mahatma Gandhi. And now - **Mahatma Michael Joseph Jackson ...**

What shall I do? The title is there ... we will see what will happen now ... It seems once again that the mind is proven inept to know where life is going. It seems as if the mission Michael Jackson is still in the beginning, not only for me, but for the whole world.

3. The Last Curtain

Early on 2nd of July I awakened thinking about Michael Jackson and full of enthusiasm. On 18th of January of 2009 I had sent an open letter to some friends, which ended: "I'm looking forward to being witness to the huge spectacle, how the sun (Source) by her presence will put an end to all illusionary forces of the I." I had not considered this thunder-like turnaround of the spectacle. I researched on the internet. There the cry of Michael Jackson, which penetrates a part of his work, was blasting out, for example in "Scream," "Earth Song," and "They Don't Care About Us." In the short film to the last of these three, hundreds of drummers in a favela, a slum area, in Rio de Janeiro are beating and braying out with fervency, full of power and a mixture of enthusiasm and wakeup call, the need and desperation of humanity into the world: "They Don't Care About Us."

Since February 2009 I myself have had lessons in samba drumming and playing the big surdo. In "They Don't Care About Us," it is teeming from these huge drums. "Michael eles nao ligam para a gente". I join the beat of the rhythm, feel how my body is in resonance with the need of the people in the film and I am drumming and drumming. Need and at the same time enthusiasm, magic and boundless joy of life. Side by side. At the same time. No opposition. All my body and mental cells are blasting, "They Don't Really Care About Us." Not about the needy, not about the jailed, not about the victims, not about the offenders, not about the ones who are calling for help, not about the underprivileged. They don't care about people, but about everything that seems more important to them. A video on YouTube shows hundreds of prisoners in the Philippines from Cebu Provincial Detention and Rehabilitation Center who are dancing and singing to this song in order to alert others about their plea and to honor Michael Jackson. Up until July 2, 2009, the video was clicked 27 million times (27,000,000). (In the meantime it is no longer available, due to GEMA restrictions). How is it possible? Only a few days after Michael's death? This would be one third of all Germans. Such dimensions make one speechless and breathless.

On August 5, 2009, I Google the name Michael Jackson and find 259,000,000 records. As I have a foible for statistics, I find in my notices that there were 2,000,000 records on June 26 at 12:00 for Michael Jackson, at 2:00 already 64,000,000, and six weeks later four times that number – and thus more records than for Barack Obama with 95,000,000, who was until now one of the "front runners." Curious as I am, I Google again one year later on June 6, 2010. The clicks for Michael Jackson are reduced to 131,000,000, for Barack Obama to

71,000,000. Michael has broken all records, ever since he entered the stage, and now he is breaking all records by simply going off the stage. After his death more than one million albums were sold in one week – again a world record. When the famous glitter glove, which Michael Jackson had worn the first time at the premiere of the "Moonwalk" in 1983, was auctioned in New York – the estimated worth lay between 40,000 and 60,000 dollars – a hotelier from Macao pays believe it or not the record sum of 420,000 US dollars. Another glitter glove from "Billie Jean" was auctioned before in Las Vegas for 192,000 US dollars, whereas the auctioneer had calculated its value at 30,000 Dollars. The taste of infinity.

I had waited like many fans and adorers for a long time for a comeback of Michael Jackson. The last years it had calmed down in relation to him, after he had got over the strain of the month-long trial for child molestation in the summer of 2005, where he was acquitted on all charges. It was clear for me that after this torture Michael Jackson was in need of time for himself, his children and family to recover and find the way again to "normal" life, as much as the term "normal" can be used at all for him. It's doubtful that someone can ever recover from such a trauma. But when Michael resumed work on his music and started new projects, all fans and friends were curious about his new album.

Totally surprising, on 9th of March 2009 Michael announced that he would give ten concerts in London. For me it was evident that I needed a ticket – at all costs. Indeed it fit my plans, because I already had planned to travel to London in 2009. I registered for the presale on the internet and waited patiently until finally I got the email with the code to buy the ticket. Immediately I logged in on the corresponding website and ordered four tickets for the O2 Arena, best category. I wanted to surprise some friends with the surplus tickets. I received the notice: "Searching, wait 15 minutes." Then it took a long time. Finally it showed "still 13 minutes waiting time," then again "15 minutes" - why? Then finally the countdown started again. It seemed to me like an eternity - then "still one minute" and then the notice: "Not available, choose another number and/or another date."

Get outta here! Once more the whole procedure ensued. Again it lasted a long time. If I don't succeed this time, I will panic. Finally it started to count down the minutes, much too slowly; this was not only fifteen minutes, but it was at least half an hour. I have the feeling that it was easier to get my Ph.D. than a ticket for a Michael Jackson concert. Then finally, still one minute and ... I've done it. Not a bit of it – "Not available, choose another number or another date."

Again the same procedure, and this time I forgot the gift tickets; now I was only in it for myself. I ordered one ticket, any category. The main thing now was that I was in. Again: "Searching ... wait 15 minutes." And this time I was lucky after an eternity, a ticket for 24th of August, and in the best category. Thanks. I booked the flight and the hotel right away and looked forward to the thrill of anticipation.

Great was the anticipation for the "Final Curtain Call," as Michael called it at the announcement on 9th of March for the "This Is It" concerts. At first I had no idea why he emphasized, "This Is It," so much, but I noticed it. This sentence can be related to different levels of understanding. Perhaps Michael sensed that early intuition could fulfill itself. On 26th of June of 2009 on her MySpace page, Lisa Marie Presley, Michael's first wife, tells us about a conversation which she and Michael had in 1995, where they among other things talked about her father's death. "At some point he paused, stared at me very intensely and he stated with an almost calm certainty: 'I'm afraid that I am going to end up like him, the way he did.'... Though she tried to deter her then-husband from such notions, Jackson "just shrugged his shoulders and nodded almost matter of fact as if to let me know he knew what he knew and that was kind of that."

Michael's spiritual consultant, June Gatlin, with whom he had met regularly since the beginning of 2008, confirms that Michael had such anticipations. It is said that June has paranormal power and "on the last occasion, in March" (of 2009), she said she sensed that there something was gravely wrong. "He wanted me to check his body....I scanned his body. I was watching his life ebbing away, but inside I was asking, 'God please let him live.' He looked at me, like, 'We know something they don't know, June.'" (http://www.michaeljackson.com)

Also music producer Rodney Jerkins, with whom Michael had often worked, confirms: "He had an intuition." Three weeks before his death Michael had asked Andrew Crouch to play the song, "It won't be long," for him on the piano.

It won't be long - Till we'll be leavin' here - It won't be long - We'll be goin' home - It won't be long - Till we'll be leavin' here - It won't be long - We'll be goin' home - Count the years as months - Count the months as weeks - Count the weeks as days - Any day now - We'll be goin' home

It won't be long -Till we'll be leavin' here - It won't be long - We'll be goin' home - Count the years as months - Count the weeks as days - Any day now - We'll be goin' home.

We shall be like Him - We shall be like Him - We shall be like Him - Any day now - We'll be goin' home

It won't be long - It won't be long - It won't be long - We'll be goin' home

4. Man in the Mirror

Will Michael's wakeup call to humanity be listened to this time, as the last curtain fell down before his comeback? Or maybe that the curtain only now was raised? Is Michael's going off the earthly stage his real comeback? As Falco already sang: "From darkness to the light...must I really die to live?" Has the time come that people finally use their ears to listen and their eyes to see instead of interpreting the world with their conditioned thinking? Now as the person Michael Jackson went off the earthly stage and there is no longer a person, how could they dull their clear vision for the message? People are inclined to look at persons instead at that which finds its way into the world – through persons as instruments. They stare mesmerized at the pen instead of studying what was written down. They criticize the pen and stay on the demand of perfection of the instrument. Is everything some kind of maneuver to divert their eyes from their own mistakes? Perhaps the instrument of the critic is even less perfect than the one he actually has an eye on. Michael's plea, "I'm starting with the man in the mirror," is rapidly discounted, and again one can point a finger toward the instrument and thereby overlook the fact that three fingers point towards oneself.

Has the time come for the awakening of humanity or will their deep sleep continue still? Is humanity ready to care about people instead of material things? To make friends instead of war? To see people and coming together as the purpose and destination of the earthly being instead of banking, business, stock and corporations? Growth, growth, growth and growth again, bombs and bombers? "I'm starting with the man in the mirror, I'm asking him to change his ways." (Man in the mirror)

Okay Michael, well and good, you started with the man in the mirror, but should we do the same? We see so many mistakes in you which first have to be eradicated before we can take you seriously. You are rich, are ugly, have too many debts, are gay, and are ill; your children are not yours biologically. You really dared to dangle Blanket out of the window of a hotel (in November of 2002 in the Hotel Adlon in Berlin). Michael, instead of cats and dogs – as it should be – you have apes, snakes, llamas and elephants on your grounds. You like to ride the carousel, you are buying expensive things, and you used to wear sunglasses, and often a face mask. You have had innumerable cosmetic surgeries. What sort of man are you? How is it possible to be like this? One like you should be put in the pillory. One like you is a great danger for humanity. If everyone were like you, where would we go?

"I'm starting with the man in the mirror, I'm asking him to change his ways, And no message could have been any clearer. If you wanna make the world a better place, Take a look at yourself and then make that ... Change!" (Man in the mirror)

Michael, I am not rich, not ugly, I have no debts, am not ill, am not gay, my children are my biological ones. I did never dangle someone out of the window, I have no animals, I don't like to ride the carousel, and I don't buy expensive things. Rarely do I wear sunglasses, never a face mask, and I have not had cosmetic surgery. There is nothing to change. The fault is on your side.

The above argument is an example of the crazy and insane logic of the dogmatic mind. Indeed the scene on the balcony of the Hotel Adlon was willingly falsified on TV. While Michael held his son for some seconds over the balustrade and held him safely in his arms, which was for sure a result of enthusiasm and not such good idea, this scene is shown on television even today as if it lasted endlessly, by simply putting together the same scene again and again and showing it as one action. Such things happen, and to many people, only with "normal" people there is no camera present. Michael himself is later interviewed about this incident by Martin Bashir, as if it were a police hearing, whereby Bashir confronts Michael with the assumption of the press that he nearly threw his son from the balcony. Michael then only asserts that he would never harm a child in any way. "I was doing something in innocence." (Living with Michael Jackson)

This example shows impressively how the media can make someone into a monster or freak due to the smallest mistake, the few seconds shown again and again and put together in a way that the viewer has the impression that the child was dangling in the air for minutes, an illusion of the senses. I know many parents who throw their children in the air and then catch them. That was never pilloried. Which is more dangerous, to throw a child in the air and to catch him then or to hold him tight over a balustrade in the arms for three seconds? We use the mistakes of an instrument only to divert us from ourselves. Because we deny putting our eyes from the outside to the inside and observing ourselves, what we are doing, we need a diverting maneuver to point a finger to the "bad" ones in order to fancy to be the "good" ones. This insane fixation on the instrument thus closes the eye for that which the instrument created, what it tells and shares with us. In no other cases are we so obsessed to discredit the instrument as in the case of Michael Jackson – to make him the laughingstock of the media. Why were people so fascinated by Michael Jackson and at the same time so provoked? Why was he the target, the prey, of a pack of hounds?

"Tell me, what has become of my rights? Am I invisible 'cause you ignore me? Your proclamation promised me free liberty.... The government don't want to see, But if Roosevelt was living, He wouldn't let this be, no no." (They don't care about us)

Which friends did Michael Jackson have? He himself said that they could be counted on one hand. In Germany was founded the "Fan"-Club, "Fanship turns to Friendship" (www.mjfriendship.de). Alex and her friends had realized that it is not sufficient to be a fan, when one is not capable of empathy with how the adored one is himself coping. Especially in the United States in the past blacks and whites never were friends.

People have been attached for a long time to outer things and outwardness, until finally in autumn of 2008 the time had come that the majority of the Americans translated the deepest longings of Michael into action, maybe unconsciously or consciously. When Barack Obama went on stage and was elected as the head of the nation, a new spirit started to blow. There was someone who listened to the blacks and to the whites, who cared, who touched people of all races and classes, who attracted masses of people and enchanted them, exactly as Michael Jackson had succeeded. Does this begin the transformation of humanity to humanness and personhood at a place where blacks and whites are recognized as equally worthy and equally entitled?

Let us follow the spectacle. The answer will show itself. "Some things in life they just don't wanna see - But if Martin Luther was livin', he wouldn't let this be." (They don't care about us, 1995)

Even Martin Luther King was taken away from his work by his death. Or maybe it is the contrary? Is the real work only initiated at death? Because man has difficulties in discarding superficiality and diving deep? Pearls are not found at the shallow waterside, but only on the bottom of the ocean, only when you dive deep. Might it be that humanity is finally ready and prepared for the dive?

5. Two Birds

Michael Jackson volunteered from the beginning as a tool and instrument that put to paper what the pen's leader made. He was ready to be the flute through which the song of the Highest resounded. That reminds us of the dark blue Krishna, who is revered in India – the author of the Bhagavadgita, the Song of the Exalted, who is figured playing a flute, while the Gopis, the maidens, are dancing to his playing. The flute is a symbol, because it is hollow so that the breath and the song can pass unhindered through it. Krishna means literally the "all-attracting." He is the one who attracts all people magically and charms and enchants them. He is one who touches people in the deepest innermost, in their soul.

Does this sound familiar to you? Everyone who met with Michael Jackson reports exactly this. Whoever got near to him was enchanted by his charisma, his song and his dance. Those are magic moments, when the song of God touches men. And it was Michael Jackson's purpose to revitalize the enchantment, the magic and the wonder. He wanted the whole of humanity hear His song that sounded through his "flute." Michael has described his feeling for Him/Her in this poem:

"Two birds sit in a tree. One eats cherries, while the other looks on. Two birds fly through the air. One's song drops like crystal from the sky while the other keeps silent. Two birds wheel in the sun. One catches the light on its silver feathers, while the other spreads wings of invisibility. It's easy to guess which bird I am, but they'll never find you. Unless... Unless they already know a love that never interferes, that watches from beyond, that breathes free in the invisible air. Sweet bird, my soul, your silence is so precious. How long will it be before the world hears your song in mine? Oh, that is a day I hunger for!" (Two Birds, Dancing the Dream)

Very young Michael Jackson has already told us in interviews that he sees himself as instrument of something that comes from above, that through him things are brought from somewhere. Thereby he is not the originator, not the source of the created, but the vehicle of something higher. An instrument, a pen does not decide, when it is used, but it acts when the one who leads the pen starts to move it. Thus also I am sitting at three o'clock in the morning at the computer.

More and more it is dawning on me what sort of sport is played on earth. Intuition slowly is changing to inner certainty. Awakening means to die, before you are dead. Michael Jackson died long before he was dead. Thereby the doer Michael Jackson has never existed. He wrote not writing, he sang not singing, he danced not dancing. He did not doing. He acted and is still acting not acting.

In my above-mentioned open letter it is said: "Finally I realized what the following chapter from the Tao Te Ching meant: 'In the pursuit of learning, something is acquired. In the pursuit of TAO, something is dropped. Less and less is done, until non-action is achieved. When nothing is done, nothing is left undone. The world is ruled by letting things take their course, it cannot be ruled by interfering.'" (Laotse, Tao Te Ching, Verse 48)

6. The Dance Lives On

It is not easy to achieve this doing in not doing and to differentiate it from business. Because looking from the outside there is nearly no difference between the doing of a maker and the doing of non-action. The physical eye only sees the dancer. But it is not able to see what moves the dancer to dance. The mover is only recognized by a consciousness with the ability of discrimination. Michael Jackson describes in his poem, "Dancing the Dream," what the wise and mystics have been saying for ages: Consciousness IS and it expresses itself through creation. Consciousness creates this world, which Michael Jackson calls the "Dance of the Creator." This dance is composed of dancers who as parts form the whole of the holy dance.

"...Dancers come and go in the twinkling of an eye but the dance lives on. On many an occasion when I'm dancing, I've felt touched by something sacred. In those moments, I've felt my spirit soar and become one with everything that exists....I become the lover and the beloved. I become the victor and the vanquished....I become the singer and the song. I become the knower and the known. I keep on dancing and then, it is the eternal dance of creation. The creator and creations merge into one wholeness of joy. - I keep on dancing and dancing .... and dancing, until there is only .... The dance." (Dancing the Dream, Dancing the Dream)

The dancer Michael Jackson is gone. The dance lives on. And with it everything that this dancer has brought to the world will also live on – enchantment, magic, love, freedom, joy, bliss. Due to wonderful encounters that have happened, I know that some people around the globe have heard God's song in his. But the masses of humanity have not yet heard it. It was not granted to Michael Jackson in his embodiment on earth to experience that humanity recognizes which breath flowed through his flute. A long time ago it was said: "Son of man you are living among a rebellious people. They have eyes to see, but do not see, and ears to hear, but do not hear, for they are a rebellious people." (Gospel, Books of the Prophets, Ezekiel 12:2)

How long will humanity walk on earth blind and deaf? And stay reluctant to true realization? And deify the mind? And claim in its hubris that the limited creations of the mind are the answer to everything? And wallow in the ignorance to be able to fill the ocean in a cup? How long will humanity still ignore the Song of the Exalted – the Bhagavad-Gita - with smart sayings like "what we cannot prove does not exist," or, "we are living in a world of duality"?

We don't live in a world of duality because we have no choice, but because we create this duality ourselves day by day, year by year. Because we made mind and thinking to be sovereign and are ignoring everything beyond mind. There is sufficient proof in history of humanity that it is possible to live a wonderful life without duality and without personality, even when this is not provable scientifically. Proofs are only a matter of mind. Spirit cannot be proved, the totality cannot be filled in a small cup named mind. Spirit is bigger than the ocean, without bounds. Spirit is consciousness, not graspable, not perceptible, not tangible, and all present here and now.

On 25th of February of 1983 at the young age of 24 years, Michael gave an interview on "Entertainment Tonight," where he talked about the origin of his creative work.

"I'll continue to put my heart into my work....I just create it...I couldn't explain the anatomy of why it happens...I put my heart in it....Songs come at the strangest times. I could be walking through a park or something and it'll just hit you... There's no set time that I write...they just come."

Question: "Where do you think the gift came from?"

Michael's answer: "God."

Question: "What is it that goes through your mind when you perform?"

Michael: "I don't think about it much, I don't think at all actually, I'm feeling it. It's not a thing of thinking or mechanics, it's all spirit and feeling...it's mainly I'm so much into the music I don't think...like I said before, I create right from the heart. There's no chemistry...I just project how I feel....I love to create...when I'm not creating I'm not as happy." (Michael Jackson Rare Interview February 25 1983, YouTube)

"So I stay in the moment and listen." (How I Make Music, Dancing the Dream)

Instead of listening to the whispering of wisdom and to soar as a butterfly into the limitless, humanity is freezing in the state of a caterpillar and crawling in the dust of earth. If this were all, it would be a pity, but not a catastrophe. The perfidious thing thereby is that the caterpillars are aiming to destroy the beautiful butterflies. Otherwise there would be too much danger that the caterpillar recognizes that in reality the transformation to a butterfly is the purpose of being a caterpillar. Instead of living its original essence – humanness – humanity is overrun by moths, critics, commentators, slanderers, enraged and disgusted people, goodie two shoes, groups of regulars, people who are always right about everything, people who put in their two cents – they all live the unnatural dharma of the moths. Dharma is a Sanscrit term for that which makes something or someone to who it or he is, what the very own essence of something or someone is. The dharma of the moth is to destroy stuff. That makes it a moth, that's the reason for its existence, that's its essence and task. Therefore it doesn't matter if the stuff is worthy or worthless. A rag can serve to fulfill the dharma of a moth – that is destroying of stuff – as well as silk or brocade. A majority of humanity is living in this state of a moth. They have to destroy and to exterminate everything. Thereby those who are different are especially the targets of destructive mockery and hate, those who don't fit in any drawer or any scheme, who are greater than their own pettiness, who don't fit into the confinement of the confined. People like Michael Jackson.

Despite this sad misery there are also rays of hope and good news. After Michael went off the earthly stage, from every corner of the world have been coming signs that the way to liberation from this miserable state is paved. In a Kryon channeling we were informed: "The potentials are there. Only the pioneers that will make them true are needed. Barack Obama is one of them. You are one of them. Michael Jackson also is one. Look at the history of

Michael Jackson, see and feel it from a higher viewpoint. Isn't there possibly hidden a great being behind this seemingly crazy man Michael Jackson? Which energies have caused the masses to exalt? Which power made this gentle human being do such strength-sapping things? Which divine energy has through him elevated the hearts of people to ecstasy? I can assure you, he was one of the very great souls. The man Michael Jackson is gone. The energy, that shared much energy of heart, has finished its service and the anchored energy stays." (Barbara Bessen, July of 2009, www.torindiegalaxien.de)

A 39-year-old female fan of Michael writes: "Every day I am amazed at what a complete person he was. What a complete and refined and superior being....And the world at its lower vibes could not grasp him. We were magnetized by his music, hypnotized by his dance. His voice touched our hearts...and still our lower nature did not allow us to SEE him for who he was. We are blessed, really, BLESSED, to have had him on this planet." (fan 2202, www.michaeljacksontributeportrait.com)

Such and similar evaluations have been reaching me recently non-stop. For years I had thought that I was the only one with my discoveries in Michael Jackson's work and that the world – with rare exceptions – was only interested in his shell. And now the reports from people who are seeing with the heart are springing up like mushrooms. Wasn't it strange what sort of craziness and insanity humanity produced in relation to an evaluation, description and understanding of Michael Jackson?

When I'm enchanted and inspired by Michelangelo, Leonardo da Vinci, Picasso, Goethe, Shakespeare, Wagner, Mozart, Beethoven, Lang Lang and David Garrett, of what interest is the color of their skin? Will I then ask questions in relation to their relationships or pets? Exactly that were the questions that reporters of the yellow press and boulevard magazines, TV and radio contented themselves with - and not only they, but also the majority of the documentaries of so-called serious journalists. Journalists should research thoroughly when following their professional ethos; reporters are mostly content with rumors and speculations.

What is the reason that the mass of humanity in the case of Michael Jackson was stuck on the level of speculations? He who is stuck on a drug after abuse of it is a case for a psychiatric hospital. But where should we house all those millions who are stuck on the level of moths? Michael Jackson was not the only victim of the mafia of moths. Also Andre Agassi tells us in his autobiography, "Open," where he describes the consequences – in this case in tennis –, the ups and downs of a superstar, with all hells and heavens. Andre gives us several examples how the mob and the moths succeed in destroying everything they encounter. After the production of a commercial for a photo camera where the sentence, "Image is everything," was done, this slogan turned in due course into a winged word that from now on was tied to him like glue. "Overnight the slogan becomes synonymous with me. Sportswriters liken this slogan to my inner nature, my essential being. They say it's my philosophy, my religion, and they predict it's going to be my epitaph. They say I'm nothing but image; I have no substance, because I haven't won a slam. They say the slogan is proof that I'm just a pitchman, trading on my fame, caring only about money and nothing about tennis. Fans at my matches begin tunting me with the slogan: *Come on Andre, image is everything!* They yell this if I show any emotion. They yell if I show no emotion. They yell when I win. They yell it when I lose. This ubiquitous slogan and the wave of hostility and criticism and sarcasm it sets off is excruciating. I feel betrayed – by the advertising agency, the Canon execs, the sportswriters, the fans. I feel abandoned." (Agassi, p.131f)

Drag performance star Georg Preuße, alias Mary, also complains in his autobiography how someone who lives in the public realm turns into a target for mockery. "When many people get excited about a thing, it suddenly turns into a negative thing without any changes in itself. In the beginning I did not understand this until I realized that there are people who want to possess an artist for them: a class that isolates itself to the outside, a certain subculture, an exclusive circle of chosen ones." (Preuße, p. 167f)

The world really is on a tightrope walk at the border between insanity and profoundness – whereby only a few people are able to recognize their situation. For the few clairvoyants the good news is that insanity can be healed. Healing starts with the recognition that there is something to be healed - and then follows the difficult step from outside to the inside. "I'm starting with the man in the mirror." Healing starts when the vision changes from the outer shell to the layers beneath. Like an onion, one by one all the layers are removed until the core is reached. Until today humanity has spent too much time dealing with the outer skin.

In the case of Michael Jackson it is apparent that most of us have not yet touched the second layer, but analyzed for centuries the outer skin. Only recently did something start to move. A change in perception and consciousness is happening which is slowly accelerating. Such shift is always accompanied by physical transformation, and there are several possibilities: When consciousness reaches a certain level of frequency the physical body is no longer able to hold the higher vibrations and breathes one's last. Then the vehicle has served its time. The physical body follows the transformation of consciousness to be able to hold the new frequency. Mario Mantese, an enlightened Master, for example no longer has a heartbeat, but his heart is breathing. The doctors are completely mystified (personal communication).

In the case of Michael Jackson, we were all witness to his physical transformation. As drugs reduce the frequency which accompanies an increase of the level of consciousness, they are able to prolong the time of a soul in the body. On 25th of June 2009 finally despite the use of drugs for Michael Jackson the time had come to leave the physical shell behind. His mission on earth was completed. The body-mind system was allowed to leave the earthly stage. But already during his years on this planet many things happened which the limited mind was not able to grasp. And to not doubt itself the mind has to invent concepts and explanations which allow it to hold on to its system and to be proved right. It is the dharma of the mind to maintain itself by its own creations. The creations of people about Michael Jackson often reached the edge of absolute insanity. It was not that Michael Jackson was insane, but the things that were spread about him for decades.

My suspicions that I already indicated in my book in 1999 are confirmed in the following message that reached me on 4th of July 2009: "A high commander has left the human energy form and entered again fully consciously the eternal circle of Being and NOTHING – Michael Joseph Jackson....Whatever the media will write now, because they are unable to grasp the energy formation Michael Joseph Jackson,...Michael was a very high commander....The commander (LIGHT) is the maker, who is creating physically in this reality....He was holding an unbelievably high POTENTIAL OF LOVE...and was no more hardly to be received in this reality....His creation, his qualities were HIGHEST physical transformation with his presence on stage through song, lyrics and dancing and through his physical body. He came as a black person and already a very androgynous being in this reality. He underwent a physical transformation from black to white...and annihilated at a blow the relevance of black and white. Ingenious isn't it? But too much for this reality and the understanding and consciousness of men. He himself believed as a human in a skin disease. It was not vitiligo; he set an example for us on physical transformation....He needed surgical support, but not as much as always is suggested, and not because he wanted to change himself through surgery. The changes happened by profound physical transformation, which often he himself did not understand.

As he already came to this world very androgynous, earthly sexuality was strange for him....He tried, but in him there was already the predisposition of DIVINE SEXUALITY. Thus he found himself again in the star children and NEW CHILDREN....As commander he wanted to have them around him physically. There never was the merest of sexuality in the earthly sense or abuse. But too much for this reality....As a human his heart was broken by these allegations of abuse, as energy form it was the beginning and the possibility to leave this reality. At the appearance in 'Wetten Dass'...one could perceive the energetic releasing of this reality....His bodily number was the 13; he went over the bridge into the NEW, he held the connection between the worlds, even when he was not aware of all this....In the end he was pure LOVE, pure soul, which the physical body was no longer able to hold permanently. His job here was completed. His soul was accompanied beautifully; between this side and beyond there is only a very thin veil." (Strebel, Botschaft in der wahren Präsenz aus dem wahren SELBST, 26th of June 2009, www.weltendienst.ch)

As is confirmed here, in the person of Michael Jackson duality was annihilated. Michael had to leave the earthly stage, because the physical was no longer able to hold the frequencies of his consciousness. Many spiritual people believe that awakening and transformation of consciousness is solely a matter of mind and that the body nearly does not matter; that is only half the truth. As the process of extinction of the "I" continues, the physical body has to transform itself or it will be burnt due to the high vibration. This fact is confirmed by other Great Souls like Master M: "I had to go through terrific, hard, nearly unbearable trials and experiences in connection with incredible suffering and pain until I could enter the kingdom of pureness. I was spun out of time by a powerful uncontrollable pull and snatched from the lower laws. Through this adventurous cosmic journey I was purified and obtained deep insights and cosmic awakening." (Mantese, 2006, p. 11)

Looking for people who were able to look through the veil of outwardness I made more finds. "Here I start to try to write...an obituary which describes the 'I AM who I AM' of this unique divine human," are the words of Johanna-Merete Creutzberg. To the life coach and expert Michael appeared to be "androgynous, nearly asexual." "It seems to me that this was not really important to him. One could say that in him the male and female were nearly balanced, nearly merged – similar as in the primal Buddha Lord Maitreya." (www.experto.de)

And like other clairvoyants, Johanna-Merete is sure that Michael went "in the full consciousness of his true greatness, his origin and full of love." "He was not alone. He was carried by the love, the estimation, respect and trust of all on this side of the veil and beyond."

One who is unable or refuses to look deeper, to empathize, to look with the heart, will miss the essential and go astray. Even if the moths are loudly praising their insane creations, they will not turn to truth thereby. It seems that Michael Jackson did not himself fully understand the dimension of what was happening through him and by him. But he spoke on a level where certain wisdom and truths soaked through crystal clearly, as is proven by the poems and reflections which he published in 1992 in "Dancing the Dream." One of my sons, who as a young boy was surely not much interested in the issues of his mother, but who himself had already dived deeply in wisdom and mystics, called in surprise in winter of 2009 – when I read to him some lyrics of Michael Jackson, "Oh he is surely awakened." Even though the media always pounced on everything that Michael said or did, I did not find any mention of "Dancing the Dream." Thus also Johanna-Merete regrets in the words of the fox in "The little Prince": "Not really many people saw Michael Jackson with the heart." That is more than evident when one reads the German edition of "Dancing the Dream." It is dripping with such ignorance that it nearly hurts physically and it is a mirror of prejudices that accompanied Michael Jackson his whole life. The one who translates the English "bliss" – which means pure joy and felicity - into German with "lust" has understood nothing, really nothing.

7. Tanners and Shoemakers

Be warned that some parts of this book are overflowing with BAD nature. How else should one react to the arrogant and ignorant way in which Michael was treated for decades? My words as prophet had come to nothing. So I'll try for once being the bad girl this time. I don't want to enter heaven but prefer to get about everywhere (reference to a German book called: Brave Mädchen kommen in den Himmel, böse überall hin – Good girls go to heaven – bad girls go everywhere). When continually provoking a lion who reacts calmly and patiently, nobody should be surprised when at some time he starts to scream and bares his teeth. Michael also did this from time to time.

"I'm giving you on a count of three, to show your stuff or let it be ... I'm telling you, just watch your mouth. I know your game, what you're about. Well they say the sky's the limit and to me that's really true. But my friend you have seen nothing, just wait 'til I get through ... Because I'm bad, I'm bad, come on, you know I'm bad, I'm bad, you know it ... And the whole world has to answer right now, just to tell you once again, who's bad.... So listen up, don't make a fight. Your talk is cheap, you're not a man, you're throwin' stones, to hide your hands. - Because I'm bad, I'm bad, come on, you know I'm bad, I'm bad, you know it ... And the whole world has to answer right now, just to tell you once again, who's bad. We can change the world tomorrow; this could be a better place. If you don't like what I'm sayin', then won't you slap my face? Because I'm bad, I'm bad, come on, you know it, I'm bad, I'm bad, you know it ... And the whole world has to answer right now, just to tell you once again, who's bad." (Bad, 1987)

"May the one who is without mistakes throw the first stone," Master Jesus said. When we deduct from the number of stones that are thrown day by day the number of the ones without mistakes then the world would be overcrowded by perfect people. We don't know if Michael Jackson completed the wheel of reincarnations or if there are lying ahead more earthly rounds, but that does not really matter. Because the legacy he left for mankind is so enormous that it will take years and decades until everything he said or did has reached the hearts of men. Due to the size of the treasure he left, we have to confine ourselves to a few of the precious pearls which are waiting to be discovered in the treasure chest.

My dream to reveal to the world a glimpse of the inner layers of Michael Jackson while he was still enchanting us on earth with his magic was shattered.

It cropped up differently, as it seemed that "God needed him more than we here on earth," as Stevie Wonder said at the Memorial on 7th of July in 2009 in the Staples Center in Los Angeles. And Reverend Al Sharpton addressed on the same day to Michael Jackson's children, Prince, Paris and Blanket, the comforting words: "There wasn't nothing strange about your daddy. It was strange what your daddy had to deal with." As of today I cannot find the answer to the question of why people are not able to see what I can see. For me Michael Jackson has radiated his whole life a grace, a beauty, an innocence and pureness which is not rivaled, and thereby his actions were a crystal clear mirror of his inner world. And all people who have met him personally confirm his outstanding charisma and his irresistible power of attraction. Why it is that despite this millions of people project something totally different on him? An explanation could be the following story of the Ashtavakragita:

There was a great Indian sage and mystic, who was according to legend the teacher of King Janaka and taught him the knowledge of how one could liberate oneself from the bond to the circle of birth and death that originates from ignorance and that came as follows: Janaka at that time was ruler in India and very interested in philosophical discussions. Every year he used to convoke an assembly of scholars, theologians and wise men. It was a contest of mastership

It happened that on that day a lad appeared in the hall of the king. He was apparently very poor and wore a loincloth. Nobody knew anything about him. The only thing that was known was that he was patiently waiting for days in front of the Palace walls until an elder scholar told the king about him and he called him to come in. His name was Asthavakra, which means the one who is crooked eightfold. When Asthavakra entered and the more than thousand scholars saw his deformed body they all started to laugh loudly. When they started to laugh Asthavakra laughed even louder.

Due to the loud laughter of Asthavakra the scholars stopped and silenced. Janaka asked him: "I can understand why they laugh – because of your body – but I cannot understand why you laugh. And you silenced their laughter with your laugh." Ashtavakra answered: "I thought that I am coming to an assembly of scholars and philosophers, but here are only tanners and shoemakers. They are only interested in skin and leather." King Janaka realized that a completely awakened Mahatma stood in front of him, a Great Soul, full of radiant wisdom and self realization. (Drucker, Al (ed.): 1997).

Have we finally reached the point where we leave the level of shoemakers and tanners behind us and see the essence instead of the skin? What is the difference between a Great Soul to a little soul? "Awakening means to be aware of what one is really *not* and to realize what one is really, namely the nameless, formless unborn Here and Now, the eternal Self!" (Mantese, 2008) This Self manifests itself momentarily in time and space, where it turns into subject and object and is able to act. While the sleeping person thinks of himself as the actor, for the awakened there is no identification with the subject, the maker. There is no separation between subject and object, no duality, no Two. By awakening, the consciousness of duality is unmasked as illusion and is thereby transcended. Looking from the outside the actions of an awakened one and of a sleeping person cannot be differentiated. One cannot see if somebody has realized that his physical and mental appearance is only an instrument, or if he thinks of himself as the creator. In both cases the action is visible in his works. But in the former case the work comes from somewhere and in the latter case there is a maker, who believes himself to be the source. What did Michael Jackson say about this?

"I am the thinker, the thinking, the thought - I am the seeker, the seeking, the sought - I am the dewdrop, the sunshine, the storm - I am the phenomenon, the field, the form - I am the desert, the ocean, the sky

I am the Primeval Self - In you and I." (Are You Listening? Dancing the Dream)

These are the words of a seer, of an awakened one, of a realized person, who has experienced Satori in the language of Zen, which means realization of the "own true nature." The awareness that is expressed here cannot be grasped by the mind, because it is coming from a realm beyond mind. Mind is also only a mirage of consciousness. How can a mirage ever understand the mirror?

And least, it is not about understanding but about realizing. This realization happens when the maker, the self-will, the ego gives up and dies. In that moment, the door to a higher wisdom opens to an intuition and clarity which gets along without thoughts, even finding expression through thoughts.

The top-heavy western man is lacking the power of imagination for this fact. He has made mind to be the measure of all things. Thus the statement "I think, therefore I am," of Descartes was put into this world and generations of philosophers turned into devotees. That statement is true for the "i" (small I), but for the "I am" it is disproved.

Michael Jackson's work is a reservoir of things that were taken from the ocean of the "I am," whereby he was always aware that the products were not "his." He made himself humbly and modestly available to serve the highest, and experienced bliss and endless suffering in earthly terms.

Michael continued to be lonesome because the world was not yet mature enough to look through skin and leather. It was too fascinated by the outer layers of the onion and too busy criticizing the instrument. Did we get excited, disgusted and entrusted long enough? Did we spill enough gleefulness, derision and mockery? Enough judgment and condemnation? Is it finally enough of arrogance, overbearance and boastfulness? Michael Jackson has been an ideal projection surface for the thick mind of the mainstream, because his ego was not very much developed. If you knew that every judgment strikes yourself you would not prostitute yourself all the time in this way.

For an awakened one there are no secrets. He looks through skin and leather! And stays silent! Michael Jackson was sure that finally the truth would triumph and not the lie: "The lie runs sprints, the truth marathons." Everyone who will witness the course can see this marathon which is not yet finished. The one who is seeking an answer to the question of who Michael Jackson really is is looking for a needle in a haystack. Better to delve into the wisdom and beauty of his poems and reflections in "Dancing the Dream" - 46 touching, inspiring and healing lyrics, twined around a hundred enchanting pictures.

"Immortality's my game - From Bliss I came - In Bliss I'm sustained - To Bliss I return - If you don't know it now - It's a shame - Are you listening?" (Are You Listening? Dancing the Dream)

In the Veda the highest transcendent reality is called "sat cit ananda" - "Being Consciousness Bliss." It refers to a state where the split between subject and object is annihilated. Bliss is a form of joy which cannot be compared with earthly pleasures, but is called by mystics as ecstasy. The Christian tradition also knows seers, who were enraptured. "Saint Teresa said, 'my ecstasy lifted me into the air.'"(Wings Without Me, Dancing the Dream)

Michael Jackson gets in the line with the purpose to share what was given to him. "...My goal in life is to give to the world what I was lucky to receive: the ecstasy of divine union through my music and my dance. It's like my purpose; it's what I'm here for." (Ebony, 2007, 2009).

"This body of mine - Is a flux of energy - In the river of time - Eons pass, ages come and go - I appear and disappear - Playing hide-and-seek In the twinkling of an eye - I am the particle - I am the wave - Whirling at lightning speed..." (Are You Listening? Dancing the Dream).

Anyone who was lucky enough to be present when Michael Jackson was acting on stage was a part of the stream of energy and could experience this spinning physically. He was sucked into the vortex of particles and struck by the wave of enthusiasm. He was a part of the game of hide-and-seek and participated in appearance and disappearance. Nobody could escape when Michael took thousands with him on the level of bliss and ecstasy – at least for some hours.

Tom Kenyon confirms that "the emotions of ecstasy and bliss create a frequency within ourselves which makes it possible to escape the levels of lower vibration of the world around us." Michael Jackson was the vehicle, the carrier of this spirit, of this consciousness, that reveals itself by "getting out of the way." People who are no longer enslaved by their mind are attracted magnetically by this light. People who have enough from these conditionings that lasted for centuries and are yearning for freedom admit that the ego is burnt in this light. When this light is embodied in someone it still radiates when the body has done its service on earth. After Michael's ceding from the earthly stage, ever-increasing numbers of people realize the light that before was only seen by a few. Elizabeth Taylor, a good friend of Michael, writes in the foreword to "Dancing the Dream": "Michael Jackson is, indeed, an international favorite for all ages, an incredible force of incredible energy....What is a genius? What is a living legend? What is a megastar? Michael Jackson that's all. And just when you think you know him, he gives you more."

Michael's reflections about reality are clear and catchy. They deal with transcendence of duality, which is only a product of the mind. Beyond mind, thinking, there is no longer an "either – or," but only an "as well as." Without "either – or" there are no more drawers. There is no longer a better or a poorer. No right or wrong. Everything is like it is. Everything IS as it IS. Period. "Don't you black or white me."

" "It don't matter if you're black or white…It's a turf war on a global scale, I'd rather hear both sides of the tale. See, it's not about races, just places, faces. Where your blood comes from Is where your space is I've seen the bright get duller. I'm not gonna spend my life being a color." (Black or White)

Michael Jackson probably did not fully understand as a human what was happening with his physical body. He himself explained his physical transformation with the disease vitiligo, a pigment disorder, where the skin is whitening slowly. In the interview with Martin Bashir he says that only God knows how his changes in appearance happened. (Living with Michael Jackson) On 1st of July 2010 Bild-online reported that Michael's son Prince was also suffering with this disorder, which is said to be inherited, as first symptoms appeared on his upper arm. Thus the question of fatherhood is clarified. By the way also Michael's sister La Toya declared in November of 2009: "Vitiligo appeared with us on the paternal side. Prince too shows it. With him you can see it at his arms and breast."

Bashir - a tanner greedy for money - was of course not satisfied with Michael's answer. He was in need of more satisfaction for his ever hungry mind, mindfucking. We can observe how a very sick mind is occupied in forcefully finding confirmations for its own projections and creations. To every attentive observer it is obvious that Bashir is not at all interested in learning more about Michael Jackson and his world, but is trying in a hypnotic way to put on Michael all the shit that was born in his own head. When someone is not able to imagine something, then that simply may not be and is not allowed to be. Human moths simply try to fill the totality in their tiny cup.

8. From Caterpillar to Butterfly

Here comes a story that Susanne from Switzerland sent to me:
"Deep inside we know that we are caterpillars. For some reasons we unlearn to pupate or we allow to be hindered to do so. That hurts. We feel guilty and inferior in some way, always searching for the forgotten, seemingly lost. In order to suppress these negative feelings, we create artificial wings for ourselves, show off with them or look down shamefaced due to our grandiose prosthesis. We admire other plastic butterflies, are envious about their terrific mockup, belittle gleefully the splendid crutches of strange jugglers, struggling and bargaining for the wings in short supply and fostering generously the construction of wings. In short, we undertake everything possible to defend our value as caterpillars and to integrate ourselves into the social fabric of caterpillars. Because the fact should not be suppressed that some caterpillars go all out and sacrifice themselves to be worth admiring for their suffering fellow creatures and their damaged prostheses. That can give much satisfaction for some time, but often in the end there remains only a feeling of endless defeat. When we are lucky enough to meet butterflies, we perhaps wallow in the mud in front of them and try fanatically to imitate them instead of getting inspired by them and let them lead us to our own butterfly being. In desperate jealousy we may even be driven to reduce them to our miserable caterpillar being by talking down about them to feel better ourselves.

Sad story. But listen! It's rustling in the wind of change, it is whispering behind every corner, singing, sounding and echoing: The time has come, the time has come ... the time of butterflies! Awake! Remember! CATERPILLARS OF ALL NATIONS: PUPATE!"

"One more chance at love, one more chance at love, one more chance at love." (One more chance)

Michael Jackson incorporated unconditional love and was giving relentlessly. A commentary to the video to the above song says: "Now we see what is directly before our eyes. That Michael is an angel sent to us by God, to open our eyes and give us the chance to change ourselves and heal this planet. The time has come to heal God's planet. Let us finally come together in peace and end the wars. Stop judging each other about meaningless nonsense...expand love which is in all of us." (YouTube, "One more chance," TheWolfPac242)

Guitarist Slash of Guns N' Roses, who often played on stage together with Michael, witnesses: "In him we find one of the last genuine super artists. He is the only one I ever met who did not compromise in relation to his style of music.... Michael and I have been friends for some time. He always gives me the necessary space to do what I want to do. Michael is very sensitive and has a palate for sarcastic humor.... Once I was waiting for him in the studio, when Michael arrived with Brooke Shields. I was already present, in one hand a butt, in the other a bottle of whiskey and the guitar on my shoulders. He didn't mind. He is different than myself, doesn't work in the same way. But he does not want me to change. He accepts me as I am." (Black + White Magazine, 1995)

While Michael never tries to change anyone else, his whole work indeed aims for "change." Long before Barack Obama made this word the mantra of his battle for election, Michael Jackson had made it a mantra in hundreds of concerts. For example, at the concert in Bucharest in 1992, in the end we hear for several minutes at "Man in the mirror" through the whole sold-out stadium: "Make that change, make that change, make that change, make that change, make that change, make that change, ..." Pure goose pimples.

"Be the change you want to see in the world," Mahatma Gandhi has invited us. Michael Jackson has practiced this all his life long with his heart and soul. On 11th of July 2009 I got a phone call from Petra Schwabe from La Palma. I had asked her via email what had happened to the Original of Michael's angel since 1999. It always has been Petra's dream to give Michael himself his soul picture. But the handing over has always been blocked. Actually it is in Los Angeles. Los Angeles means "the angels"; then it is probably at the right place. Why it never should reach Michael himself will continue to be a secret.

Then Petra added: "Michael is an avatar, a Mahatma." I was staggered. I did not yet tell her about my new book project. How mysteriously things integrate and comply, when you simply follow what is rising from the ocean of wisdom, when you withdraw the dominion and control of the mind! Michael's soul picture is full of symbolism, in the region of the heart the inner child and perhaps Paris, who came later to earth. Striking is the huge crown chakra, the seventh energy vortex, which serves as an antenna to receive the higher wisdom. Michael Jackson's life work is a wonderful proof that he was a fantastic receiver and that his radio was tuned to the right frequency.

During the evolution of human consciousness the chakras open one after the other, from the root chakra to the crown chakra, until the full potential of being can express itself through the physical instrument. The life energy – the Kundalini - rises, when the instrument is cleaned from mental blockades, when the pen is willing to be led or the flute willing to let the divine breath – the Song of the Exalted - flow unhindered and undiluted through it. The higher chakras of tanners and shoemakers, of moths and caterpillars are yet closed, as the flute is clogged. The higher dimensions are closed to them – until the day when spring cleaning will happen and they end their living as "cluttered" and turn themselves into pure instruments. When Michael Jackson calls the highest as God he is not talking about something male. In his poems he uses both forms for the divine, "He" and "She."

"It's strange that God doesn't mind expressing Himself/Herself in all the religions of the world, while people still cling to the notion that their way is the only right way." (God, Dancing the Dream)

One-sidedness, ignorance and assertiveness block the door to the levels where joy and bliss are at home, which Michael incorporated and irradiated. Assertiveness allows a limited mind and a blown-up ego to feel important, to make oneself cocky and to proudly press one's breast – the existence being as miserable as it might be. While tanners look at the skin, seers look at the content.

"For me the form God takes is not the most important thing. What's most important is the essence. My songs and dances are outlines for Him to come in and fill. I hold out the form, She puts in the sweetness." (God, Dancing the Dream)

While religions have their own ideas or pictures of the form of God, these are obsolete on a level which transcends religion. We pass through all steps of development from kindergarten to school and eventually university. And then there are steps which transcend even the highest grades of university. In relation to levels of consciousness this is the state beyond forms and names. Michael's reflections are based on this perception.

"But for me the sweetest contact with God has no form. I close my eyes, look within, and enter a deep soft silence. The infinity of God's creation embraces me. We are one." (God, Dancing the Dream)

Many awakened masters and mystics talk about this land of stillness. The door to this space is open to everyone who no longer allows himself to be bewitched by the mental level. "There are no bounds between the manifested and the unmanifested, nowhere separation, all is one – you! In the totality, the breathless stillness of Here and Now radiates a gigantic energy, shines an I-less holy love, and this inexhaustible graceful glory is what you really are." (Mantese: 2008, p. 78)

Michael Jackson incorporated and lived all his life this I-less love. For material people, those who only believe the material to be real, this high energy of love is hardly bearable. And they shun it as the devil the holy water. In this state the separation between I and you, between ego and nonpersonality, between you and the world, is annihilated. This separation, which we create with our senses and our thinking, is in reality an illusion and is called Maya in Sanscrit.

"We're all in line, waitin' for you. Can't you see? You're just another part of me...." (Another Part of Me)

This Maya enchants us and casts a spell over us in a way that we are no longer able to escape its fascination. As the human mind and intellect is not capable of recognizing this illusion, the same way as it is not able to see through a fata morgana, man stays imprisoned in this room until the door to the para-mind, to that one beyond mind, is opened. A fata morgana seems totally real to the senses and the mind, only when we get near enough that there is no longer a distance between us and the phenomenon, the illusion of the senses dissolves to what it is – hot air. But as most people don't come close enough, the illusion continues. Only a few search really seriously the closeness, which threatens the life of the ego. This closeness comes with stillness, with stillness of mind. In this room of stillness the reality is revealed as totality, no limit, no separation, I and you one.

The illusion is the diversity, which is perceived as separate forms. Thereby the assumption emerges that there exists my self and an other. We see inevitably certain characteristics in the other and think him to be different from us and our characteristics, without realizing that this is an illusion of the senses. In reality we can only perceive things in the other that have a resonance in ourselves and our characteristics. Without this resonance no perception exists. That means in good English: The other one is always only a projection surface for our own inner selves, the mirror in which one can recognize one's self. Due to ignorance, we project the perceived in our counterpart, whereby we think about him as being an other. The perceived world appears and superimposes the consciousness. That which you are in reality is not the appearance but that which firstly enables this appearance.

Michael Jackson's lyrics describe the real and the unreal. When a spark of this truth is lit up in yourself, your belief in a difference between inner and outer, between I and you, between subject and object, between self and other, goes out. After I and you have died, and the self and the other went out, the dance will live on. Then there is no longer a dancer, but only the eternal dance of creation.

"...Grinning, ducking my head for balance, I start to spin as wildly as I can. This is my favorite dance, because it contains a secret. The faster I twirl, the more I am still inside. My dance is all motion without, all silence within. As much as I love to make music, it's the unheard music that never dies. And silence is my real dance, though it never moves." (Dance of Life, Dancing the Dream)

Mario Mantese tenderly calls those who live in this state of consciousness the blossomed ones. "The whole universe is a guest in the heart of the blossomed ones, and despite the big agitation in the world, the heart of the blossomed ones remains still, carried by divine reason and love." (Mantese, 2009, p. 48)

True stillness is not the absence of tones and sounds. On the contrary, stillness comes often when we listen to music and get ourselves into the higher frequencies. Michael Jackson often swept across the stage like a tornado, loved to swirl around himself in such unbelievable velocity that one could hardly follow him with the eyes, and at the same time was totally still inside. "Whether it was conscious or not, Michael had started really getting in tune with his spiritual energy. I noticed how he was moving Chi energy during his dance. When you observe others imitating his dance the Chi movement isn't there. That is what set Michael apart and made him so attractive for others....The Chi movement explains the smoothness of his Moonwalk and his fluidity of dance." (Denny Lyon, http://thesocialpoets.blogspot.com).

Whoever is still inside radiates this "thoughtlessness" of the whole being and attracts people magically. This stillness elevates the hearts and souls and is the reason that works and brings about everything, whereby there is no worker. That is the secret of the influence which Michael Jackson had on so many people worldwide. Countless reports prove that Michael Jackson had more influence on the life of some people than even their parents and teachers. (It's All About L.O.V.E., 2010) Stillness, also called presence, is understood in the whole world in the same way. It speaks all languages and is at home in all cultures and all nations.

"...The presence rises, shimmering with light. I could be in it forever, it is so loving and warm. But touch it once, and light shoots forth from the stillness. It quivers and thrills me, and I know my fate is to show others that this silence, this light, this blessing is my dance. I take this gift only to give it again." (Dance of Life, Dancing the Dream)

Even in young years Michael Jackson felt responsible and obliged to keep on giving what was given to him. To see that the holding back of a present or a talent due to false humility or shyness is egoism may surprise you. But we can already read about this obligation in the parable of the talents in the gospels. A master gave to one of his slaves five talents before starting on a long journey, to another two, and to a third one talent. The one with the five talents had made ten when he returned to the master, the one with the two had made four and the one with one talent had not used it, but buried it and could only show his master one. In the parable the master applauds the first two slaves, but was angry at the third one: "For to everyone who has, more will be given and he will grow rich; but from the one who has not, even what he has will be taken away." (The Gospels, Matthew 25:29)

Michael Jackson has truly increased his talent to the immeasurable and thereby flooded the whole world with love and joy.

"...I want to continue to grow. To me, the biggest sin is to be given a gift, a talent, because it's actually a gift from God, to take that and not cultivate it and make it grow, that's the biggest sin in the world." (Ebony, 2009)"

"I have a tree on my property, and lots of times, I go up and sit in that tree alone, and I'm peaceful and still and I meditate. And very often, God gives me the creative spark that I need to do the work that I excel in." (Jones, p. 27)

We can see this tree, which Michael rarely used to show, in his song "Childhood." In the same way Michael Jackson revealed the secret of the giving tree to Martin Bashir, who was completely unable to appreciate this trust. Michael was always generous with his treasures and has thrown tonnes of pearls to swine. Aphrodite Jones tells us how much Thomas Mesereau, Michael's attorney, tried to correct the distorted image for the jury members that the public had of Michael due to the agitation by the media, during the trial in 2005. "'We will prove to you,' Mesereau said, 'that Mister Jackson will often wake up at three o'clock in the morning at Neverland. He will walk out of his house alone, and he will walk under the stars, under the moon, under the sky. He will meditate on his own way, and wait for ideas and inspiration to come.'" (Jones, p. 27)

Michael himself often told us that "children, animals and God were his sources of inspiration." He was most fascinated by the "magical stuff" during dawn and dusk. Michael knew that dusk facilitated reaching the so-called level of alpha. This state corresponds with a certain frequency of brain waves, which opens the creative and inspirational realms of consciousness. Michael loved this other world, where he found happiness and bliss. He himself called this want "escapism," which can be understood as a desire to escape the insanity of this "normal" world. Nobody can force us to adapt to the top-heavy heartless thinking and doing and to trot along like sheep. Michael Jackson has held on to his original perception, which made it possible to increase his talent to the immeasurable.

Why ever should an exceptionally gifted artist and human being follow the stupid insistence of the media greedy for sensation and lose thereby himself? Michael always stayed true to himself and has followed his inner guidance. And he was not the only one in history of mankind who made a fool of himself. History tells us about many awakened souls who were called fools. The wise Ramakrishna was called the "holy fool" in his time. "This type of spiritual teacher startles us by their shocking and eccentric behavior compared to our usual rut and turn upside down our moral ideas....The spiritual and holy life is based naturally on a basic reversal of conventional values and attitudes.... In Tibetan buddhism this orientation is known as 'mad wisdom.' We find the phenomenon of holy foolishness in Buddhism, in Hinduism, in Sufism, in Christianity and in natural religions." (www.wegdermitte.de) Such humans are masters of disguise - and Michael Jackson was the master of masters.

"In infinite expressions I come and go - Playing hide-and-seek - In the twinkling of an eye - But immortality is my game... Deep inside - I remain Ever the same" (Are You Listening? Dancing the Dream)

The fact that the world was not able to raise the veil seems to be more likely a problem of the world than of Michael. The fact that mass and press failed to value Michael as a human being and to recognize his part as someone who brings light to the world and instead derided him in the way of moths does not diminish Michael Jackson's excellence, but only proves the inability of mass and press. As now the form Michael Jackson which walked on earth is one with music and dance, the world has to decide if it will finally accept his legacy and rectify what it neglected to do. It is due to the world to honor this legacy, to cultivate and to practice it. Even if the world denied Michael Jackson during his lifetime his human rights, it will be an even greater shame to deny to him even now the one human right to leave him alone. But as the name already says, gossip press are nuts (wordplay in German „Klatschmedien" = gossip press, „einen an der Klatsche haben" = be nuts).

Even when the old rumors and flights of fancy are still circulating, there can be observed an interesting change. The number of people who take a good look and no longer let themselves be led astray by ignorance is growing day by day. Many people awaken suddenly and abruptly and realize that they have overlooked something in the past. And already the door to the essence of Michael Jackson opens, to that which he really personified. And not seldom this realization is accompanied by a profound fright and is related to feelings of guilt – as, for example, Madonna confessed publicly during the memorial in Staples Center. Whoever does not rely on the "old" media, but researches the internet, may observe that worldwide there is a peeling of onions under way. "The internet is a big chance: When the truth can expand without subvention, it will beat the subsidized lie." (Baader, 2008)

From Margit I received the following message on 8th of October 2009: "When I was reading 'Dancing the Dream' after his death, I was tremendously terrified. My first thought was: 'Oh my God – he was an awakened one' (whatever that means). I have looked at him only as a singer and humanitarian. I was truly affected and did not yet digest it til today." Michael has written long before what many people are only realizing now.

"...A star can never die. It just turns into a smile and melts back into the cosmic music, the dance of life." (Dance of Life, Dancing the Dream).

Also Michael's star will never die. His star has already outshone everything when he inhabited the earthly body and now he will shine even brighter after having discarded the weight of the body. And always more people will discover his light and splendor – perhaps we will detect him one day in the sky as a supernova. Anyhow everyone can find the light and his star in his own heart and follow on their search the advice of the wise and awakened ones: "Die before you are dead." (Mantese, 1994) The person Michael Jackson and the personality Michael Jackson died long before the body quit his service on 25th of June 2009. The energy form Michael Jackson had transformed long before into a smile and has merged with the cosmic music and the dance of life. "Smile" with the music of Charlie Chaplin wasn't in vain Michael Jackson's favorite song.

"Smile, though your heart is aching - Smile, even though it's breaking - When there are clouds in the sky, You'll get by. - If you smile, with your fear and sorrow - Smile, and maybe tomorrow - You'll find that life is still worthwhile - If you'll just... Light up your face with gladness - Hide every trace of sadness - Although a tear maybe ever so near. That's the time you must keep on trying - Smile, what's the use of crying? - You'll find that life is still worthwhile - If you'll just...Smile." (Smile, – Words John Turner and Geoffrey Parsons)

A video that fans and friends of Michael Jackson already knew for 25 years, in July of 2009 suddenly made it around the world, the film from a horrible accident in January of 1984 in the Shrine Auditorium in Los Angeles that occurred while shooting a spot for Pepsi Cola. Michael was dancing and continued dancing down stairs even when his hair was already on fire. In his autobiography, "Moonwalk," he downplays the incident as a terrible mishap. Friends indeed know that since that time he now and then had suffered terrible pain because of the serious burn on his head. As also his hair had burnt and did not grow again, and he from then on wore a wig. We all know that he nevertheless showed us all his enchanting and spell-binding smile, even though he was often surely close to tears. The press quickly forgot such things and returned to its work of destruction. History repeats itself even after thousands of years – again and again. How long will this continue?

"Unless ... Unless they already know a love that never interferes, that watches from beyond, that breathes free in the invisible air. Sweet bird, your silence is so precious." (Two Birds, Dancing the Dream)

Rumi expresses it like this: "Beyond right and wrong there is a garden. There we will meet." (Cited in Tina Turner: Beyond) Tina Turner herself says to this: "Begin every day singing like the birds. Singing brings you beyond, beyond, beyond, beyond." We can see that there are people on this planet who have left the material hamster wheel and found with the heart the door to dimensions, which tanners and moths are not interested in. Whoever opens the eyes of the heart will meet other Seers at every corner. But also here is held true that one can only perceive the things that are in resonance with oneself. When the frequency for purple is not present inside, then I will not be able to recognize this color, even when taking a bath in it.

9. The Search

"I'm searching for the world that I come from - 'Cause I've been looking around, In the lost-and-found of my heart. No one understands me.
They view it as such strange eccentricities - 'Cause I keep kidding around - Like a child, but pardon me. People say I'm not okay - 'Cause I love such elementary things - It's been my fate to compensate - For a childhood I've never known. Have you seen my childhood?
I'm searching for that wonder in my youth - Like pirates and adventurous dreams - Of conquest and kings on the throne. Before you judge me, try hard to love me - Look within your heart, then ask - Have you seen my childhood? Before you judge me, try hard to love me - The painful youth I've had." (Childhood)

In this way only speaks a holy fool, who realizes full of empathy that the world in its blindness and deafness is so used to its dark dungeon that it seems to have forgotten that there is light. Michael Jackson takes himself as model and example in his work and his message to lead the awareness of people to certain things. That, fools and good artists have in common. The intrinsic value of art is not dependent on the understanding or lack of understanding of the observer, but on the proximity to spirit. Michael's longing was directed to healing the world, whereby the worldwide problem of a lost childhood plays a vital role. A child that is not allowed to be a child, that does not feel secure, that has no home, will inevitably go painfully astray.

The media did not understand this message and according to their narrow mind argued that Michael was incessantly complaining about his own bad childhood. People with certain experiences are always in a better position to support others in this issue than theorists who only know about its from books and make their own thought about it – and invent stories. Blindness and shortsightedness fail to recognize that the truth always has the longer wind than the lie.

Michael Jackson, for example, never made himself the King of Pop, as the media have been claiming mantra-like for the past twenty years, but he was predestined as such from his management and others. He never felt like a king, but like a prisoner, as he told Barbara Walters in the year 1997 in an interview: "You feel like you are in prison." On the inner portal to Michael's Neverland

Ranch we can read: "Dieu et mon droit." This sentence has been the motto of the British monarchy since the 15th century and means "God and My Right," which says that the right of the monarch to rule is coming from God. It was funny to see how easily fans were misled, when they translated this motto to "God and my Will" – that's really right off the mark. (It's all about L.O.V.E., 2010, p. 62) Right off the mark is also off the mark. The expression "King of Pop" says rightly – when we recall the life of Michael Jackson from his sixth to fiftieth year – that the artist Michael Jackson was King. But it fails to recognize that the human being Michael Jackson was life imprisoned, to give the King of Pop day release when it was convenient to the ones who were interested in it. Michael was not let out on probation after fifteen years due to good conduct – as some criminals in Germany with lifelong judgment - but his imprisonment amounted to 44 years. Who is surprised when Michael sings,

"Take me to a place with no name, She said don't worry my friend, I'll take care, take my hand, ah, take it there, Oh take me to a place without no name."

This song, which was not released before his death, appeared on the internet on the 16th of July, 2009. (Thank you for the information, Antje!) Even the American news channel CNN presented it during prime time. The 24 seconds were already, on the first day, available in more than fifteen versions with 379,000 clicks on YouTube. Michael, now you abide at a place with no name. There you are no longer the King of Pop. There you are only a Great Soul – a Mahatma.

Saturday morning, 18th of July 2009, raining, cold, I go shopping, full of energy, feel the dance of life in my cells, the song of stillness, lovely, wonderful. Thanks! This place without name is here, is everywhere, where the "I" died. It is there, where one thinks about things no more. Where the cause of problems is extinguished. The Ashtavakragita fell again into my hands. *"There are the ones who believe that the world exists and is real. Then there are the ones who believe that the world does not exist and is not real. There are only a few blessed ones who don't think about it but always rest still in the being."* Even though this being cannot be described in reality, there is much written about it. Because even those who rest in the being try at times to couch the unspeakable in terms.

"You and I were never separate - It's just an illusion- Wrought by the magical lens of Perception - "There is only one Wholeness - Only one Mind - We are like ripples - In the vast Ocean of Consciousness." (Heaven is Here, Dancing the Dream)

This magical lens is the magician Maya, the delusion, the illusion. The wave believes it exists separate from the ocean and imagines it can take control and decide about its direction. What hubris! A small wave tries to direct the ocean with force of will. The majority of people believe in this arrogant thought.

Michael Jackson had a different view. Instead of trying the impossible, to revolt against God's will, he preferred to dance and to celebrate life. Isn't this ingenious?

"Come, let us dance - The Dance of Creation - Let us celebrate The Joy of Life" (Heaven is Here, Dancing the Dream)

When heaven is here, then it is pointless to hope for a future hereafter. And why do we believe that it will be better hereafter than here? What is it that nurtures the hope of people in a better hereafter, when they are not even able to create a better here? False teaching far and wide. Misleading interpretations of wise words and teachings, because the cup cannot hold the ocean per se. A trial that is foredoomed to fail from the beginning. The only possibility for ending the tied-up trials is the realization that one disposes only about a mingy cup, the mind. When the mind and the intellect render with humbleness, in this moment of realization one also will be able to fall on the knees in humility and to raise the hands and fold them with true devotion to a "Namaste" – "I bow before your divinity." Thus one lines up in a dance with the nature spirits – the fairies, salamanders, gnomes, undines and sylphs. Totally void of thoughts and free. Heaven is Here. With a Namaste Michael Jackson always welcomed his guests and even at public appearances he showed this sign of humility.

"To know who you are, You are much more, Than you ever imagined." (Heaven is Here, Dancing the Dream)

"The infinity of God's creation embraces me. We are one." (God, Dancing the Dream)

The one who dives deep to the bottom of the ocean will no longer find waves. These only ripple at the surface, where we can also find massive waves, but even thus they don't get deeper. Depth and waves are contradictory. In the depth the wave dies. Depth is stillness, silence, motionlessness, peace. Wave means movement, uproar, noise, dispeace. On the level of the wave we are creator; there we find multiplicity, there is existence. On the level of depth we are One, Wholeness, only Being. Nothing exists, there is nobody, no body. I cannot reach there, because I have always been there. There I am and there I will be, because "I" will be destroyed, as soon as "I" reach the depth. Michael Jackson describes the activities on the level of the wave, the creation very vividly.

"Curving back within ourselves - We create- Again and again - Endless cycles come and go - We rejoice- In the infinitude of Time" (Heaven is Here, Dancing the Dream)

Then Michael changes to the level of the depth, where everything is as it is.

"There never was a time – When I was not – Or you were not – There never will be a time – When we will cease to be." (Heaven is Here, Dancing the Dream)

When the identification with the surface ends, a change of levels can happen very quickly, because one no longer sticks to a certain step. While you have tears in your eyes in one moment and are overwhelmed by deep sadness, some seconds later you can be overwhelmed by the joy of the depth. It equals a quick, always changing, ascending and descending. For the wave and "me," the quick ascending is not life-threatening, but the quick descending. In the depth there exists neither me nor you nor I. But immediately afterwards infolding is happening, unfolding, development, and whatnot, anyhow creation, and again "I" am there.

"Infinite Unbounded – In the Ocean of Consciousness – We are like ripples – In the Sea of Bliss... "Heaven is Here – Right now in the moment of Eternity – Don't fool yourself – Reclaim your Bliss" (Heaven is Here, Dancing the Dream)

The holy fool prompts us to not make ourselves a fool. By the symbol of the zero – the 0 – he has no beginning and no end, cannot be measured and cannot be counted. It is and stays zero – no matter how often you take it or how often you put it down.

The words of wisdom Michael Jackson wrote down will only flow through a pen when all the layers are peeled to the core. What remains is nothing. This nothing is the zero, is THAT from which everything comes and THAT to which everything goes. From this nothing, never something came into being and in this nothing never something entered. Paradox? No, only for the mind. The mind is part of the layers. When the last layer is taken off, the mind is deleted. Then we have admission to the spheres beyond mind, to pure intuition, to awareness. Then we can see with the heart.

Brooke Shields cited the words of the little fox from the "Little Prince" at the memorial: "You only see good with the heart; the essential is invisible for the eyes," and added: "Michael has always only seen with the heart." In an open letter that I had sent in 2009 to some friends, I describe my experience:

"Most of you know some outer incidents of my agitated life – the mind-body-system 'Margott' abides by now more than 61 years on this planet. Today I want to give you a little glimpse into awareness. Early on I headed off to search for something (I don't know what), driven by a longing for homeland, sense and emotional security. As I could not find this in my family of origin I continued searching in my first marriage. When I did not find it there either I looked for it in books. I read everything that came amiss about world religions, esoterica (= secret teachings), ancient wisdom teachings etc. Then I searched outside in the world and went from Germany to Brazil. There the search continued in a second marriage and foundation of a family, which led me all the more through hells and heavens. The less I found the more intensive my search turned out to be. In the meantime, having returned to Germany, I searched with gurus and spiritual teachers, visited ashrams, workshops, trainings etc. Here and there I found inner peace through exercises, but it was not permanent. Until one day I realized that the problem was the searcher herself, the doer, the maker. As if an iceberg would think that it had to do something to melt. I realized that all my activities had only resulted in the fact that the searcher, the doer, the exercising person felt even more forceful and important. Finally I realized what the following verse of the Tao Te Ching meant:

> *'In the pursuit of learning, every day something is added.*
> *In the pursuit of the TAO, every day something is dropped.*
> *Less and less is done until you come to action without striving.*
> *When you follow this practice, nothing remains undone.*
> *All under heaven is done by letting things take their course.*
> *Nothing can be gained by interfering.'* (Tao Te Ching, verse 48)

The longing vanished; the search had reached an end. There is nothing to be done. 'I' takes place by devotion to the 'Source.' As the iceberg melts in the sun, so the doer, the I, melts, by integrating with, tuning into the 'Source.' There is no longer a fight, no resistance, no more desires, no goals. Is is as it is. It is done what has to be done. I look forward to being together with you the witness of this great spectacle, when the sun ('Source') deletes by its presence all illusionary forces of the 'I'."

Michael Jackson was doubtless the embodiment of unconditional, I-less, holy love. His mantra "I love you" was not an empty phrase – as malicious tongues claim - but an expression of his deep sensing: "I love you, I really do". These words have made thousands and thousands human hearts leap for joy at every concert, in every speech, in each encounter. They have at last and for some time lifted lonely souls onto the peaks of Olympus. And when then the masses chanted, "Michael we love you," he upped the ante with, "I love you more."

Fans report that they got to know the feeling of emotional security and being accepted, what they had searched for in vain with their parents, the first time they met Michael. Acceptance, and to transmit the feeling of being seen, is the basis for stability in life and the development of self-confidence. A complete stranger like Michael Jackson with only one sentence comforts sick souls and heals old wounds. A complete stranger like Michael gives people what they searched for in vain in their family and in their immediate environment.

For this reason the death of Michael Jackson touched me to the quick, more than would the death of a family member. As my real family I don't count the ones with the same physical genes, but the souls to whom I feel akin, not the bodies which were born from the same mother, but the souls which came from the same spirit. Michael's love, free of prejudice, and his childlike innocence have helped me not totally lose my faith in mankind. He has helped me to find my own childlike innocence again, which was literally beaten out of my body in my youth. It took years of painful work to discover it under solidified and gluey conditionings, truly a work of Sisyphus.

The mind which is separated from feelings cannot imagine how an adult man could embody childlike innocence. And exactly at that point the paranoia of media and moths begins – hordes of attorneys, profiteers, power-mad, greedy for money, parasites, exploiters and envious people took part in the campaign of destruction against Michael Jackson. What these little minds did not consider: He who is without ego is invincible.

Michael is invincible because "There never was a time, When I was not, Or you were not. There will never be a time, When we will cease to be." (Heaven is Here, Dancing the Dream)

Besides some rare awakened souls, children have easier access to the enlightened levels of being. The mind of children is not yet sucked with lovelessness and obsession to control everything. Their thinking is without malice. Of the total of forty six stories in "Dancing the Dream" eleven are dedicated to children: Magical Child Part 1, When Babies Smile, Children of the World, The Boy and the Pillow, Children, Innocence, On Children of the World, Wise Little Girl, A Child is a Song, Child of Innocence, and Magical Child Part 2. They all are a declaration of love for the children of this world – therefore the age is not important; there are children from zero to more than hundred, and represent an inexhaustible fund of inspiration, deep insights and wisdom. Whoever gets oneself into depth feels how it gets "under the skin" – a realm which is of no interest for tanners, because they are satisfied with flayed skin.

"It's easy to mistake being innocent for being simpleminded or naive.... To be innocent is to be 'out of it'. Yet there is a deep truth in innocence. A baby looks in his mother's eyes, and all he sees is love. As innocence fades away, more complicated things take its place.... Then life turns into a struggle." (Innocence, Dancing the Dream)

The endless conditionings are a part of these complicated things which were inseminated into our mind since birth and which are not conscious to most people. As they are jammed into unconsciousness it is not easy to discover and remove them. Even superglue can be dissolved easier than the demands that were repeated endlessly: you may, you should, you must, you may not. They become second nature in such a way that we accept them undoubtedly as truth without thinking for one second of bringing them into question. Some of the most frequent conditionings are, "I must do everything right," "I am not allowed to abandon my family," "I should not disappoint anyone," "I must be polite and nice," "What will the neighbors think about me?", "I have to carry it off well," "First work, then pleasure," "Money has to be hard-earned," "Money stinks," "Children don't understand this," "When adults are talking children have to keep their mouths shut," "Adults should not be disagreed with," "I am not allowed to say no," etc. etc. These are only some of the thousands of convictions which impress our soul deeply and which we follow unconsciously, unquestioning, day by day. If we don't we feel guilty.

Besides the individual there are also the collective conditionings and group rules. Michael Jackson was raised in a Christian environment as a Jehovah's witness and did not know Christmas or birthdays. He did not blow out birthday candles with sparkling eyes and breathe a birthday wish. There was no list of wishes, no Santa Claus, no Christ Child to bring presents. Instead little Michael had to do service, when he with a copy of "Awake" rang the bells of doors together with his mother, trying to evangelize the neighborhood.

Michael tells us in the "Home Videos" on YouTube how the Jackson brothers stood at the window during Christmas time admiring the Christmas lights outside with the longing wish to be a part of this celebration. This wish was only fulfilled for Michael at 35 years of age, when his friend Elizabeth Taylor insisted on transforming his home Neverland into a Christmas celebration in 1993. In the video we see both looking very normal in dressing gown and pajamas, Elizabeth knocking at Michael's bedroom door and calling him to the handing out of presents. Michael enters the room with the Christmas tree hesitantly and approaches it at the same time curiously and uneasily. Carefully he touches the tree decorated with lights – like a child that makes a new discovery. Michael's comment:

"I have met a lot of people in my life and very few are real real real friends, you can probably count them on one hand. And Elizabeth is one of the most loyal, loving, caring people that I know. She decided to transform Neverland into its first Christmas...."

Elizabeth adds: "It is 1993 and this will be Michael Jackson's very first Christmas. It has taken me five years of talking him into celebrating Christmas at Neverland because I understood that if you were a Jehovah's witness they don't celebrate Christmas. When he quit being a Jehovah's witness I said to Michael, 'I think Christmas is a wonderful way of celebrating love. It's a celebration of love.' And I can't see Christmas without Michael or Michael without Christmas."

Michael adds: "I had no idea she was planning this....At the same time it's exciting, I feel guilty too at the same time. I remember going in the bathroom and crying later, because I felt I had done something wrong."

Exactly such feelings arise if one proceeds to disbelieve the old conditionings and convictions and tries to free oneself of them. Only after having unmasked this feeling of disloyalty or betrayal as an illusion and having confidence in our deeper wisdom will the knot dissolve. These old impressions are so deeply dug into our innocent souls that attempts to free oneself of them can lead to a fierce fight with painful emotional confusion. A wild determination is necessary to not give up the fight too soon. Exactly that is the reason why the majority of people will not free themselves from these brainwashing until the end of their earthly life. Tied once, tied forever, regardless of whether the ties are of rusty iron or of golden chains. Chains are chains. In the mentioned film we can witness how Michael and Elizabeth have fun unwrapping their presents – four times there appears a "Super Soaker," and every time broad laughter.... Michael's comment: "I love Super Soakers so much,...It's a rule when you come to Neverland you are bound to get wet, either be thrown in the pool, or you have a water balloon fight or a Super Soaker fight." (Home video 2)

10. The new Children

Michael Jackson in private – as far as we are granted access – gives us an idea of what he means with magic and a glimpse of its meaning for psychic health. Magic has nothing to do with tricks but more with enchantment, is fragile, a structure woven from innocence, which should be handled like fine porcelain.

"When you get right down to it, survival means seeing things the way they really are and responding. It means being open. And that's what innocence is. It's simple and trusting like a child, not judgmental and committed to one narrow point of view....You miss the freshness and magic of the moment. Learn to be innocent again, and that freshness never fades." (Innocence, Dancing the Dream)

"Child of innocence... Come fly with me far and above - Over mountains in the land of love- "Child of innocence, messenger of joy
You've touched my heart without a ploy - My soul is ablaze with a flagrant fire - To change this world is my deepest desire." (Child of Innocence, Dancing the Dream)

For some time, so-called new children have been born in this world, also known as star children or indigos. These beings embody in a special way deep wisdom and innocence. Michael Jackson had an immense sensibility for the jewels among man and used to have friendly contact with them. The children, with whom he surrounded himself, were in some way special and radiated a freshness which inspired and energized others. Michael Jackson looked for their proximity to take from their huge creative reservoir, to realize his ideas and visions.

Michael is not the only artist who realized this secret of innocence. Reamon sing: "Sweet innocent child with your open eyes, you've seen us for who we really are. And I know that there'll be tomorrow. So that hope can have its glory day. And I wish that this world would embrace you from magic stars and mystery. My open heart … Why did you make it so hard? This life is so complicated, until you see it through the eyes of a child." (Eyes of a Child)

This song of praising the child Michael Jackson sang with every fiber of his being.

"With a child's heart nothing can ever get you down, With a child's heart you've got no reason to frown, Love is as welcome as a sunny day, No grown-up thoughts to lead your hearts astray." (With a Child's Heart)

Why don't artists, musicians, dancers and fools finally overtake, so that politicians, managers and public authorities can take their well-deserved vacation? Susanne Sejana-Kreth has done much research on these new children: "For some years new children have been born. These children are different than we were in the past. The energies on this planet have changed. We stand before an evolutionary leap, are stepping into a new age. In this new age there must be new people….The new children are the first humans of this new age….These children are known as 'Indigo children.' Indigo because an American therapist, who dealt with the life and aura colors of people, saw a new color in 1975, which was not found in humans before: She saw indigo blue in babies….They come to earth with full consciousness and knowing why they are here and how long they will stay on earth….They come to earth feeling that they are royal majesties and often behave like one. They have self-confidence and have the feeling that they are deserving being on earth….They have absolutely no fear, because they believe in themselves….They express things which we have thought about before but not dared to speak out. They see truths for which we have no antenna. They are, when allowed to unfold, loving and caring people, who are extremely smart and have an impressing charisma, with eyes that show how old is their soul. Indigo children look at us openly and knowingly, while 'normal' children in the same situation would look away….An examination of the DNA of the Indigos showed that is not the common one….Now this new DNA was also found in adults….Moreover it is reported that Indigos have master parts in every one of their twelve soul parts, while we only have three master parts in our twelfth soul part." (www.energie-der-sterne.de)

In these children Michael Jackson has found his master, not in ossified, solidified adults full of prejudice. In the presence of the children he was allowed to be a child himself, who had free access to the divine richness. Among these children who were not wedged in a corset of rules and conditionings and who didn't want anything from him besides love, Michael Jackson was only himself and not the King of Pop. And he gave them never-ending love. Thereby he was beyond measure. He was an endless giver. Ghata told me on 8th of July 2009: "I met him personally, we hugged each other...and instead that I could give something to him...I was blessed. There is no other way to put it."

The color of Indigo also dominates Michael's angel picture, especially at the two dolphins and in the huge crown. Michael set an example for us in limitlessness, which comes when you let go of the mind. Not in the sense of disregarding rules and laws, but as the chance to take advantage of the possibilities that are available in abundance without the filters of the conditionings, to unfold our potential and increase our talents. In relation to his creative work Michael overstepped the unconscious rules and brainwashing that were passed down by generations due to anxiety and fear and which obstructed our possibilities of expression and repressed our creativity. Inherited conditionings tie us to the past, to old experiences and remembrances, and prevent us from living the freedom of the moment, to be in the Here and Now, to experience the richness of the presence.

"That's what I love about being with kids. They notice everything. They aren't jaded. They get excited about things we've forgotten to get excited about anymore. They are so natural, too, so unself-conscious....They energize me – just being around them. They look at everything with such fresh eyes, such open minds. That's part of what makes kids so creative. They don't worry about the rules. The picture doesn't have to be in the center of the piece of paper. The sky doesn't have to be blue. They are accepting of people, too. The only demand they make is to be treated fairly – and to be loved." (Moonwalk, p. 274)

Let's rejoice that there actually is taking place a transformation on the planet, which is even accelerating. The flower buds are beginning to unfold their leaves and in due time everything is shining in full blossom. And by this shining other buds are encouraged to open up too. Michael Jackson was open for everything that entered his life. He was inspired by every culture and all peoples. He was very literate and knew the work and the mindset of all the masters. In his innocence he was indeed so open that he was abused by wicked minds which projected everything onto him that was born in their insane brains. Even today we are led astray by the persecutors of true humanness, and submit ourselves without complaining to the dictate of ogres. Sometimes we indeed meet someone who is different, and sense it, touched and moved: "He/she is so human."

Why are such encounters so rare? Why are only a few humans really human, that which a human is indeed due to its essence? Why does the description "human" not fit for all humans? Do we only say about some trees that they are tree-like and about others not? Are there swine-like swines and swine-unlike swines? Are there dancer-like dancers and dancer-unlike dancers? No, because a swine is a swine and a tree is a tree. But seemingly not every human is a human, otherwise we would not only call a few to be human. What about those who are not human? Why were they born as humans, when they are not what they are?

The solution for this enigma is in my opinion the solution of all problems of humanity. When all humans are human, then heaven will be Here, as Michael Jackson has described it. Until now unfortunately the inhuman are in charge on this planet and in their ignorance systematically sully everything that makes a human human. A world which puts everything upside down and itself stands on its head, as Michael Jackson expressed it on his cryptic expressive cover to the album "Dangerous." When these inhuman discovered humanness in Michael Jackson, they leapt on it like moths and used their whole inventive spirit to comment in a disdainful way from turgid to kitschy until artificial and untrue. A moth has no idea that its own stupidity, or better, inability to empathize, is creating the bad state of affairs.

Michael Jackson's staging of "Heal the World," "Earth Song," "I'll Be There" and "You Are Not Alone" will only reach those who have already been visited by humanness. The reason for the arrogant and assuming critic is the fear of light, for humanness is pure light. Light is the death of the moth. Moths are attracted by light, but when they get too near, they are burnt merciless in it. And exactly this will happen to human moths when they approximate the light that Michael embodied. When they want to stay moths, they have to stay long from the light. But who says that the dying of moths should be prevented? When the moth dies, humanness will arise from the ashes like the Phoenix. Actually there shines ever more light on the planet; the time of moths has gone. The time for butterflies is near. Butterflies are not interested in stuff, they fly freely in the invisible air and dance in roundel the dance of life together with all other butterflies. When we dance we hear the voice of the heart, and the voice of the mind silences and submits to the heart. Michael Jackson gave a speech on 21st March 2001, at the University of Oxford, which can inspire us:

"Human knowledge consists not only of libraries of parchment and ink – it is also comprised of the volumes of knowledge that are written on the human heart, chiseled on the human soul, and engraved on the human psyche. And friends, I have encountered so much in this relatively short life of mine that I still cannot believe that I am only 42. I often tell Shmuley that in soul years I'm sure that I'm at least 80 – and tonight I even walk like I'm 80 (alluding to the crutches he was using because of a broken foot). So please harken to my message, because what I have to tell you tonight can bring healing to humanity and healing to our planet. Through the grace of God I have been fortunate to have achieved many of my artistic and professional aspirations realized early in this lifetime. But these, friends, are accomplishments, and accomplishments alone are not who I am.... Tonight I come before you less as an icon of pop...and more as an icon of a generation, a generation that no longer knows what it means to be children....It is not just Hollywood child stars that have suffered from a non-existent childhood. Today it's a universal calamity, a global catastrophe....Today's children are constantly encouraged to grow up faster, as if this period known as childhood is a burdensome stage, to be endured and ushered through, as swiftly as possible. And on that subject, I am certainly one of the world's greatest experts."

11. Human Rights of Children

Then Michael points to the importance of unconditional love for a healthy development of mind and character. He calls those who have everything on the outside – richness, success, clothes and cars - who are "in" and nevertheless are feeling a painful void, the generation zero. And from this not only children suffer, but also adults who have no more access to their inner child.

"Love...is the human family's most precious legacy, its richest bequest, its golden inheritance. And it is a treasure that is handed down from one generation to another....I would therefore like to propose tonight that we install in every home a "**Children's Universal Bill of Rights**," the tenets of which are:

1. The right to be loved without having to earn it.
2. The right to be protected without having to deserve it.
3. The right to feel valuable, even if you came into the world with nothing.
4. The right to be listened to without having to be interesting.
5. The right to be read a bedtime story, without having to compete with the evening news.
6. The right to an education without having to dodge bullets at schools.

7. The right to be thought of as adorable – even if you have a face that only a mother could love."

Then Michael continues: "Friends, the foundation of all human knowledge, the beginning of human consciousness, must be that each and every one of us is an object of love. Before you know if you have red hair or brown, before you know if you are black or white, before you know of what religion you are a part, you have to know that you are loved." (Oxford 2001)

Besides the right to unconditional love, Michael has always stressed how important it is that every child gets the opportunity for an education. And so he was already a pioneer in this realm, before it came to the limelight by PISA studies. "An education opens a person's mind to the entire world, and there is nothing more important than to make sure everyone has the opportunity for an education. To want to learn, to have the capacity to learn and not to be able is a tragedy." (1 March 1988, UNCF)

I learned recently that Michael Jackson's tireless admonitions later bore fruit. In 2010, Bill Cosby, at the age of 73, put forth an initiative aimed at strengthening the rights of children and eliminating destructive habits. His book, "Food, Family and Fitness," explains the devastating effects of fast food, which are in his view only a symptom of the neglect of the rights of children (CNN, Larry King Show, 10 Feb. 2010). Michael calls at the end of his Exeter speech to immediately begin the change:

"We have to stop the prejudice, we have to stop the hating, we have to stop living in fear of our own neighbors. I would like all of you now to take the hand of the person to the left and to the right. Go ahead! Right now! I mean it! Right now! Go ahead! Don't be shy. Do it! Do it! Now tell the person - tell the person next to you that you care for them. Tell them that you care for them. Tell them that you love them. That is what makes the difference. Together - together we can make a change of the world. Together we can help to stop racism. Together we can help to stop prejudice. We can help the world live without fear. It's our only hope. Without hope we are lost." (YouTube: Michael Jackson speech about Freedom and Love. Don't forget his words! Rest in Peace Michael)

The call to end hatred, prejudice and fear must not go unheard. Michael does not call to fight against something on the outside, but the abandonment of the lower emotions to ourselves. This is Michael's alarm clock. It is not an empty shell or just lip service, but he was always a role model when it came to becoming active and caring. In an interview with "Ebony," he said in 1988: "I feel very fortunate to be blessed with recognition for my efforts. This recognition also brings with it responsibility to one's admirers throughout the world. Performers should always serve as role models who set examples for young people."

Before the BAD Tour in 1989 Michael was visited at home by a deathly ill young boy and his parents. Michael told him that he would come to his city three months later for the opening of his tour and that he wished the boy to attend his show. He gave him a jacket that he had worn in a video, whereby the eyes of the boys started shining: "You want to give it to me?" "Yeah, but you have to promise me that you will wear it to the show," was his answer. Moreover he got the legendary glove which Michael usually does not give away.

The boy was on cloud nine. And really heaven was already near because when Michael came to his city he just had died and been buried with the jacket and the glove. "God knows I know, he tried his best to hold on. But at least when he died he knew that he was loved, not only by his parents, but even by me, a near stranger, I also loved him. And with all that love he knew that he didn't come into this world alone, and he certainly didn't leave it alone." (At this point I have to pause for some minutes until my tears are dried).

Then I ask myself why did humanity – besides some few friends and fans – not return the love that he gave us so generously? Why did one of the purest and greatest souls of this world have to leave this world with the feeling of being alone and not understood? Michael speaks thereto in his Oxford speech: "If you enter this world knowing you are loved and you leave this world knowing the same, then everything that happens in between can be dealt with."

He continues to speak about the neglect of children, about their anger and desperation in America and Great Britain, of drug addiction and violence and the childlike cry for help to finally be seen. Indeed the failure lies on both sides.

"I have discovered that getting parents to re-dedicate themselves to their children is only half of the story. The other side is preparing the children to re-accept their parents....I'm calling upon all the world's children... to forgive our parents, if we felt neglected. Forgive them and teach them how to love again....I pray that my children will give me the benefit of the doubt. That they will say to themselves, 'Our daddy did the best he could, given the unique circumstances that he faced. He may not have been perfect, but he was a warm and decent man, who tried to give us all the love in the world.'" (Oxford)

At least at the memorial we know from Michael's daughter Paris, who was 11 years old at the time, that Michael's humble wish was surpassed in all respects. In front of millions of people before the screens she confessed: "I just want to say, ever since I was born, Daddy has been the best father you could ever imagine, and I just want to say, I love him so much." (Memorial 7th of July 2009)

That there is no need for Michael to grieve over his fatherhood from heaven, millions of people could realize impressively at the 52nd Grammy Awards in January of 2010, when his three wonderful children together with their three cousins went on stage and Michael's eldest children – Prince Michael I and Paris – proclaimed before the whole world how much they loved and missed their daddy. Everyone who was ever present when Michael was together with his children confirmed the close relationship between them and the loving contact that Michael used to have with his children. At that awards ceremony Michael got a Grammy, this time for his life's work.

In total Michael won 18 Grammys during his lifetime, the first in the year 1971, the last in 1995. On 31st of January 2010 he was posthumously awarded his 19th, which was received by his children. In addition Michael has reaped four Black Gold Awards, four American Video Awards, three MTV Awards and the People's Choice Award. But more than awards, the welfare of children was to Michael near and dear. His Oxford speech ends with a vision:

"Shmuley once mentioned to me an ancient biblical prophecy which says that a new world and a new time would come, when 'the hearts of the parents would be restored through the hearts of their children.' My friends, we are that world, we are those children. Mahatma Gandhi said: 'The weak can never forgive. Forgiveness is the attribute of the strong.'...] conclude my remarks with faith, with joy and excitement. From this day forward let a new song be heard. Let that new song be the sound of children laughing. Let that new song be the sound of children playing. Let that new song be the sound of children singing. And let that new song be the sound of parents listening. - Together let us create the symphony of hearts, marveling at the miracle of our children and basking in the beauty of love....God bless you and I love you."

How long yet will people waste their time finding differences between them and fighting themselves to be right? Why are they more interested in the differences instead of the similarities? What is so fascinating about being right and being proven right? Even in court it is not sure that your demand for justice will be fulfilled; instead you are judged. That can also be a blatant injustice, as judges in case of doubt depend on experts. But who is the one who verifies if the experts are really experts? Experts also are trapped in their conditioning cocoon and often not able - even having the best intention - to look deeper to find out the truth. Many experts too have a blind eye of the heart. Especially when dealing with psychopaths, trained clinical eyes are required together with a great ability of distinction - viveka in Sanskrit - to realize who is hidden behind the mask of the charmer. Viewed superficially, such people radiate an unbelievable charm, which can easily be mistaken as charisma at first look. When in such a situation, someone without distrust, totally innocent like Michael, meets someone like Martin Bashir, he is an easy victim of smooth-talking words and opens his soul to a hypocrite.

Michael Jackson was treated unjustly all his life, not only by dubious figures, but often by well-meaning contemporaries. In our society attributes like pureness and innocence are suspect, as they serve more simply as projection areas for egocentric, sanctimonious, heartless minds. When these minds realize that they can make money with their news, they take up the course of everything that brings money. Naturally the truth then falls by the wayside. It is interesting to observe how many of the media who taunted and derided Michael Jackson during lifetime now make money with quotes and false hymns of praise and quickly assembled tributes. In 2005 I myself had a dispute with the private music radio station Antenne Bayern, because they refused to play Michael Jackson songs during the trial. To my complaint that this equaled a prejudgment and that in Germany the presumption of innocence is valid until the contrary is proven, I received the answer that the radio station has to take into account their listeners and that they did not want to be confronted with angry protest from their audience. A radio station without backbone, slave of their audience, without civil courage. The reason? Fear of losing cohorts of stupid sheep? The competitive radio station Bayern 3 did not submit to public pressure and continued to play Michael's songs even during the trial. Now after Michael's leaving, many stations and media have again a halo, or better, a hypocritical halo. Why is there nobody with the courage to bring documentation about their own dubious coverage in the past and review their own omissions? Why is there nobody to admit that he missed the truth during Michael's lifetime?

At least one of the 2400 media representatives of the whole world, who daily stayed out in 2005 in front of the court in Santa Maria for five months to report about Michael's trial, has shown this courage. Aphrodite Jones, an American journalist and author of crime novels, was at the time responsible for the trial news on the TV channel Fox News. After the judgment on 15th of June 2005 she came courageously and unexpectedly to realize that her reports – and that of all 2400 colleagues – during the whole time had totally missed the truth. A collective trance had had its grip on the whole press. In chapter "Innocent" of her book, the shameful outing of the representatives of the moths is described. In reports and documentation, facts, views and opinions are rarely clearly distinguished. When I lift my arm only I can know what this means. It can be a greeting, I may be winding up to beat someone or express my joy or do exercises, etc. An observer can only see the lifting of the arm and projects his own meaning to it and takes this for the truth. But this is not necessarily identical with my intention. An accurate assessment is more than likely a coincidence. Ignorance about the motives of actions is the reason for misunderstandings and the impossibility to ever clear them out. As long as we insist that only one of two can be right and that the second is in the wrong the world will remain torn.

Who is right in the following example? The one who says: "God is nowhere!" or the one who says: "God is now here!"? In reality both are right: "God is nowhere" is right, because there is no place where he is. And "God is now here" is also right, because God is in all places. But as people are not able to imagine that both sides can be right at the same time, enemies and wars are created. Whoever looks through the emptiness of being right may one day follow the hope and vision of Carl Sandburg: "Sometime they will give a war and nobody will come." (The People, 1936, Wikiquote)

Perhaps we will still experience this day, because the number of warriors who make war is slowly diminishing worldwide, while the number of "warriors of light" ("Krieger des Lichts", song from Silbermond) is increasing. Also the number of people who are dancing life and are tired of strife is increasing. On 8th of July 2009 at 15:21 o' clock on the "Sergels

Torg" place in the center of Stockholm a flashmob took place, which was organized by the Swedish street-dance troupe "Bounce" (www.bounce.nu): "A Tribute to Michael Jackson"! A flashmob is a performance in form of a flash, a relatively new form of art, where a larger group of people appears suddenly at a public place, starts an action and disappears after some minutes as if nothing had happened. That day, 300 dancers met, rehearsed for an hour and then performed as an ensemble to the sounds of "Beat It" a dance to honor Michael Jackson. The video of four minutes (with more than 5,122,600 clicks in June 2010) speaks for itself. Thousands of Swedish people were admiring this breathtaking performance. The "Boston Blade" comments two days later, "Either times are changing or Michael Jackson really holds influence on Swedes, because I wouldn't have believed you could get people to dance in central Stockholm. Definitely not as an ensemble. And yet, the proof is unmistakable in this....A truly amazing performance....Back to my surprise. Swedes aren't public, collective dancers. They don't get up and volunteer to do flash mobs....They're rather low-key, shy and reserved people....I now believe anything is possible." (www.thelocal.se)

"All is possible" is the mantra of Michael Jackson and "Yes we can" is the mantra of Barack Obama. And both mantras combined result in "Change." These mantras in unison unfold a force that can move mountains. I get the proof day by day on my table. Here follows a small selection of the feedback of people who got to read this manuscript before publication:

"I was never a direct fan....I liked his music, but until recently I never thought much about him. But what this man evokes in me in the moment is frightening." (Bettina, 18 July 2009)

"There are so many parts of the book which evoke an AHA-reaction...I can only stress again and again how important it is that a TRUE report about Michael is published instead of this disrespectful claptrap: The world needs YOUR BOOK!" (Antje, 18 July 2009)

"Finally I can find a confirmation of my thoughts and feelings in my encounter with Michael Jackson, which were never related to a 'shimmering star.'...Finally someone talks about the love which blossomed in him and which his heart tried to expand." (Stephanie, 18 July 2009)

"Michael Jackson was the most known and at the same time most misjudged person on earth. His love to humanity was impressing and touches me deeply. I believe that he was a great soul." (Christine, 17 July 2009)

"The book speaks out of my soul." (Angelika, 16 July 2009)

"The vision (of a snake of light) lives in the hearts of the awakened ones in the whole world. In me it arose shortly after a concert of the superlatives of Michael Jackson in Hamburg in relation to the energy of love. The vision, that we all could really be connected in love and light." (Hayron)

"I was not a real Michael Jackson fan. I liked his music and also visited the HIStory concert. But what I am feeling now is not explainable with the normal mind. From the first day of his death I fell in deep sadness when I saw his pictures on TV and looked into his eyes. Something touched my soul so deeply that I started to search....Your book ("Das Mysterium von Michael Jackson und Sathya Sai Baba") has now helped me in my search to get closer to the man Michael Jackson." (Karin, 13 July 2009)

"I am sure some people have heard God's song in his. But the mass of humanity does not. G. also says this, but I (and I am now a fan for 22 years) believe the number is now increasing every single day! What I actually see in the internet and also in private circles can nearly not be expressed in words. I am sure that momentarily something is happening on earth that is accelerating by the death of this Jesus-like energy which Michael embodied for a long time." (Antje 11 July 2009)

"The being of Michael Jackson has peeled out of the usual description and there appeared a shining and glance....You succeeded at something unbelievable with your powerful words." (Aldegunde, 9 July 2009)

"His leaving of the body is like a new order of creation. For me he is the most misunderstood being on this planet...and indeed many have realized his LIGHT." (Gabriela, 9 July 2009)

"You have a very close connection to Baba and Michael...there are certainly not many people on earth who knew for a long time, how 'THEY' are." (Heike, 8 July 2009)

"The music of Michael Jackson shaped my childhood. When it calmed down around him,...I was distracted from him. Only after the 25th of June 2009 the news hit my heart directly. I cried endlessly and started doing research....His books, interviews and speeches, his song lyrics, his charity gave a deep insight into his spirituality. His presence is still here. I am sure I am not the only one who is perceiving him." (Angie, 8 October 2009)

"I read the 'Mysterium' with great enthusiasm and goose bumps and discovered the new title full of joy. Such viewpoints are rarely published and even in German. My heartfelt thanks for your courage." (Karin, 16 August 2010)

"I have read your book, "Mysterium" and want to compliment you. I have never been fascinated by a book so lastingly. You inspired me to reflect more." (Sabine, 13 August 2010)

"I am very glad that there are people like you, who dedicate their talent, their wisdom and knowing to make it possible for others to understand Michael and to see his message. And I wish that Michael's children could read your books, perhaps later. I believe they would be very happy that there are people who saw and understood their father in such a way." (Petra, 3 August 2010)

"Thanks to your book I started to really understand Michael's messages, respectively found explanations for many things. I am anxious to read your new book." (Renate, 25 July 2010)

I thank the source, which taught me to "step aside" and to share its richness.

In a press release dated 26th of June 2009 from the Bollywood Group of Companies, board member Kamal Dandona stated: "I am absolutely devastated at this heartbreaking and totally shocking news of the tragic demise of Michael Jackson. He attended our very first Bollywood Awards and so graciously accepted our request to not only attend but even to wear an Indian Kurta designed by Manish Malhotra especially for the occasion. When I later met him and his children for dinner, my feelings were reinforced that this was a good man, who was incredibly misunderstood by the public....Michael Jackson's unsurpassed creativity and immensely loved music, brought happiness to every corner of the world....It was a true privilege and honor for me to have met him and known him as one of the most talented superstars in the history of music. We shall all miss him greatly." (www.mahiram.com)

Michael Jackson gave thanks for the Humanitarian Award, which he then received, under endless applause with the words:

"Thank you very much. Thank you very much for this honor you have awarded me tonight. I've always believed that the real measure of a celebrity's success was not just how famous he becomes, but what he does with that fame and fortune....The attention and fortune showered on an individual celebrity is oftentimes immensely disproportionate to his or her achievements. Today a person can literally become a celebrity overnight throughout the entire world, and that kind of attention can be difficult for an individual to handle. But I have also learned that such fame can also be an enormously effective medium to focus attention and mobilize resources for a worthy cause. I have been blessed with so much and have an opportunity to do what few others can. But I believe it is more than just an opportunity, but a duty. I feel to reap and enjoy the fruits of my talents for myself would be selfish, irresponsible and unconscionable. In these days of such abundance and advancement in what we can do, it pains me to think that we do so little for our children. In some ways I feel undeserving to receive an award for doing something that is my duty. I accept this award as a gesture of encouragement from the people of India and a commission to do more for mankind. I love you very much. Mahatma Gandhi knew how important bringing the world's attention was to gaining freedom for India without using any weapons. In some ways he was the first person to truly understand the importance and power of the public. He has always been an inspiration to me and it gives me even greater joy and pride to be recognized by his people....We have the same mission to bring world peace...." (YouTube: Tribute to Michael Jackson – Bollywood Award Show, 1999).

12. Judgment - Ur-Teil

The question of the "Boston Blade," of whether times have changed or if Michael Jackson has influence on the Swedish, is perhaps not a matter of "either/or," but a matter of "as well as." It is inarguable that countless people have had experiences and realizations since Michael's earthly form has been gone whereby they were shaken to the core and which are rattling at their beloved bastions. Whoever refuses thereby to trust the accelerating flow of life and tries to control the direction of the boat will suffer, experience crisis of meaning, be at times completely at a loss, fall into a deep hole and feel weak and empty. Control freaks and fanatics of security will not only be washed in the washer, but certainly also spin-dried. What's the reason for "me" to maintain the control? Because "I" fancy to know where the journey goes. Our educational system emphasizes the pure imagination too much. It sees some journeys as valid and other journeys as harmful, even all journeys leading to Rome. We are living in an era where old supposed truths will reveal themselves as illusion, where we get more and more conscious that our image of the world thus far is constructed on sand. Master M reveals the reasons for this development to us. "The 'I' appears on the stage of the big world theatre, but neither the world theatre nor the actors who are playing their roles on the stage are real." (Mantese, 2008, p. 121)

In the abysses of time where brute force and lovelessness reign, the instruments of force for the "I" are forged. The sharpest instrument is judgment. It dissects the whole, dissects the "Ur" (in German Ur-teil = dissect the Ur). It separates the common, creates opposites. It manipulates, oppresses, blackmails. It creates the past, present and future, where in reality is only the Now. Judgment creates superiority and inferiority, where there is only equality. It cuts the totality, which you are in reality, in endless particles, until you miss the forest for the trees, and don't know anymore who "I" am – until the seer is discovered. "Inside your heart sits a Seer." (Magical Child Part 1, Dancing the Dream)

This seer is the vista, he is able to lift the veil, disillude the illusion, dis-illude. Despite the contrary impressions of the physical senses, the seer is able to recognize with his non-physical senses that the fata morgana is a mirage and that nothing that we see with our physical eyes exists.

"As long as love is in my heart, it's everywhere." (Love, Dancing the Dream)

"Look into your hearts. What do you see? Not you and I, but only We." (I You We, Dancing the Dream) "If we could for one moment BE - In an instant we would see - A world where no one has suffered or toiled." (Quantum Leap, Dancing the Dream)

Michael speaks here about the one who I really am, about the realization of the absolute. About that which creates multiplicity and enables all forms and names, but by itself is not the multiplicity and is untouched by its creations.

Pain and suffering only exist on the level of manifestation. They are created by the mental activity of the "I." Without thoughts there are no emotions. Emotions are the result of the process of thinking. Let's take an example: We are sitting in a café and see how at the table beside ours someone is tapping on the table with his fingers. What do you see? Someone who is nervous? Someone who is insecure? Someone who is tense? Someone who taps the rhythm of a song that he hears inside? Someone who is training for the timing of a song? Someone who tries to discover what material the table is made of? Someone who makes uncontrolled finger movements because of a motor handicap?

Your answer will be that which you project on the situation, and that means that it is only valid in your world. It says nothing about the world of the one who is tapping and whom you are only observing. The other one is only the mirror, the mirror of what you created by your mental activity. When you transcend this level of projection, the doors to Being will open themselves, where the whole multiplicity of forms and names has no more importance. Where only beauty, wonder and magic prevail. As they reveal themselves in nature, when we come directly in touch with them.

"We would see...a world...Of pristine beauty never soiled, Of sparkling waters, singing skies, Of hills and valleys where no one dies...you still have promises to keep, Just take that plunge, take that leap." (Quantum Leap, Dancing the Dream)

Whoever does not understand the change of levels can easily get the impression that Michael contradicts himself permanently or is talking paradoxically. How can he complain about the suffering of the world and at the same time talk about a world where there is no more suffering? These statements describe different levels of consciousness with an ability of discrimination - in Sanscrit viveka – for the frequencies of vibration for each level.

Our perceptions and statements change depending on what layer of the onion we are focusing on. The outer layer is brown, the following layers are white and when all layers are peeled off, nothing remains. Nothing is not nothing, but being, pure consciousness, stillness. This totality is called sat, cit, ananda – being, consciousness, bliss in Sanscrit. On the level of being there is neither subject nor object nor that which creates subject or object. When thus there is nobody, no body, then there cannot be suffering either. Without subject there is no object, because the one is necessarily the condition of the other.

Michael knew this door of bliss and passed through it. Few people have looked behind this door and therefore one is quite alone there, all one. Alone anyway when it is about using words to describe the space beyond the door.

"In your beauty I've known the how - Of timeless bliss, this moment of now." (Planet Earth, Dancing the Dream)

Michael calls the part within us with access to this space, "magical child."

"His invincible armor was a shield of bliss." (Magical Child part 1, Dancing the Dream)

"In the bliss we're floating awhile." (When Babies Smile, Dancing the Dream)

"We'll do it with song and dance and innocent bliss." (Children of the World, Dancing the Dream)

"In this bliss we cannot feel fear or dread." (Heal the World, Dancing the Dream)

"I was born to never die, To live in bliss, to never cry." (Ecstasy, Dancing the Dream)

While there are no tears and no suffering in the being, the stay in the physical body ties us to massive dark forces of the I, which suck us like massive powers of nature in the dimension of suffering. Only by permanent awareness do we avoid being lost in the suck and vortex. In the beginning of the journey of awakening we are successful only at times. That means that also with an awakened consciousness we may be lost in the "dark night of the soul" until the light at the end of the tunnel appears again. In these times there can be present both, pain and suffering and peace and bliss.

"From bliss I came - In Bliss I am sustained - To Bliss I return." (Are You Listening? Dancing the Dream)

"We are like ripples in the Sea of Bliss,...Don't fool yourself, reclaim your Bliss." (Heaven is Here, Dancing the Dream)

"Your angel is a speck of light perched at the very center of your heart. It is smaller than an atom, but just wait. Once you get close to it, your angel will expand. The closer you come, the more it will grow, until finally, in a burst of light, you will see your angel in its true shape, and at that very instant, you will also see yourself." (Angel of Light, Dancing the Dream)

Awakening means to realize the Self and to unmask the self as an illusion. As this Self was given different names in various cultures, religions and spiritual traditions, many people have difficulties in understanding, because they believe that different names indicate different things. That's a trap which we easily step in. A woman named Mary may be called Mrs. XY, Miss AZ, daughter, mother, child, aunt, niece, grandchild, great-grandchild, grandmother, wife, lover, friend, etc. And yet it is always the same person who reacts to each name. Also when the example is a little bit flawed it nonetheless makes clear that the countless names of the absolute all indicate the same. For the awakened consciousness, the different names are like traffic signs which show us the way, but which are not the way itself.

One who enters the space of stillness and the land of bliss is not **indifferent**, as at times it seems from the outside, but for him all is **without difference, equally valid** (wordplay in German: gleichgültig = indifferent; gleich gültig = equally valid). He acts in loving service when acting arises from the ocean and stays inactive as long as there is no impulse arising. Even the doer has died, as everything that has to be done is done in not doing. There is nobody who says that something should be done, but doing happens. In the moment when the doer appears, there also appear hubris, intervention and boastfulness. In the moment where there is only doing, everything happens from the wholeness of joy, from inspiration – that means led by spirit - and committed to the Self.

There is no helper and nobody who needs help, but only help itself. There is no giver and no receiver, but only giving. There are no opposites, but only different views due to different angles of seeing the One. One who describes the front side of a medal is not more or less right than the one who describes the back side. Both are right, each one in his way and at the same time. The all-knower is in denial of the fact that he describes the same medal as his supposed contemporary. In reality it is not even clear who sees the front side and who sees the back side, everything only a question of the angle of seeing. All these are arbitrary descriptions. When awareness happens, every "either/or" turns to an "as well as." Then I am black and white, good and bad, honest and a liar, then I am holy and a whore, victim and offender. In the Nag Hammadi, scriptures that remind us not to get stuck in duality, it is written:

"I am the first and the last.
I am the honored and the defamed.
I am the whore and the saint.

I am wife and virgin.
I am the knowing and the ignorance.
I am the shame and the impudence.
I am shameless, I am shamefaced.
I am the power and I am the fear.
I am the war and I am the peace.
Become aware of me.
I am the humiliated and enormous powerful one." (Joan Borysenko, 1995)

And in the apocryphal gospel of John, "Dancing Song of Christ", we find the following lines:

"I want to be saved and I want to save. Amen.
I want to be hurt and I want to hurt. Amen.
I want to eat and I want to be eaten. Amen.
He who does not dance at that does not know what it is about. Amen."

And: "The grace dances. The purpose of all things can dance. He who doesn't dance does not know what happens." (Thanks to Rena)

Christ dances, Osho dances, Krishna dances, Shiva dances, Michael Jackson dances. I dance. When do you dance too?

As long as people deny their dark side and only believe in their sun side, they cement and create the problems of the world. In the moment I believe that I have to defend myself I create the attack. Before this thought appears in consciousness there cannot be an attack and no aggressor. And equally valid is that in the moment I attack the defense is created. When I am against something I enforce exactly that what I am against.

This knowing is the basis of the Asian martial arts and therefore they are much more effective than many western fighting forms with brachial force. Everyone can try out this for themselves first hand. When someone approaches you and tries to push you back then you will immediately put up resistance and push him back yourself. On a large scale such a situation results in war. When you, on the other hand, follow the pressure smoothly when someone tries to push you back, then his impulse gets lost in the void. Only through resistance can an impulse against something increase in force and power. When it is not energized and there is no resistance, it will peter out and has no chance to survive.

As long as we have a minister of defense there will be attack. Due to ignorance about the energetic causes of manifestation, we unconsciously create war and then unconsciously hold it alive. The only energy that does not give birth to its opposite is pure unconditional love. True love never interferes, as Michael describes in "Two Birds." It knows no difference and no separation. The sun shines on everything and all equally. It does not separate out right from wrong, just from unjust, or good from bad. It warms up everything and all – without difference. The sun is equally valid, disinterested in whether its light shines on a saint or a criminal. As well, the screen doesn't mind if the most touching romance is projected on it or the wildest butchering. The screen remains untouched by the content of the spectacle and drama. It does not know anything about the pain and joy of the actors.

That which you really are is this screen. The actors, the film and the drama are only a passing phenomenon. But that which you really are remains unchanged and untouched by the film and the story. Man lives in the illusion of being the actor and the role and to really experience the drama. Thus he identifies himself in his ignorance with the spectacle. By this identification, all suffering and sorrow of the world is created.

Why does man not reflect about this, not lift the curtain and not get to the bottom of the things with which he is confronted day by day? Is a life without problems too dull for many, so that they don't know what else to talk about, when they awake in the morning in bliss without a reason? What would then be the issue at the regular's table or gossiping at the bakery round the corner? Man needs action, and in having problems there is more action than in being content in stillness. Man is searching for the kick of adrenaline, is fixated on the senses and fascinated by everything that arouses the senses and is exciting.

The screen does not experience highs and lows. The screen does not complain or extol. As is said in medical reports: "The patient is complaining about an ache in the back or about a stomachache." Why am I complaining or lamenting when I give the doctor the information that I have an aching back? By such phrasing we only are cementing the complaining and lamenting in the world. I never complained to a doctor; I only tell him what the matter is and where I have pain. People are totally insensitive to what monsters they are creating day by day with their use of words and language, which is only an expression of our way of thinking – a hodgepodge of horror products. And when these products then inhabit our universe we start to fight against the not-wished-for products, and thereby empower them even more. If that is not insane, then what else shall be insanity? I produce something I don't like and then do everything to get rid of the unloved product, I unconsciously energize it all the more.

Humanity lives in complete ignorance of what it really does and has no idea about its absurd behavior. By the realization of the screen the way through heaven and hells ends. **Then everything is as it is.** Period. The screen knows no attribute. IT IS.

13. The Searcher

Man pretends to search for bliss and peace or God. But instead of really being interested in finding, he actually prefers the search itself. He fears nothing more than the end of search, because thus the searcher also will end. Without a searcher there is no search, without search there is no searcher. The Indian mystic Tagore makes clear this unwritten law in a story:

"A man is searching for God his life long, he is searching for him everywhere, in every corner of the world. Finally he arrives at a long stairway and goes upstairs. Arriving at the top he is standing in front of a big gate where it is written: 'Here lives God.' Lifting his arm and wanting to knock at the door, he realizes in one moment: When this gate opens and he enters, everything has ended, his search, his philosophical ideas, his longing, simply everything. After realizing this he quickly takes his shoes under his arms and goes downstairs noiselessly and is now searching for God more intensely. But now he knows that he may search everywhere and everything, but this gate has to be avoided by all means, lest everything will be ended."
(Mantese, Lichtfokus 11, p.33)

Now is the time to end the search. The alarm clocks are ringing so loudly that they are even heard with earplugs. The time has come. Now. On 24th of July 2009 I sent the first chapters of this book to some people who happened to be in my mail address book. Three hours later I realized that I had forgotten the attachment. This happens to me at times, and being well organized and structured, even now I have not succeeded in overcoming it. To a friend I wrote after that: "Without attachment one lives better." This morning her answer came: "Now it's getting comical, I wrote to my sister right now in relation to your answer, 'without attachment one lives better,' because I found it so BEAUTIFULLY ambiguous. Now I found your second mail with the attachment, even from the time it was sent before....so the universe wants to say I should clearly receive the broad hint again without knick-knack (segmenting) and without distraction."

Did you too already perceive that your attachment makes your life more difficult? Or, better stated, that you have attached yourself to many things? With attachments and adherents it is difficult to navigate; at times the adherents swing out or go into a tailspin, and at times they get so heavy that our forces are lacking. You have to pull the attachment, it is not able to move itself under its own steam. Perhaps it does not even want to go where you do. And especially the attachment is tied to you and you to the attachment. Let go of the attachment and the adherents, free them and yourself. Only then can you care for your own advancement and the attachment is free to care for itself. Only thus you can empower yourself, only thus you can **respond** to life instead to the attachment, you can take **responsibility.**

I repeat myself because every day I am newly stunned by the immense powers that were freed by Michael's death. Karin wrote to me: "I have (like many others too) felt that Michael Jackson was special, something the soul loves! Nevertheless until now I did not grant myself to study the King of Pop. With the time of his death I woke up and bought all CDs and the autobiography to find out now what exactly it is that I have always loved somehow in relation to him."

A direct view into Michael's soul is given in his book, "Dancing the Dream." I am utterly amazed when reading in a Michael Jackson forum from a fan: "This book is not so important, because it contains no facts." Facts relate to form and skin, but to get the message you have to dive deep. Many fans are unfortunately shallow swimmers and splash about in the shallow banks. Michael Jackson himself referred to "Dancing the Dream" as more autobiographical than his autobiography "Moonwalk." Michael Jackson fans who followed him for years everywhere and did not get tired of bathing in his light and his aura are still struggling to perceive the "Great Soul" and to recognize, as the second step, that they themselves are this Great Soul too. They are fascinated by the shimmering bird, which "catches the light on its silver feathers" and don't hear His song in his song, exactly as Michael Jackson has prophesied. "Oh, that is a day I hunger for!" (Two Birds, Dancing the Dream)

Why is it so hard to hear God's song in Michael's songs? The fans adore the form of Michael Jackson as an idol, and they sap his energy. They took from him who was an eternal giver until in the end he was totally dead on his feet. Also when they returned a little bit to him, most of them escaped his essence by the skin of their teeth. Michael Jackson was surrounded his life long by vampires who sucked his blood.

"Being mobbed by near hysterical girls was one of the most terrifying experiences for me in those days. I mean, it was *rough*....it *hurts* to be mobbed. You feel as if you're going to suffocate or be dismembered." (Moonwalk, p. 90-91)

The initiative of some fans – thanks to Alex, of "Fanship turns to Friendship," has only found a little echo in the fan community. As friend one should be a giver, and there the phase of hunter and collector ends. As friend one no longer follows an idol but an ideal. "Slowly we are reaching the realization that true energy is coming from a universal source. There is no need at all to get it from other persons." (Redfield, 1995, p. 106)

The tendency of people to tap the energy of others, Michael Jackson has named and shamed in a genius way in his masterpiece, "Thriller." Lyrics and music are from Rod Temperton, who was the former keyboardist of the pop group, "Heatwave," to which the formerly cited Mario Mantese belonged. Thriller was originally called "Starlight." The short film was mentioned in 2006 in the Guinness Book of World Records as the most successful music video of all times – and still today this is valid.

"This is the end of your life, they're out to get you. There's demons closing in on every side. They will possess you....Creatures crawl in search of blood.... The foulest stench is in the air, the funk of forty thousand years....for no mere mortal can resist the evil of the thriller." (Thriller)

The song describes on the one hand how Michael Jackson lived as a chased one, sucked one and obsessed one. On the other hand it paints a picture and is a genius description of the state of the world and humanity. In 1968 we at times boasted loudly, "Behind their robes only the fustiness of a thousand years,..." and had the vision to finally free ourselves from this fustiness. We are always the last member in the chain of humans, which reaches back forty thousand years and more. The only chance to release from the chain and to get rid of the attachment starts with awakening from the state of dreaming. As long as we believe in the existence of the past we have to pull it behind us. Past is only that which I remember, nothing more. It has no existence of its own, only in my mind. The world is what I think and believe in. There is no world without mind. When thoughts end, only Here and Now remains, pure Being, the totality. THAT from which is created everything and THAT in which everything immerses. "And I keep on dancing and dancing...and dancing until there is only...the dance." From the dance comes the dancer and the dancer immerses in the dance. Then there remains no trace of the dancer and no marks.

"He had lived in the desert all his life, but for me it was all new. 'See that footprint in the sand?' he asked....I looked as close as I could. 'No, I don't see anything.' 'That's just the point.' He laughed. 'Where you can't see a print, that's where the Ancient Ones walked.'...'Where nothing is missing, that's where the Ancient Ones harvested the most.'" (Mark of the Ancients, Dancing the Dream)

In the same way wise men and mystics have expressed it for ages as Laotse: "A good walker leaves no marks," because he walks on earth without being a walker. He comes to the world as a temporary phenomenon in consciousness. "Marks point out towards living beings. But the one who reads the marks as well as the marks themselves and all living beings that left the marks behind only exist as phenomena in the garden of God, because God does not leave marks and he never entered the garden." (Mantese, 2009, p. 45)

During the whole "time" nothing has happened besides that the wave arose and again immersed in the ocean. "We are like ripples in the Sea of Bliss." (Heaven is Here, Dancing the Dream)

What's the reason that this book is crawling with repetitions? Indeed not for the reason that Ernst Horst assumes in the critique of my first book, "Das Mysterium von Michael Jackson und Sathya Sai Baba": "As missionary writings like this are addressed to simple minds a certain redundancy makes sense for sure." (FAZ, 13th of June 2000) Redundancy is indeed not so much for simple minds, but more important as Jesus already mentioned for the intellectual and so-called knowing ones. One who knows much has much more trouble in leaving his corset of mind than someone who is comparably green. A fuss that is replete with knowledge can only be filled after it is emptied. A fuss only filled a little bit can reach the goal faster. The ties of conditioning in which we are trapped for centuries don't break loose when we pluck them a little bit. The breaking loose of a gordic knot needs more attention and effort. "Repetition is the key to masterhood." (Kenyon, p. 120)

The knowledge about the absolute is sinking in as a drop on a hot stone in the dense layers of matter, only very slowly, and sublimes the materiality only peux à peux. It is a journey from the gross to the subtle, from the dense to the fluffy, from flesh over mind to spirit. Spirit is everywhere and does not leave marks. Nevertheless everything is accomplished by spirit. The spirit that Michael embodied already worked wonders during his lifetime, but since he is no longer embodied the whole potential can unfold. His physical death is acting as a break in a dam, where the waters are not only overflowing but are flooding the whole environment.

And why should a book about awakening not be directed to simple minds? Simple minds are per se not so stodged as the minds of the so-called literates, who, as the name already says, pride themselves in their collected pseudo-knowledge (wordplay in German: "gebildet" = literate; "Einbildung" = pride onself"), without realizing that they don't know, know nothing. "I know that I know nothing," said Plato.

True knowledge is not a collection of mess in the mind, but an absolute void, free from concepts, ideas, convictions and creations of the mind, so that spirit can flow through it unhindered and sing the song of life. The creations of the mind on the other side are pure illusions, phenomena like a fata morgana. The more creations are stored in our mental stock, the more stodged and impermeable is the flute. "Blessed are the ones who are poor in spirit, because heaven is theirs." (The Gospels, Matth. 5:3)

The less literacy in the sense of deformation the less delusion and the lesser hubris in the sense of making oneself the measure of all things (wordplay in German: Bildung = literacy; Verbildung = deformation, Einbildung = delusion). The ones who are poor in spirit, the modest and humbled ones, have less difficulty in directing themselves inside and in listening to the butterfly than those who always have a smart answer to everything and put in their two cents.

To realize who you really are you have to be still. That does not mean that you may no longer talk. The noise of the world is not produced by words which come out of our mouth or by sounds. The noise of the world is produced by the permanently active mind, by the thinking which creates endless concepts, produces thoughts incessantly, revivifies imaginations without interruption. The noise of the world comes up because the mind is not able to let a fact, an incident or an observation simply be, be as it is. In the moment of observation the mind starts obsessively to analyze the observed, to measure and to classify.

In the moment that Roger Federer was victorious at Wimbledon in 2009, he was supposed to give account to reporters as to how he succeeded in winning - as if there were a plan to adhere to. The joy about the victory had not even penetrated each cell of Roger's body, as top-heavy analyses were required, as comparisons and explanations were wrested from the champion. Comparisons to others, comparisons with himself, comparisons with earlier times. What is this all about? For what does it serve?

During football's world cup in 2010 the coach of the Germans, Jogi Löw, was asked in the first press conference after the victory of 4-0 against Australia, what he could say about the prolonging of his contract after the WM. But hello, which planet do reporters live on? How insane must be a mind which never can stay here. Do those penetrant pushies really believe that a coach in the midst of a four-week long, demanding, concentrated and focused football tourney is lying in bed at night awake and thinking about questions about the future?

The mind is so insane that it is always occupied with when-what-where-why-how, how long and since when? How often, when better or worse, when will be what, where and how and why will it happen again or even not? In the midst of insanity the mind is in its element – and people follow it willingly like cattle to the slaughterhouse. The mind analyses, explains, measures, compares, judges, criticizes, praises, flatters, adulates, destroys, assumes, scores, evaluates, complains, argues, grieves, asks, requests, never listens, understands nothing, doubts, wonders, grasps nothing, grasps everything.

Enjoying is a strange thing to the mind, is not part of its essence and unknown terrain. Man could enjoy if he only was willing, but it seems that he prefers to follow the mind rather than joy and enthusiasm. The mind is also incapable of simply resting and being still, because this would be a death threat to it. A still mind is no more a mind. Instead it willfully makes everything into what it wants it to be, and thereby leaves nothing as it is.

It's a poor world in which everything must be cut into pieces. What a cannibal makes with the human body and which rightfully is disgusting to us, the same the mind is doing endlessly with the world. The mind dissects everything. Its being is like that of Prokrustes, an ogre of Greek mythology, who puts everything forcefully into a given scheme. Every man has these solidified schemes in his head. They are the sum of everything he has ever experienced, undergone, thought or felt. And as two people in the world have not experienced exactly the same things, there are not even two identical schemes in the heads of men.

With other words: There are more than 7,000,000,000 (seven billion) schemes, in which the world is pressed. Therefore the question is justified of whether there is only one world or more than 7,000,000,000 worlds. One world will only be when the billions of worlds in the individual heads are extinguished. Without taking the head out and getting thoughtless, there cannot reign unity, cannot be lived oneness, cannot be peace. Only when men start to question the validity of the schemes in their heads, when they empty their mental vessels – or at least don't mistake them to be the ultimate wisdom – will the door to unity open. When all mental vessels are emptied – when all seven billion humans are poor in spirit - and provide their vessels for the highest to fill them, so that the "Song of the Exalted" – the Bhagavadgita – can flow in, then unity will be realized, then only One breath will run, one spirit reign, remains One taste. (Wilber, 1999)

In that moment all addictions vanish. First of all longing vanishes because the searcher died. Without searcher there is no search and no addiction (wordplay in German: Sucher = searcher; Sucht = addiction). Not because the searcher has left this earth but because the quality of searching does no longer exist. The searcher dies when he stops searching, not when he finds. And man continues to live joyfully without being a searcher – relief and easiness arrive. Only being is unbearable for the searcher; without a searcher being is lighter than a feather. Indeed there are only very few serious searchers who really are ready to find. Most searchers want to be and remain searchers – like we were told in the story of Tagore. If the searcher were ready to find, there would not be so many addictions in the world: addiction, binge eating, sexual dependence, kleptomania, computer addiction, alcohol addiction, drug addiction, gambling addiction, cigarette addiction, television addiction, workaholics, addiction for sugar, coffee addiction, helper syndrome, attitude of the gossiper, longing, jealousy, profit addiction, addiction for more etc. In Germany, for example, millions of youngsters suffer from the WOW addiction, - the World of Warcraft addiction.

And the actual finance and economic crisis – which in reality is a system crisis – was primarily created by addiction, by greed and avarice, the obsession for money, the obsession for power, the obsession for sex. Money is sexy. Only when the primal self is realized, then bit by bit all these addictions and thereby more than the seven billion egos will melt like ice or snow in the sun. In the presence of the sun, melting happens without the necessity to do something. The iceberg melts alone by being exposed to the sun. The one who stays in the shadow has a chance to keep "his" addictions and will never smell release and freedom.

The biggest long track of humanity is the glorification of personality. In seminars and trainings of personality development, an unfolding the personality is celebrated and paid court to. Simply overlooked is that personality is the same as ego and thus egoism. All these efforts around the personality are nothing but a gigantic ego trip. When we substitute the word personality with ego, we will abruptly become conscious of this trick of the ego to avoid its own unmasking. The ego is indeed extremely inventive to secure its survival and is not shy to use ever new tricks. In its perverted efficiency, it invents one more teaching and another exercise and yet another method to supposedly satisfy the searcher. The one thinks by itself: I don't know this yet and that is indeed something new and that one I must also know. All these shifty exercises are only made from egos for egos.

Only when the ego dies, you are immune to the creations of an insane mind. Then you awaken to the glory of being human, which is not different from the glory of divinity. Every fatalism and each fanaticism vanish. The view clarifies to perceive the glory and majesty of creation and nature, finally to truly see it (wordplay in German: wahrnehmen = perceive; wahr nehmen = truly see) – as the face of the One, the All-One. The getting conscious of how narrow and tight-laced are the conditioned ties of thinking is at first a gigantic shock, the realization that every second, every minute, incessantly you are thinking things which are holding you in prison and jail you in a self-created dungeon. Never have you examined if the countless thoughts that you are following automatically are the truth. You adopted them all unchecked as inherited from your ancestors. You are dragging in your mind millions of years. Do you wonder when you are exhausted, feel weak, are without energy? Only when you reject this inheritance and empty cellar and attic of the collected mess will there be room for life force, joy of life and love of everything. Due to this richness you will succeed on subjects you before thought to be impossible. You will always have enough time, because all matters will be settled by themselves. Only a nice vision? No, reality, the moment the ego comes to an end. Then there will be no more personality and you are no more a personality.

When you read "The Unpersonal Life," (1993) or do the 365 lessons of a "Course in Miracles," then the scales will fall from your eyes, that you until then had only lived in a world of illusions and followed a fata morgana. When you see through this illusion there is nothing left that has to be secured, nothing to defend, nothing to develop, nothing to unfold, nothing to change. You are the fool, the zero in Tarot, the jester at the royal court - and you enjoy the privileges of fools. You can live your lifestyle. And exactly at this point, a perverted mind will surely put into my words what fits in his stuff. You can do what you want does not mean that you don't follow rules and order anymore, but it means that the self-will has died and you follow His will. That one only wants that which arises from the flow as a result of the natural order. When you don't exist anymore you follow the leader of the pen. Then you are not a slave, because you no longer exist. How could nobody be a slave? You will not do anything that your mind may fear at this moment to do, when the dams will break. This fear comes from the ego. When the ego dies, its creations also die. What resounds through the purified vessel, through the hollow flute, cannot be outnumbered in loveliness. Instead of passing time with learning of measures and numbers and cramming dead knowledge, we pass time with dancing and celebrating life, listen to the songs of dolphins and rocks, dive into a world full of magic.

"Cold as a rock without a hue - Held together with a bit of glue - Something tells me this isn't true - You are my sweetheart, soft and blue. Do you care, have you a part - In the deepest emotions of my own heart. Tender with breezes, caressing and whole - Alive with music haunting my soul." (Planet Earth, Dancing the Dream)

14. Magic

When we believe we know everything or are always right, we are killing the unspoiled magical child within and create a conditioned robot, someone good, well-behaved, who does nothing what adults could disapprove of. Thus beings are produced who run amok within – and as we have experienced painfully, do it sometimes also in the outer world. Only by suppression of innocence and joy are such destructive forces produced, which some time or other are directed to the destruction of the suppressor.

"Once there was a child and he was free - Deep inside he felt the laughter - The mirth and play of nature's glee - He was not troubled by thoughts of hereafter - Beauty, love was all he'd see - "He knew his power was the power of God.... - This power of innocence, of compassion, of light - Threatened the priests and created a fright.... - "Don't stop this child, he is the father of man - Don't cross his way, he's part of the plan - I am that child, but so are you - You've just forgotten, just lost the clue." (Magical Child part 1, Dancing the Dream)

The seed of this magical child is laid out in everyone and only in later years is the veil of oblivion laid upon it by the creative force of mind. The time has come to break the charm, to raise the veil and awaken the remembrance of that which I really am. Remember who you are, that's all one has to do. Don't give credit to the rules your parents, educators and teachers drummed into you and forget all social conditionings. And ask yourself at each thought which starts with "you must" or "you should" or "you may not" if that is really the truth. And don't be satisfied with a quick superficial "yes," because this "yes" is a habit and coming from the shallow mental waves at the banks of the ocean. Dive deeper to the bottom of it and there ask yourself if the thought that is trying to lead you is the truth or not.

Byron Katie has described this method of self-exploration in her book, "Loving What Is," in detail. It supports us to debunk the projections and conditionings which we think to be the truth due to ignorance. The way to your Self, which in reality is not a way, because you already are there, is self-exploration, no less and no more. Throw all exercises and methods overboard, which were only invented to arrive somewhere, sometime, or to find something. End the search and remember that you already are what you are searching for. You are already seated in the armchair at home and only dreaming of being in search of your home. In the moment you awaken the search has an end.

The best is if you start immediately to dance, sing and play – and that which was sunken in the past will be raised to the surface from the depths of the ocean, and mankind will arise in unison to One Song. The first forerunners of what life will be, we can find everywhere, where people are coming together to sing and dance instead of protesting and reclaiming. Look at the flashmob "Glow" from Madcon during the European Song Contest 2010 on YouTube, where Lena Meyer-Landrut got the magic twelve points for Germany.

Things fall into line of the natural order itself in a wonderful way when dancing life. There are innumerable examples for a new spirit of departure, all of which you can find on the internet. Here are some examples: the concerts "Live AID" on 13th of July 1985, "Live 8 Make Poverty History" on 2nd of July 2005, and "Live Earth" on 15th of February 2007. At the same time rock and pop bands gave concerts in various cities all over the world to address together the urgent problems of the world.

The first action from 28th of January 1985 came indeed from Michael Jackson – who at that time was called Smelly by his colleagues due to the wonderful fragrance that he emitted - and Lionel Ritchie: the project "USA for Africa" (United Support of Artists for Africa). Forty-five artists came together to produce the song, "We Are The World" under the direction of Quincy Jones. The purpose was to help fight the hunger of people in Africa. Most of the participants came directly from the American Music Awards to the recording in the Lion Studio and worked all night until early in the morning without honorarium. As part of the party were Dan Aykroyd, Harry Belafonte, Lindsey Buckingham, Kim Carnes, Ray Charles, Bob Dylan, Sheila E., Bob Geldof, Daryl Hall and John Oates, James Ingram, Jackie Jackson, LaToya Jackson, Marlon Jackson, Michael Jackson, Randy Jackson, Tito Jackson, Al Jarreau, Waylon Jennings, Billy Joel, Cyndi Lauper, Huey Lewis & The News, Kenny Loggins, Bette Midler, Willie Nelson, Jeffrey Osborne, Steve Perry, The Pointer Sisters, Lionel Ritchie, Smokey Robinson, Kenny Rogers, Diana Ross, Paul Simon, Bruce Springsteen, Tina Turner, Dionne Warwick, and Stevie Wonder.

"Let us realize that a change can only come when we stand together as one," is said in the "Making of" Video. Immense power is released when people come together and fight together for an issue.

The single with the song was published with an edition of 800,000 copies on 7th of March 1985 and immediately reached first place on the charts and was sold out within a few weeks. At the door of the recording studio was a plate, "Leave the ego outside." The video documentary "We Are The World – the story behind the song," proves that this is really possible: "We stopped being individuals," "There was an immediate feeling of belonging, there was an immediate feeling of oneness."

As of 2010 the song had sold seven million copies and brought in 60 million US Dollars for charities. Still today there is an organization with the same name, which not is connected with this project, but honors Michael Jackson equally. Their statement after Michael Jackson's death says: "The loss of Michael Jackson profoundly saddened all of us who had the honor of working with him over the years. We at USA for Africa and the many programs we funded were particularly blessed to be the beneficiary of his extraordinary talent as he joined with Lionel Richie to create one of the greatest humanitarian anthems ever written. 'We Are The World' not only raised tens of millions of dollars for relief, recovery and development in Africa but inspired and helped to educate people all over the world to the issues of hunger and homelessness and the abject poverty that is so much a part of that equation. As part of Michael's legacy those efforts will continue for years and years to come." (www.usaforafrica.org).

With the football world cup ion South Africa from 11th of June to 11th of July 2010, the African continent was finally honored for all that it is, an equal part of the world community and a continent of joy of life – the cradle of humanity. On 1st of February 2010 the song was recorded again under the title "We Are The World 25 for Haiti" with more than 80 artists in the same studio as the benefit project, "Artists for Haiti," under the direction of Quincy Jones and Lionel Ritchie, and published on 12th of February, the day of the opening of the Olympic games in Vancouver. Involved were Celine Dion, Barbra Streisand, Pink, Akon, Usher, Janet Jackson, Mary J. Blidge, Enrique Iglesias, Orianthi, Carlos Santana, as well as Michael's nephews Taj, Taryll and TJ. Material from the original version from 1985 was cut into the song and the video. There also exists a Spanish version, "Somos el Mundo 25 Para Haiti," which was produced by Emilio and Gloria Estefan and published in March 2010.

In the meantime, bigger or smaller projects with the purpose to "Change the World" have sprung up like mushrooms so that one loses track of them. On www.playingforchange.com you find a multimedia movement which originated in the United States with the goal of creating "Peace on Earth" via music.

I am writing this part of the book on 27th of July 2009 and this day I am hitting the way to the musical, "Thriller Live," that was performed successfully for many years in London and premiered on 22nd of July in Munich. I am sitting in the first row, seat 33 (for the numerologists among you). The two and a half hours are hot, breathtaking, magic. And MJ Mytton-Sanneh, the ten-year-old Michael singer really looks a little bit like little Michael – and is also called MJ.

Michael's spirit fills the room, reaches every cell of the body, mind and soul. The musical ends with "Man in the Mirror":

"If you wanna make the world a better place take a look at yourself and make a change ... and no message could've been any clearer, if you want to make the world a better place take a look at yourself and make that...Change,...make that Change."

For some seconds on the screen Barack Obama appears. The mantra "Change" has taken over the mantra "Hare Krishna" in the Western world. And those who are conscious of the power of the word know that "Change" will reach a momentum which will be followed by the quantum leap. "Michael's spirit will always be with us," says Adrian Grant, the producer of "Thriller," in an interview. Michael's spirit is spirit itself. There is no individual Michael Jackson, but the energy form is like all great souls an expression of the One. Rejoice that the process of transformation is in full swing, everywhere, in all hearts, worldwide: Until now solidified dense wafting masses of energy are starting to move, turn into fluid and transparency. Dark, threatening massive masses of clouds saturated with hate, aggression and brutality are opening wide and giving room for rays of light which struggle through and lighten up the blackness. It is not necessary to have 2000 watts to expel the darkness in a room; a candle is sufficient.

"We are now prepared to take you to the next level." (2000 Watts)

And already the next proof for my unbelievable statements is dropping in. As I am no longer a believer I am visited by the unbelievable. Reality doesn't care about obstacles, penetrates and bypasses walls and transcends borders. Borders are products of the human mind. Why should the truth fail due to a limited mind? Why should a butterfly ask the caterpillar where to fly? Why should freedom ask the imprisoned for permission? Why should the awakened ask for the opinion of the dreaming one?

Elke describes in an article, "The true legacy of Michael Jackson to the world," '"The last comeback of a megastar!' or 'The wave of connectedness?'": What is it – that the masses actually ask, what moves us so much, provokes us, touches, stirs us up, affects us, reminds or awakens? A megastar has left the stage of life. So what, many ask themselves, there are things much worse. Is it necessary to make such hype? Exactly! Is there nothing better for them to do? Why are so many touched, even those who were not fans of Michael Jackson – like myself? What is he triggering within us right now with his change of states, which apparently was not there before? For three weeks now, the comeback of the megastar rages worldwide – no continent is omitted! What has this being Michael Jackson by his death initiated within us with his specialness, eccentricity, outlandishness, unworldliness? Is there after all a more important legacy for us besides his music, his innovative dancing, his performance, his wonderful mostly profound lyrics, which were written from the soul and are more than mere words in a beautiful dressing? Why do we only now realize them? Why do we read and hear them right now - and apparently understand them only now? These are questions that come to me, when again and again I feel new waves of love, connectedness and joy, as soon as information, the lyrics of a song, a YouTube video of Michael reaches me. I never was his fan! I nearly did not perceive the lyrics, as also happened to me with the lyrics of the Beatles....Only now many recognize: Michael Jackson was a phenomenon! He succeeded with his courageous always-changing outer appearance to connect opposites as no human before had succeeded in such a drastic and worldwide way. He was loved or he was hated – that's human nature. The fact is – he provoked and made conscious prejudice, deprecation, joy and total ecstasy/devotion, in any case strong feelings as no one before had done. As man/woman/child and black/white he touched taboos and seemingly incompatible opposites of this world and overcame them and united them by himself. He has made public the crime and abuse of children and sacrificed and suffered himself! He was seemingly perpetrator and became victim! He has simply only loved – that was his crime! Deep within an innocent great soul of a child, which only wanted to stir the world and remind it of the pure love between humans, and actually succeeded therein at times – always freshly and now after his death more than ever! That is what also now splits the world - so many that didn't believe him – that too deeply he touched the beloved mechanisms of resistance and fight of the mass consciousness, the separating, evaluating, especially deprecating, the lust to talk someone down to feel better about oneself, to be above such things – standing as the 'good one' before oneself to polish the inner lack of self-appreciation a little bit. He served and is still serving in an outstanding way as a screen of projection for the self-rejected parts and inner fights against love in each of us - Michael, what did you move and bear for us? What great light-filled soul is hidden behind all this? He connected us all and everything – poor and rich, black and white, men and women, masses, peoples, nations and in the end – the whole world! He wanted to bring together the opposites, the separated - in himself he succeeded in a grandiose way; he sacrificed his body and finally himself. His legacy to us is a brimming-over wave of connectedness, which embraces the whole planet. It's not sadness which prevails, no – it is a feeling of commonness, of joy, of love, which overcomes all borders and separations. He achieved with his death what he sang about in his songs as a utopia or deepest wish in all hearts – by his transition and the never-ending flood of media messengers, this profundity in the human light-filled nature was resurrected. Hearts have opened by fresh feelings and also by the confusion that one death was able to trigger something like that. My memory of the death of Lady Diana is just awakening. She too has achieved similar things for the world – her greatest legacy too was the unifying, connecting, the love, which reminds us that in the end we all are One, that we are love - as Michael sang about. If you look around, the whole world is coming together - NOW! Can you feel it? We are indeed all equal! The blood in you is the blood in me. Can you feel it? The world should be love – love each other wholeheartedly. We decide, each one of us, if we want to surf on this wave of connectedness and the joy of sharing, the uniqueness of each individual wonderful being on this earth, and want to be carried by the remembrance of the soul of what we wanted to bring to the world – like Michael. 'When you succeed to dance in hell – then you are in heaven! (Osho)'." (Elke Antara Minerva, 15th of July 2009, asked for distribution)

15. Birthright

Everyone who is ready to let go of prejudice and judgment is able to realize crystal-clearly the true essence of Michael Jackson. Thomas Mesereau addressed the dominating prejudices plainly when he declared: "I didn't want race to be an issue in this trial. I feel that Michael transcends race. When I learned about who Michael was, when I learned about his life and his world, I concluded that Michael has a very rare quality, and that is – he brings people of all races together." (Jones, p. 19)

Thomas Mesereau is lawyer and was Michael's attorney during the trial in 2005. He belongs to those ones who immediately realized after meeting Michael Jackson personally who he really was. Whoever is not able to do this has to adjust his receiver to the right frequency. "There comes a time, when we heed a certain call, when the world must come together as one. There are people dying and it's time to lend a hand to life, the greatest gift of all." (We Are The World)

Instead of supporting Michael Jackson and his friends in this gigantic task to do something for the world, the media have pounced on his person with speculations and sensationalism. For decades we were supplied with the ego trips of reporters. While pure journalism means communication of facts, many reporters make their money with speculations. Facts are mostly boring as shit. With facts there is not much money earned and one cannot inflate one's ego. Only reports which produce an outcry of the whole nation sell well. The sentence, "Michael Jackson has had an operation because his nose bone was broken," has no worth as news. Nobody is interested in something like that. There has to be invented something more so that the sanctimonious can be indignant, disgusted and cry loud, "Ugh," or "Baah," like sheep.

We need stories and tales to take our minds off things. And to make the story believable also for the non-believers experts are brought in. These experts are on their own ego trip and don't want to disappear again too quickly from the spotlight. That means that they need a story: "Michael Jackson's nose is starting to crumble away." Wow, I need to know more about that, quickly buying a journal. What is written therein? Some suppositions, some assumptions, some banalities, and for every common sense item only bullshit. Some pictures added so that everyone can see it. Have you already heard about photo montages? And already the chumps have their proofs. Michael called it "trash". .

Everyone who knew him better, because of personal knowledge or by doing research, can only laugh in the face of such stories. But the money is already rolling in and the reader has paid dearly for the trash. Have you heard about picture manipulation in the digital age? Michael has warned all of us: "It's trash, don't buy trash."

In the interview with Ed Bradley on Christmas 2003 he said: "It's people with a dirty mind who think like that. I don't think that way. That's not me."

Ed Bradley inquired: "And do you think people look at you and think that way today?"

Michael: "If they have a sick mind, yeah, and if they believe the trash they read in newspapers, yeah.... Just because it's in print doesn't mean it's the gospel. People write negative things 'cause they feel that's what sells. Good news to them doesn't sell."

Also Georg Preuße reports about painful experiences with the trash that was produced by the media. "It's really bad...that the lies from the Springer house will become more real in the end than reality. They construct their worlds according to their will and from that realities form which are believed by everyone. And suddenly it's true – crazy." (Preuße, p. 283)

I myself have had the experience as a greenhorn in my profession in the 1970 that you have no chance individually against these monopoles of power. During my work as media abstractor with the German broadcasting station Süddeutscher Rundfunk I had accomplished a research project about the "Effect of brutality in television investigated in the example of the comic series Speed Racer" and published the results. The German Bild succeeded, actually only using citations from my report, in claiming the contrary of what I had written. By simply ignoring a little "not" or using similar tricks, they represented me as a supporter of such brutal comics. When I tried to defend myself, colleagues advised me with a worn-out smile only to desist – no chance to succeed.

Nowadays it is possible to get stinking rich with trash and garbage. You perhaps know some stinking rich junk and scrap dealers. When it is about sensations, common sense is no more in demand. We need kicks and adrenaline. The realization that our mind is insane is sinking into our consciousness only step by step. Until now we have cared more about our body and looked after its booboos. The health of the mind does not bother most people. We all have a more or less insane mind; in reality we all are mentally ill – not only those who for that reason were put in a psychiatric hospital. We are dreaming and accept the dreamt things as true. While dreaming one is completely persuaded that one is awake and all that one experiences is real.

Only ***after awakening*** is it suddenly crystal clear that all before was a dream. There is also a good message: "Change" – Change is in full swing – and indeed more rapidly than some prefer. Thereby the forerunners and pioneers are always ahead of the mainstream. Pioneers always go through absolute hell – at least when they are active in the outer world. Pioneers are as seeds. Once seminated the seed will sprout when it is watered and has fallen on fertile ground. Pioneers throw little stones in the lake and then it makes ripples. Even these becoming weaker as they move from the center and in the end are nearly no more perceived, the impulse continues, in-visible, un-hearable, un-sensable. It expands step by step in the whole physical universe and well beyond. When the number of pioneers increases, the vanguard is already forming itself. And day by day more people will follow. Every day, every hour, every minute, every second there are souls awakening and joining the army of the warriors of light. This army transcends the mind and the senses and follows the heart, realizes the essential, the intrinsic, the truth. This transformation from head to stomach, from mind to heart is accompanied by an inner fight in the phase of transition, because the old ruler – the ego – will not give in. It has had the power for centuries, has been obsessed by it and has fended off every attempt to overturn the throne. Self aggrandizing, the old ruler has derided the power of love, defamed and taunted, has tried to kill the child of freedom and magic. Even when he succeeded temporarily in bringing it to its knees, the attempt to kill the magical child was not successful, because in reality it is immortal.

"Deep inside, you know it's true. Just find that child, it's hiding in you." (Magical Child part 1, Dancing the Dream)

History shows that the withholding of childhood is the most severe crime that can be done to a child. Often the parents are not even conscious of what they are doing and what consequences their actions have. Often they themselves have been victims of this crime, as their parents as small parts of the human chain have suffered the same. One who was not given love in childhood is often not capable of giving it to others. One who is empty himself cannot fill another vessel. Thus behavior and feeling patterns have propagated themselves for centuries, and in endless rows victims become offenders and offenders in turn victims. Whoever sees through this pattern no longer has prejudice toward others who are only a link in the chain, and judges others no more. For him it is clear that everyone is only a link in this chain and he is more interested in finding out how this fatal chain can be burst through. "He who is without fault may throw the first stone," Master Jesus said. Jesus himself was surrounded by those who were condemned and outlawed by society. He was a friend of the outcast ones. Until today most Christians don't follow Jesus and his teaching as example, but only their own perverted minds. I don't deny the right of anyone in the world to adjudicate and to judge, but it should be clear that judgment and adjudication are an expression of an enormous amount of arrogance, boastfulness and hubris. Who has the right to raise the sword against another human? Who has the right to decide about life and death of another human? Whoever takes this for granted is engaging in competition with God and challenges His role.

"Love was taken from a young life and no one told her why....She innocently questioned why, why her father had to die, She asked the men in blue, how is it that you get to choose, Who will live and who will die, Did God say that you could decide?....Only God can decide, who will live and who will die....There's nothing that can't be done, if we raise our voice as one." (We've had Enough, Dancing the Dream)

When I deny here the right to judge I am not talking about court where a judge in a judicial process has to decide. There it is the case of finding the just sentence for someone who violated the law. It is a judgment in the sense of a decision of which consequences someone has to suffer for his actions. It is not a judgment about a human being, but a judgment about what he has done. Here I question the right to judge people, judge the person, her being and humanness. Nobody has the right to judge this. How easy is it to judge children as stupid and ignorant. Thank God ever more voices rise who want to give children back their rightful place in the world and recognize that children stand nearer to higher wisdom than most adults. Ever louder sounds the call of those who see with the heart. The heart does not judge. There is a lobby slowly forming for those who were denied the birthright of every human for unconditional love. Thereby we are dealing with a love that does not interfere, that claims nothing and expects no service in return, but is simply poured out over everyone from the horn of plenty. People with lost or traumatic childhoods will be healed in this way and then will be able under their own power to take their rightful places in this world with dignity.

16. Armband

Who (besides the fans) has ever noticed that Michael Jackson had the custom of wearing an armband on his right upper arm? For example in the video "Black or White" (1991) – by all means look at the 11-minute version of the "Panther Dance," which was banned at times; the video "Smooth Criminal," at the NAACP Awards in 1994; and in "Teaser" (Album HIStory), at the MTV Video Music Awards in 1995. On 16th of July 1996 Michael performed live in the Sultanat Brunei for the 50th birthday of Sultan Hassanal Bolkiah in the Jerudong Park Amphitheatre in Bandar Serih Begawan, where the royal family (not the Sultan himself) was present and entrance for the 60,000 attendees was free. The last song of the concert was the premiere of "Earth Song," and there Michael wore a red armband.

A comment on YouTube says: "He is the embodiment of philanthropy." Even seeing the performance years later one senses the same intensity, such that it produces goose bumps. One who is well versed with mudras can see that

Michael is also a master in this realm. The term "mudra" is Sanscrit and means, "that which brings joy." It constitutes symbolic hand gestures/poses which express that one wants to please the gods and give something. In his masterpiece, "Jam," Michael is wearing a golden armband, in "Dangerous" a white one, in "Smooth Criminal" a blue. Michael is also wearing an armband on 27th of June 1999 at "Adventure Humanity - Michael Jackson and Friends" at the Olympic stadium in Munich. One sees this as well on 7th of November 2001 in Madison Square Garden in New York, in celebration of his 30-year anniversary on stage as a solo artist, at the performance of "Black or White" with the legendary Slash.

This concert in New York was the third that I attended personally and it belongs to the highlights in my life. A part of it was shown on German 3Sat television on New Year's eve in 2009. It started with various artists who honored Michael. "Wanna be Starting Something" was sung by Usher, Whitney Houston was one of the performers, and we could witness an Africa show – the word "Makkosa" from the song "Wanna be Starting Something" comes from Cameroon. Usher and Luther Vandross then sang together "Man in the Mirror." Michael was seated at the side of Elizabeth Taylor that evening in the audience and also his mother Katherine was present.

As a highlight, followed the performance of Michael himself, first together with his five brothers, so that in 2001 the Jackson Six were on stage for the first time and scintillated as thirty years before with a "salute to vocal groups." The "Jackson Five" plus Randy brought a medley from songs of the Mills Brothers, the Andrew Sisters, the Coasters and the Supremes. At that time the eight-year-old Janet sang together with Randy as a duet – and then all together sang in German, "Bei mir bist du schön" (for me you are beautiful). That evening at Madison Square Garden, Michael performed in shining white with golden gaiters. The six Jacksons succeeded as always to produce goose bumps with "Can You Feel It." Then followed "ABC," "The Love You Save," "I'll Be There", "I Want You Back," "Dancing Machine" with 'N Sync, and "Shake Your Body." Further highlights included "Billie Jean," "You Rock My World" with Usher, and "The Way You Make Me Feel" with Britney Spears and Chris Tucker. At the American Music Awards on 9th of January 2002 Michael also wears an armband, and again on 29th of August 2002. Also in the short film "Jam," where the King of Pop tries to teach the King of Basketball Michael Jordan to dance, and the King of Basketball tries to teach the King of Pop to play basketball. One can sense that the two have fun.

At the press conference with the announcement of the "This Is It" concerts on 9th of March 2009 in London, Michael Jackson appears for the last time in the public with a black armband and red jacket. But also when rehearsing for the tour he did not cast it off, as is proven in the film "This Is It." Until now there is still no reason to cast it off. I have had the experience that nearly nobody knows why Michael wore this armband, and in fact most people did not even notice it.

How is it possible that serious journalists for decades did not care about the meaning of this gesture? The only explanation is a lack of presence.

The number of information units that hits us every second is so huge that we only can perceive a tiny part of it. Besides we perceive less, the more conditioned thought filters we have in our mind. That is called lack of presence. Presence perceives without filters. Michael himself told us that he would wear the armband as long as there are poor or abused children in the world.

A shocking destiny of year-long abuse by his own mother is told us by Andreas Marquardt in his biography "Härte" (hardship), where he speaks about the sexual abused by his own mother for many years. As a sort of unconscious compensation he later changed from victim to perpetrator and passed on the suffered brutality and violence to everybody he met. After eight years of clinks the transformation began, and he heard again the quiet whispering of the butterfly within. His life partner, who herself had become victim of his excesses of violence, has held to her vision for 27 years that there was another core hidden under the shell. What wonderful ability of discrimination! Andreas confirms that to him was denied the only human right: "The worst was that I was not left alone." In the meantime he cares for neglected children at the edge of society and holds readings in high-security prisons, so that others can profit from his experiences and find again the faith in them that once was lost. "Children must be put again in the focus of our society and not at the fringes of society. We don't care enough about children." (Oliver Geissen Show, 21st of April 2009)

The real meaning of the fundamental right, "The dignity of men is not unimpeachable," has only revealed itself to few people. The others don't appreciate the fight some people fight with their destiny, how arduous it is to follow the call of one's own lost soul and to free oneself from the mire of brutality and violence which one got into as a child. As an adult, Andreas turned perpetrator to unconsciously take vengeance for all the injustice that had been done to him. But instead of looking deeper and giving this man a helping hand, most people only see the surface and immediately the hatchet of judgment has fallen.

Andreas is an example – which I have come upon by chance – that the impossible is possible when we hear the call of our hearts and deliver ourselves to the pain which accompanies the process of transformation. Otherwise a lost childhood ends in a lost life. Like always the media in the case of Andreas don't report about the attempts of people who engage themselves and support a good cause, but they talk about the ex-pimp. To put a label upon on someone is easier than to look closely. People tend to keep us in the drawers we were once put in. It is not easy to stay in the Here and Now and to see someone as he really is now, but easy, without questioning them, to take out again the stored data of the past. What would we say when someone would talk about someone of fifty years as an ex baby, or talk about an "ex primary school pupil" when someone is by now professor at a university? Why do we put a sign on somebody for years when he has stolen something in a supermarket as a child? Most people live only in the past; they don't get much of the present. They are not conscious that life takes place only in the present.

17. Below the Belt

Labelers are only content when they have put a label on someone. They are not much concerned that this label will stick to the person her whole life, like slaughterers who label dissected halves of pigs in the slaughterhouse. What otherwise should a labeler do if he would not label? Can you imagine refraining from labeling? Not to put a brand on other people anymore? To dispose of all drawers? Hardly likely because the labeling and the sorting are wonderfully distracting. As long as you are occupied with labeling and branding there is no time left to mind one's own business.

Instead of starting with the man in the mirror, labelers prefer to look at others. To question how corrupt, dishonest and twisted one is oneself is difficult. We are here to develop and grow. Development does not mean to add something new, as is falsely taught even by psychology, but it means unwrap (wordplay in German: development = Entwicklung; unwrap = ent-wickeln). That means to remove that which has hidden the essence, to discard the outer layers until we have reached the core. To develop oneself means to un-wrap until the true essence is un-veiled and un-covered. We are all wrapped in the conditioned patterns of thinking and behaving, which have nothing to do with our selves. The cover has nothing in common with the content. The shell surrounds the core, but is not the core itself.

Humanity is unconsciously identified with the shell, with the skin, with the body. Do you seriously believe that you are the body, when you say for example: "I am thick" or "I am thin" or "I am beautiful" or "I am ugly"? Is this really you? Aren't you first of all a human being?

Most people want to be free and are seeking freedom their whole lives. Thereby they see that being free is their true essence. We are like someone who is sitting at home on the sofa and thinking about and asking himself how he can find the way home. Michael would have loved to free himself from the shell of the "King of Pop" and would have liked to be simply a human being. Look more closely what you see, when the King of Pop is dead.

Michael is and was always a Mahatma in the shell of the King of Pop. In www.mahatma-haus.ch I find the following definition: "Mahatma means Conscious Being. It is the way to the true freedom of mastership, the way to divine consciousness."

"The master is gone," writes a fan on 17th of July 2009 in an internet forum. A clear view. But what is the purpose of the mindfuckers and self-satisfiers? Do you feel the judgment behind the question of Diane Sawyer to Lisa Marie Presley in an interview in the year 2003: "Why did you marry Michael Jackson?" In which sort of world do we live where I have to justify and explain to journalists why I marry whom? Unschooled ears don't pay attention to the unspoken implications of statements. In this case they mean: How can you do such a thing? Lisa Marie answers: "…I fell in love with him, I did." Diane Sawyer insists: "In love?" The unspoken part of this question says: I can't believe that. Lisa Marie answers: "Yes, I fell in love, at the time. Now…"

Diane Sawyer continuous with her investigation: "Sexual attraction?" Hello, how deep under the belt do the moths still go? Under the guise of serious journalism that's nothing but voyeurism. Lisa Marie nevertheless continues surprisingly calm: "I told you. Everything I said was the truth." But Diane Sawyer's greed – inquisitiveness we call it when making it seem harmless – is not yet stilled: "Sexual attraction?" And Lisa Marie confirms: "At the time, yeah." Diane Sawyer continues to needle: "What did your mother say?" Lisa Marie was 35 years old at the time. Hello! Must I ask my mother for her opinion if I am 35 years old when I marry?

For me it's cool when Robbie Williams shows the world – unfortunately not Diane Sawyer – his naked butt and says kiss my ass. But Diane is not yet sated. The glutton continues to persist: "And you did live together?" Lisa Marie answers with a simple: "Yeah." Do you realize that Lisa Marie is well educated? We urgently need bad girls and bad boys to finally put a stop to the game of the moths instead of nicely providing information. Diane Sawyer continues: "I didn't believe that." Why then did she ask the question? When she then does not believe in the answer? Not to know something, but to get a confirmation for her own belief? That means it's only about self-satisfaction of her mind. And slowly Lisa Marie has had enough: "Well, let's just put it this way: If he was in town he was at my house." (http://www.youtube.com/watch?v=g0E7EfN9iGA) Diane's intrusive behavior is a prime example of how far journalists go with their hypocrisy and corruption: "Again, you can slug me on this question, but I gotta go back. So these were like romantic nights?"

Diane Sawyer is by the way not a reporter from "Bild," but besides Oprah Winfrey one of the most influential talk masters in the United States, with regular shows on prime-time television.

When this type of coercion to strip the soul is part of our civilization and culture, then I prefer to live with the natives in the Amazon jungle. Rumors, once put out in the world, are rarely exterminated. They turn about themselves as soon as the stone is thrown into the water. The same is valid for all impulses. It's strange that we don't use this phenomenon to realize our vision of peace, joy and freedom, but primarily to satisfy our sensation-seeking.

As psychological evaluator for driving ability, I was, for example, for more than fourteen years, confronted with the rumor that this so-called "test for idiots" – I don't know who shall be the idiot, the customer or the evaluator – can only be passed when someone is able to pile up three balls. Once put in the world, this say-so survives intractably, but as of yet I have never met someone to whom this really happened. That's only an example that we do not believe things based on common sense, but that which the believer wants to believe. Believing distracts us from looking at ourselves, because thus one is too occupied with the search for the guilty one and with one's own indignation.

When in 1993 the first investigations of child abuse of Michael Jackson started, the media had their story of the century. Serious allegations were made that Michael had sexually abused the then thirteen-year-old Jordan Chandler. One year later the civil lawsuit and the whole issue ended with a settlement, where Michael paid to the family a reported sum of two-digit millions of dollars. The numbers that have been circulating since then are rumors, because the settlement was accompanied by the agreement of secrecy on both sides. At that time Michael Jackson agreed to the settlement due to his lawyer's advice. These had held out the prospect that a regular lawsuit would take years and that something like a second O.J. Simpson case could be expected. But Michael wanted simply to make music and feared he would not be able to stand such psychological stress for a long time, and of that he was indeed right.

Michael's attorney during the second allegations, Thomas Mesereau, called this settlement later Michael's biggest mistake, as he let himself be manipulated. In retrospect one always is more clever than before. But to start then with statements like what would have been when, is only silly. When it would not have rained, the street would be dry today. Every being behaves in a certain moment according to what he deems right in that moment. Period. When things afterward display otherwise or develop differently than one had believed, then one's state of consciousness has changed, one has had new experiences, has new information or another way of thinking. In that state one would perhaps decide something different, but at the time of the original decision all this was not yet there. "What would be when?" is one of the favorite questions of reporters and journalists, and in reality they are only swirling hot air. The smart-aleck "wisdom" of the mind in retrospect are empty and substanceless. They only serve to appear more interesting and to secure the survival of the "ego." When you hear or read "when-then," then you may prepare for a comedy evening, but nothing more.

18. The True Story

Here is the true story that Mary A. Fischer published in October 1994 under the title, "Was Michael Jackson framed?" in the magazine GQ und was later published as a book: "It is a story of greed, ambition, misconceptions on the part of police and prosecutors, a lazy and sensation-seeking media and of the use of a powerful, hypnotic drug." Also Geraldine Hughes published in her book "Redemption" in 2004 the truth about the unparalleled hounding of Michael.

Evan Chandler, Jordan's father, was an unsuccessful dentist, who used the friendship of Michael Jackson with his son to fleece him to the bitter end. In his dental practice, he gave his son during a treatment the drug sodium Amytal, which is known to produce false memories and has a hypnotic effect. There exist documents which prove that Jordan's mother had rehearsed with her son to fix the story. Michael Jackson's odyssey started in May 1992, when his van broke down on Wilshire Boulevard in Los Angeles. He came to the car rental office of David Schwartz, who was married to June Chandler, the divorced wife of Evan Chandler. David called his wife to come immediately with her six year old son Jordan, who was a big Jackson fan, to the office. Thus Michael got to know Jordan and his mother. June gave Michael her phone number and Michael actually called Jordan later. There developed a friendship and from then on the whole family was regularly guests at the Neverland Ranch. During the following year, Michael showered the Chandler family with presents and benefits. He financed their journeys to Disney World, Monaco and Paris.

From March of 1993 on Jordan stayed also overnight at Michael's house, which nobody from the family objected to. Michael had created Neverland as place of retreat for himself and at the same time opened this place for children to enrich their lives, make them happy and to fulfill the last wishes of terminally ill children. Evan Chandler was more or less successful in his profession as dentist, which he only performed due to family obligations, and really wanted to be a writer. The marriage with June had ended in 1985. Friends told that the reason for separation was his fiery temperament. June received sole custody. Later it was known that Evan in 1993 had debts of alimony to her in the amount of 68,000 dollars. Until then he never had cared very much about his son; that changed when Evan got to know Michael. From then on he boasted about it to his friends and colleagues. He also invited Michael with Jordan to his home and made the proposition that Michael should build a new house for him.

When June and Jordan flew with Michael to Monaco he got more and more jealous. There exist tape recordings of a conversation from July 1993 between Evan Chandler and David Schwartz, Jordan's stepfather, where Evan can be heard saying: "This man is gonna be humiliated beyond belief. He will not believe what's going to happen to him. Beyond his worst nightmares. He will not sell one more record....If I go through with this, I win big-time....I will get everything I want, and they will be destroyed forever."

Those who know something about personality disorders have no difficulty in realizing that these are the words of a psychopath. Psychopaths circle only around themselves. They manipulate others in all respects without any respect and abuse them for their purposes. They completely lack a sense of guilt and empathy. Their emotions are shallow and dull, whereby they radiate a superficial charm, which is not easily seen through. This world is filled with psychopaths, more than most may suppose. Among them are chairmen of banks and securities worth several millions, chiefs of corporations and trusts, managers, businessmen and naturally also mafiosi and many small crooks.

Evan Chandler then joined with his attorney Barry Rothman to stay the course. Evan said about him in a phone call with David Schwartz: "He's mean, he's very smart, and he's hungry for the publicity." The clients of Rothman confirm that he is a character of deceit and manipulation. A former employee even called him a demon. His company was bankrupt in November 1992.

When Michael learned of the allegations, he consulted his then attorney Bert Fields, who himself brought in a certain Anthony Pellicano to pursue investigations. On 9th of July 1993 David Schwartz and June Chandler played the tape to Pellicano. The same day Pellicano visited Jordan and asked him directly looking into his eyes, "Did Michael ever touch you? Did you ever see him naked in bed?" The answer to all these questions was, "No."

On 11th of July Evan asked his ex-wife to send Jordan for a one-week visit to him. After that Evan kept the boy without the agreement of the mother and started to fight for custody. From then on the boy was isolated from his friends, his mother and his stepfather. On 4th of August 1993 Evan Chandler with his son and Pellicano met with Michael Jackson, where they read the report of a psychiatrist to him, who mentioned the possibility of abuse. Jordan looked at Michael as if he wanted to say, "I did not say that." And Evan pointed his finger at Michael and said: "I'm going to ruin you." The same night, during a meeting in Rothman's office with Pellicano, twenty million dollars were demanded. Until now Jordan himself had not accused Michael. Some time later Jordan was then given the drug sodium Amytal during a dental treatment in the presence of Evan Chandler and Mark Torbiner, a dental anesthesiologist. After that the boy accused Michael the first time himself. Dr. Phillip Resnick, a psychiatrist, confirmed: "People are very suggestible under it. They can say things under sodium Amytal that are blatantly untrue....It is quite possible to implant an idea by the mere asking of a question. The idea can become their memory, and studies have shown that even when you tell them the truth, they will swear on a stack of Bibles that it happened."

On Sunday the 22nd of August 1993 the media learned of the accusations of Jordan and from there on a witch hunt began in which the yellow press as well as all serious media participated. Some former employees of Michael also incriminated him. Later it was discovered that they had offered their story for money. They had to confess under oath that they knew everything only from hearsay. The investigations by the police were done extremely aggressively, whereby children were bombarded with lies, as for example, that there existed incriminating photos, or the policemen stated that they had been abused themselves, or they forced the children into a corner with suggestive questions. Investigators even flew to the Philippines to investigate a supposed case, but they did not find incriminating material. In the end, Michael Jackson and his accuser came to the well-known civil settlement, which included maintenance of silence for both sides. There was never a charge made by the prosecution, or a trial, because despite extensive investigations of about thirty children and after hearing of 200 witnesses, as well as an unbelievable financial effort, there could not be found any clues for abuse.

Mary Fischer has described the details and personal entanglements in her research in an elaborate way. Everyone can read her report since 1994. So far I cannot find in any media article about Michael Jackson a report about these findings. At times there is mention or hints that the whole issue was a lie, but no background, no details. Why should a corrupt world care to debunk its own corruption? More likely they will continue to wallow in the trash and make cash. The media are really not interested in the truth, because with the truth they cannot make cash nor profit. Reports about Michael's innocence would diminish their editions and bring lower ratings on television. Tanners and shoemakers must suppress the truth, because otherwise they would have to saw at their own chair. The truth does not fit the image of Michael Jackson that was cemented in the public's mind for decades. To write the truth it would be necessary now to dismantle the whole house that was constructed so laboriously. In the past I often have thrown my hands up in horror when friends of mine – honest authentic lovely people – came with their stories about Michael Jackson and believed them in all seriousness, only because it was written in the "Süddeutsche Zeitung" or another serious magazine.

19. Cry for Help

At the time Michael Jackson was confronted with the first allegations, he was on his Dangerous world tour. The tour had started on 27th of June 1992. After 69 concerts with more than 3.5 million attendees, Michael terminated it – as was said due to health problems – on 11th of November 1993 in Japan. On this day my youngest son, in whose Dangerous album I had found the crucial lyrics for Michael's awakened consciousness, had his tenth birthday. And at the same time on the other side of the globe things happened that seemed unbelievable.

Here is the story of Inesita from Chile: "OK this is the story, 1993 – at that time I was over forty – I knew nothing about a singer or musician named Michael Jackson. I had not even seen a photo nor read a comment or heard something else about him. ... That was nothing unusual, because since my 16th year I traveled a lot and stayed most of the time in the mountains, in the jungle or in the wilderness, distant from any radio, television or magazines, which I always had refused to read. Finally I decided to settle down in Valdivia in the South of Chile. I lived in peace, comfortable, no problem during this phase of my life....

But one night there happened something that changed my whole life. I lay in bed sleeping and at the same time awake....I could hear the tiniest noise in the huge house in which I lived, was aware of my body, quiet like a mummy while at the same time sleeping. Suddenly there appeared a man in my room, radiating bright with a golden halo around his head and he came to my bed. WWWoooWWW you will say, but not at all wow, because the man-angel-spirit – or whatever – talked to me as if he was really in the room, with a soft, smooth, melodic voice, which frightened but also calmed me....He called my name and said: 'The time has come that you go out and look for me. Please help me, remember our promise, help, help, listen to this music I composed for you.'

And still dreaming I heard music that was so loud that I finally had to open my eyes. The music I learned weeks later was, 'Will You Be There,' by Michael Jackson. Now it may sound silly, but in that moment I was shocked.

Two weeks passed with the same dreams and I was completely insane and in love with a 'spirit'....Somewhere I suddenly caught a look at a TV at the moment that it was announced that a great entertainer would come to Chile, with his image (note: Michael was on 23 October 1993 in Santiago de Chile) and I was really shocked and cried in front of everyone, 'THAT'S THE MAN OF WHOM I DREAM.'

I want to keep the story as short as possible. From then on for two years, Michael Jackson was called in my daily life and daily in my dreams and at night: 'Help me, come and look after me, and something like, THEY WANT TO KILL ME'.... It was overwhelming, but at the time my love and my confidence in this man grew every day....He also told me...always dreaming...everything about his life, about his family problems, his passions, his fears and things in his marriage that were happening. I knew it a month before it actually happened and the news began to report on it. I heard loud and clear, 'You are not alone'...All the melody and the lyrics six months before the HIStory album was released.

But the important thing was what really happened. Was Michael aware of the telepathic connection that he had? I went to a psychiatrist, who told me that I was not crazy, but I needed a parapsychologist. The craziest thing was that I started painting angels, magic angels with Michael's face, body and hands...Michael dancing, Michael flying, Michael angels everywhere. There came a time when I really wanted to know if Michael also dreamed of me. He showed me in a dream the plan of his home in Santa Inez Valley (my name is Ines and I thought that this is some kind of message ... or whatever) near Santa Barbara, and he said that everything would going very easily for me. So one day I took a plane to LA and went to meet Michael.

The first step at the airport in Los Angeles, I was connected to Michael and also the next and the next. (I had left the house, the furniture, the dogs, chickens, trees, cats, left all of my friends back, my son (17) with his father, and moved to the United States alone, with no one waiting for me, an utter madness).

I lived first in Santa Barbara, and then in Montecito. I decided to write about this experience in a book for others who may have had the same unusual experience. When the book was finished, I had to go with the idea to Michael to show him the book and to ask him if he dreamed about me. Isn't that crazy? I met the horrible Chilean journalist who started the gossip that hit Michael so hard. I met relatives of the Arvizo family (grrr), one of the judges and a Spanish translator. I met people who really hated Michael. I met very few who respected him. I met true friends (I hope) as Deepak Chopra.

Before I talk about my encounter with Michael, I must say that in those incredible two or three years, I had so many many strange spiritual transmissions and I learned so many things about life and I became aware, that I need another tribute site to write them down. I have learned so much about souls before being born on earth...amazing. I became a defender of Michael with my brain, body, heart, my soul and my nails...with my art, my paintings, my poems and the whole universe. Michael was my Guru,...the light on my way....You, my friends, Michael's beloved ones, consider that I have read no newspapers, no magazines, no tabloids. I had no cable, no internet (it was 1993 to 1995).

Then finally, the day...I took my book, asked a friend to steer the car and we drove to Los Olivos in Santa Inez Valley, where Michael himself had told me that his home was there: the Neverland Ranch....We arrived, parked the car and my friend was waiting for me down the road from the ranch. It was three o'clock in the afternoon, very warm. The gates were open and I went in. A nice lady in military dress came over and asked me what I wanted. 'Is Michael at home?' I asked. She laughed and said, 'Yes.' 'I want to give this book I have just written for him.' The military lady said, 'OK, come in.' I walked a long way along a narrow road, my mind was blank, no thinking, just going. After a while I came to meet a lot of people, and MICHAEL!!! He came up to me; between us were a couple of meters. We looked for a long moment...Oh yeah, I saw those eyes again, the same eyes that I had seen the day when the angel first appeared in my dreams. His energy was so intense, pure, beautiful, POWERFUL...I felt the energy with my body, my heart beat faster....

I can say Michael Jackson really was a powerful man, an interdimensional being, BUT ... but he was trembling, astonished, frozen....We stared for a second, a minute, a lifetime, an eternity. I cannot say. The people around him came and suddenly grabbed him with anger. 'He is not feeling well,' said one, and pulled him into the car. He almost fell...he continued looking at me...and then I saw the world turning up and down ... I had an extreme panic attack and ran as fast as I could to get to the road, and ran ... without breath, with the feeling that I could die at that moment ... and ran!

I was inwardly very ill, so I returned to Chile. Well, now I'm exhausted ... I miss a lot of situations, but I can say that the first part of the book is published, the second is ready to print, but is still in my desk. The book is not in libraries and bookstores, the reason is...simple. Too many people make profit with Michael's talent, first in life and now after his death....I do not, Michael, I love you, protect you, share my soul, my spirit, my mission with you, and I want to do with your life no commercial profit. So it is. I am sure that the same applies to most of the friends on this tribute page. True love for all of you."

This report I found at the end of August 2009 on www.michaeljacksontributeportrait.com. Afterward, please note afterward, I read the news in my profile and found there Inesita's invitation to read her report. Exactly that I had just done without her suggestion. Coincidence? Coincidence is only an expression that is used when one has no explanation. Please note that explanations are a type of self-satisfaction of the mind – mindfucking. Is there someone out there who still believes that there is a separation between us? Inesita is living in South Chile; I am living in South Germany. On the Tribute Portrait site there are thousands of users every day.

Inesita and I started an intense exchange via email and later I asked her how she came about inviting me. This is her answer: "I looked at the list of members and saw your name which jumped immediately in my heart and I clicked 'add as friend.' Your name simply jumped." The mentioned website is a common project of Jerry Biederman and David Ilan, an American artist, who uses a technique called pointilism – his paintings are only made of dots/points. It is planned to produce a portrait of Michael consisting of one million dots whereby every dot represents a fan who has registered as a part of this huge project.

On 29th of August 2009 the project was initiated in Hollywood with a ribbon cutting ceremony. Also present were some honor guests who knew Michael personally: Azia Pryor together with Chris Tucker, Don Wilson, the producer of the short film "Man in the Mirror," Allan 'Big Al' Scanlan, who for fifteen years operated the amusement park in Neverland, and Brian Friedman, choreographer and dancer. Dot Number One, the first point of the portrait, is Michael Jackson in the center of the heart, the second dot is his son Prince Michael, the third daughter Paris and the fourth Prince Michael II; all three are parts of the heart too.

I am dot 9266, a part of Michael's nose, undoubtedly the most controversial part of Michael Jackson. That is not a coincidence for sure, as will be confirmed after the publication of this book. In the meantime the site turned into a Mecca for Michael Jackson fans and is used for intense communication and sharing. People all over the world make friends and gather in groups according to certain issues. By September 2009 there were 20,000 "dots" registered and in August 2010 more than 300,000. You are not required to be a fan. You can also be a friend who wants to honor Michael Jackson and use the great power of transformation which is actually circling the globe.

In an interview on the day of inauguration of the site, Big Al answered the question, "What was it like to work for Michael Jackson?" Big Al: "When I am old and grey (not too long from now), I will look on my time at Neverland and my experiences with Mister Jackson as some of the fondest and most cherished memories of my life." Question: "Mister Jackson always exuded such a beautiful spirit when he performed and was interviewed. What was it like to be around his energy? What was Mister Jackson like as a friend?" Big Al: "For the first part of that question...as for spirit and energy in person...it was one hundred times more powerful than you can imagine. For the second part...I always tried to be realistic and remind myself that I was the employee and he was the employer. That was hard at times because he treated me better than many friends treat each other. He was always very polite, respectful, honest and compassionate. If you find a friend that is like that one hundred percent of the time, do not lose that friend....It was a very rewarding and humbling time for me. The impact that a day at Neverland had on the inner city children and the children who were dealing with life-threatening illness was beyond belief. To represent Mister Jackson and to help make his dream come true for those children, to be part of that magical day and the memory those the children will hang on to...was a blessing."

The complete very insightful interview – and additionally one with Brian Friedman – can be found when you google, "Allan Big Al' Scanlan and Brian Friedman remember Michael Jackson: honored guest at MJ Tribute." Through summer 2010 also many celebrities joined this portrait as dots, for example Diana Ross, who was Michael's friend since childhood, his brother Jermaine, the civil rights activist Jesse Jackson, talk show host Larry King, Dr. Maya Angelou, Michael's attorney Thomas Mesereau, the mother and the sister of Ryan White.

20. False Stories

In the years from 2003 to 2005 Michael's life was teeming with parasites with their outrageous fictitious and twisted stories. Parasites suck the blood of their host. They can only survive when they are fed by the energy of their host.

"Creatures crawl in search of blood....your body starts to shiver, for no mere mortal can resist the evil of the thriller." (Thriller)

Michael describes here vividly the goings-on of those who are nourished from the life blood and soul energy of others. The verdict of not guilty on 15th of June 2005 for Michael Jackson was the result of proved innocence and due to a lack of evidence. But the public did not want to accept this. The media adhered to their stories and doubts and continued to circulate the label of pedophile. In an interview with the late Ed Bradley on Christmas 2003 Michael commented on the allegations of ten years before.

Ed Bradley: "What is your response to the allegations that were brought by the district attorney...that you molested this boy?" Michael: "Totally false. Before I would hurt a child, I would slit my wrists. I would never hurt a child. It is totally false. I was outraged. I could never do something like that." Ed Bradley: "This is a kid you knew?" Michael: "Yes." Ed Bradley: "How would you characterize your relationship with this boy?" Michael: "I've helped many, many, many children, thousands of children, cancer kids, leukemia kids. This is one of many." Then Ed Bradley states: "That British documentary last February, which you didn't like." Michael: "Yeah I didn't like it." Ed Bradley: "You said in that documentary that many children have slept in your bedroom. You said, and I'm gonna quote here, 'Why can't you share your bed? The most loving thing to do is to share your bed with someone.' As we sit here today, do you still think that it's acceptable to share your bed with children?" Michael: "Of course, of course, why not? If you're gonna be a pedophile, if you're gonna be Jack the Ripper, if you're gonna be a murderer, it's not a good idea. That I am not. That's how we were raised. And I didn't sleep in the bed with the child. Even if I did, it's okay. I slept on the floor. I gave the bed to the child."

Even Ed Bradley, contrary to Diane Sawyer, having a true wish to understand Michael, does not succeed because "normal" adults have lost their innocence. If I had had the chance in my childhood to sleep in the room of my idol who even makes his bed available for me, I would never have descended willingly from cloud nine to earth. In the mentioned documentary of Martin Bashir, "Living with Michael Jackson", Michael stresses the relevance of the consciousness of men to understand the behavior of people. Those who peruse it attentively and are not blind and deaf like a church mouse can see clearly that Bashir is not at all interested in learning more about Michael or in hearing the truth, to get to know about him and to understand. He is only anxious to find a confirmation for his own (insane) mind and preconceived opinions. He is totally incapable due to his self interest to debunk his own projections, prejudices and judgment. Instead he is trying to squeeze and force a man who is "greater than life" – as Elizabeth Taylor calls him – into the narrow bed of Prokrustes. Truly spoken, I wouldn't let my child go even to an amusement park in the company of Bashir, much less in a room, but I would entrust my child to Michael without hesitation, and I assure you that my capability of distinction is quite sharp.

I remember well that I preferred to pass my time in the late sixties during my college days with gay friends. Thus we could talk the night long about God and the world without fearing that someone would try to strip off my clothes. For the majority of men sexuality is limited to the root chakra. That means that their level of excitement depends greatly on outer or inner stimulus and that they have difficulty controlling these impulses. The creative force of the sexual energy is wasted in orgasm and by ejaculation or used to procreate a child.

With progressed souls, in contrast, the sexual energy is led to the upper parts of the body. With an opened heart chakra it expresses itself as empathy, capability of discrimination and unconditional love. When it rises further to the crown chakra, the concerned one is directly connected to the divine power of creation. Thus the impossible becomes possible.

Undoubtedly Michael was already on this level as a child and later reached the zenith of creativity. One who lives his sexual energy bodily and lives it out will never reach this level. The genius of our world, people with charisma and presence, always have long phases where they are not active sexually. It is a myth to believe that someone who is not sexually active needs medical treatment. It is widely known that Michael Jackson was not one for whom sexuality was important. Accordingly from this aspect the allegations lack a basis and logic. One does not need to be a prosecutor to find out about the absurdity of these statements, but only be a little bit willing and capable to look beneath skin and shell. For this the capability of discrimination is necessary – in Sanscrit viveka - that is the ability to discriminate between true and untrue. But basically the interest in this is not great.

"They wanna get my ass, dead or alive. You know he really tried to take me down by surprise. I bet he missioned with the C.I.A. He don't do half what he say. Dom Sheldon is a cold man. Dom Sheldon is a cold man. Dom Sheldon is a cold man." (D.S.)

One needs not be a detective to find out whom Michael is talking about. This Thomas W. Sneddon, Jr. worked as a prosecutor in Santa Barbara County in California; he was known as "Mad Dog." And this mad one really succeeded in completely destroying the life and career of one of the greatest artists and most wonderful human beings of our time. Michael was thrown to the wolves, or better said the moths. Sneddon was obsessed with convicting Michael Jackson somehow. Nobody thought of driving the devil out of Sneddon. He conducted the investigations against Michael in the year 1993 as well as 2003 and brought the charges of sexual abuse of children, deprivation of liberty and other crimes in the year 2005. The whole thing is as absurd as it would be to bring charges of aggravated battery against Mother Teresa. The district attorney of Santa Barbara was known to have the press in his hands. Whoever has eyes to see and ears to hear realizes very clearly what motives are driving and moving him. Our inner impulses and psychic undertones dig in our face during life as life lines. Look at the physiognomy of Sneddon when he talks. Would you entrust your children to him? Did you ever see him smile heartily?

"Smile though your heart is aching, smile even though it's breaking." (Smile)

Smiling is not the same as laughing. Laughing is a momentary expression of joy. Smiling is a sign of an inner permanent state. "Imagine if all people of the world would smile at the same time for one moment. In this moment the whole of humanity as a whole organism would experience an enlightenment which would change the whole consciousness." (Mantese, 2009, p. 67)

Michael's charisma and the effect of his smile transmit very intensely to the viewer in the video on YouTube, "Michael Jackson, very emotive video, to cry!!!!" that is underlaid with the song, "Find Your Silver Lining," from Steve Gooden. The comment from 10th of February 2010 of Shahparah says, "Something very divine surrounds him." Michael Jackson has contributed considerably to the enlightenment of the world.

"I'm the light of the world." (This Is It)

On 21st of Dec. 2009 I heard Master M saying the same sentence at a meeting in Winterthur in Switzerland: "I am the light of the world." "The self-willed acts bound to his drives. The selfless does not act, because what operates through him is the holy, all-encompassing cosmic course, with which he is living in harmony. He is stillness, universal ordering power, the light of the world." (Mantese, 2009, p. 69/70)

One who observes what Michael triggered alone by appearing, with his radiating smile, by his blown kiss, through one gesture, feels the operating power of light through the form. Take the film, "Teaser," in "HIStory on Film, Volume II." The term "teaser" is ambiguous and means scriber, enticement, difficult task, rascal or stirrer. For this reason Michael's message in "Teaser" was not clearly deciphered until now. Such carrots are the ideal projection surfaces and screens for the observer. Look what you can discover in "Teaser" and you know what is uncovered in you.

For me it deals with the unfolding of the Self, it shows how with a thunderbolt all shells crumble away and the radiating core appears. Michael's body is only used as an art form. What other forms could he have chosen without pledging himself to some group? Therefore only he himself remains when dealing with the Self that belongs to nobody and to nowhere. "Teaser" shows the attraction of light on people and shows the never-ending army of soldiers of light. No weapons, no tanks, no guns, but trappings, which only serve to salute.

On the internet we find the proof how Michael with his smile performs the miracle of a smile on the faces of deadly ill children. Often they even didn't know who was visiting them and stood before them. "Smiling is not something that you do consciously. Smiling simply happens. That's the unmeasurable beauty of a smile....Smiling happens in the magic of a moment, unwilled and unexpected....When the pure heart of divine power is enlightened then the smile of man reflects this light." (Mantese, 2009, p. 67/68)

Michael Jackson was the embodiment of this light, which revealed itself in his smile. When on the other hand the ego tries to smile, because it believes it must use gimmickry, the effects are unpleasant or often even threaten us. There lie worlds between the levels of consciousness of an awakened one and the one who is in deep sleep. On 19th of November 2003, District Attorney Thomas Sneddon said in a press conference: "Within a short period of time, there will be charges filed against Michael Jackson," sounding confident, cocky and gloating. He is often described as pugnacious and tenacious. With laughter he added: "Like the sheriff and I really are into that kind of music."

What is the relationship of such a statement to the issue? Later he was told to apologize for the light tone, which to my knowledge he never did. Many observers describe Sneddon as combative and obstinate. "I believe the people feel that he is a person with a mission....He's a law-and-order guy who sees the world in black and white. There's bad guys and good guys, and he sees himself as the good guy." (Tatiana Morales, CBSnews.com/stories/2003/12/17/)

A good guy with the mission to destroy Michael Jackson? In this matter he did his utmost. This sheriff Sneddon from Santa Barbara even succeeded in bringing about a change in California law which facilitated the realization of his paranoia against Michael Jackson. Who gave this order to him? Was perhaps the hand of God in the pie?

People project their own unreleased monsters on others and believe erroneously that this enables them to free themselves from them. It's an impossible undertaking but it explains the existence of whippers and slave drivers and the motivation of investigating officers and prosecutors. More often than most people believe, the choice of profession serves personal concerns and provides a chance to take one's anger out on somebody else. The result can only be unjustness. Thank God Sneddon was stopped. Perhaps a better choice for him would be mafiosi. Why he chose the most innocent man will remain a mystery forever and enter the annals as cosmic joke.

From my own experience I can say, be on your guard in front of self-proclaimed good people. They are the wolves in sheep's clothing. A true good person will never call himself as such. Did you ever slip into the shoes of someone who is in the dock innocently for nearly five months? Are you really able to imagine? And now consider that this is not happening in an anonymous court with perhaps three reporters, but in front of more than 2000 representatives of the media, who cover day by day the news about you in press, radio and television to all corners of the world. Besides some indigenous people there is nobody in the world who does not know Michael Jackson. This torture is rarely imaginable by anyone, even approximately, who has not experienced it himself, because we lack the necessary capacity of discrimination to do so. After such an experience you are scarred for your whole life. For this sort of hell the soul is not prepared and even less when it is a sensitive and sensible soul like Michael, who is not even able to deal ill with a fly.

At that time the murder began, the murder in installments. Involuntary homicide by his personal doctor Murray is not what took Michael's life, but the treatment by the mass, the public and especially the press. Michael was not a monster and not an "ubermensch." But he was after the acquittal a broken man. To be confronted for months with lies, greed, hate, envy, falsehood and hypocrisy may perhaps in some way be taken by a cold-hearted blunted monster, but for a fine soul full of compassion and empathy is that the death blow.

And nevertheless the smile also after all that did not totally disappear from Michael's face. What greatness of a man, who continues dancing in hell!

By the way, Michael Jackson had gotten to know Martin Bashir on the recommendation of Uri Geller. Uri had surely meant well, to acquaint Michael with a journalist who had previously interviewed Princess Diana. But he had no sufficient capacity of discrimination to realize that this was not a good omen. With that he had put a moth and a hypocrite on Michael.

Bashir spent eight months with Michael at Neverland and accompanied him on journeys. The premiere of "Living with Michael Jackson" in particular set the allegations in 2003 rolling. Bashir supposedly wanted to correct the image of Michael Jackson in the public. Perhaps it all had to be like this, so that the plan for Michael's stay on earth could be fulfilled. In any case, the friendship between Michael Jackson and Uri Geller was history after that (1st of August 2009, RTL Explosiv).

Uri related that once he hypnotized Michael and – without his knowledge – asked the question, if he ever had done something inappropriate to a child. And Michael's spontaneous answer was at that time: "No, never." One who would put such a question himself has doubts and does not trust the assertion of innocence of the concerned. When I am persuaded of the credibility of a statement then I don't need any proof. There exists a knowing due to a capacity of intuitive discrimination instead of a knowing due to conclusions from collected information. People with sharpened capacity of discrimination – viveka – have access to the quality of energy of a living being and can feel their essence directly. Viveka happens when the flute is hollow and pure, at a void free from thoughts and mental constructs. Thus the intuition can flow through it unhindered. Ever more people reach this state, where step by step all mental trash is disposed of.

The 1938 born author Ishmael Reed gives a statement to the cause of Michael's death in "Counter – America's best political newsletter": "In my opinion it was the prosecution of Jackson by this District Attorney, who, among other things, violated Jackson's fourth amendment rights, and made disparaging remarks about the star during a press conference, and the side-show pro prosecution media coverage that killed Jackson. In my lengthy examination of the trial printed in my book, 'Mixing It Up, Taking on The Media Bullies,' I concluded that though millions of Jackson's fans celebrated his acquittal, the District Attorney, who was allowed to squander the California taxpayers' money so that he might humiliate a rich black man, whom he felt had sassed him, was the victor. At the beginning of the trial, Jackson was dancing on top of a van. During the trial he had to be hospitalized. At the end, he was a frail, emaciated wreck."

Reed calls Sneddon's charges a revenge campaign, where he used the whole power of the state.(www.counterpunch.org/reed06292009.html)

Thomas Mesereau also confirms that the behavior of the district attorney was exclusively motivated by revenge since 1993. One who knows a little bit about reading body language can see for himself. The film documentary from Larry Nimmer shows how Sneddon invades Neverland with his sheriffs and a search warrant in the absence of Michael Jackson. Sneddon went so far that he even wanted to show photos of Michael's genitals to the grand jury during the trial in 2005, which was even to the two presiding judges overdoing things and was denied.

Reed also reveals the arbitrary coverage of many prejudiced journalists. "All these opinions indicate that the bosses of the television networks had adopted the task of declaring the verdict of the jury null and void whenever it pleased them. This white electronic jury has put itself above the law." According to him also the coverage of Jackson's death in American television was ignorant and salacious. In the "Today Show" it was discussed what happened to the money of the "nigger" – please note: nigger. Michael Jackson's philanthropic activities and his support of more than forty charity organizations, which brought him a listing in the Guinness book of world records, were at most mentioned marginally. Michael's honest and everlasting efforts to support the poor, ill and weak people and to better their life conditions and life quality, are not recognized. On the contrary, his love for humanity and special love for children turned to be a disaster for him – as Master Jesus was accused about his contact with those at the edge of society.

Cory Rooney, producer and songwriter, who was appointed as vice president of A&R in 1998 at Epic and was a friend of Michael, tells us in an interview what Michael had told him about the background of his relationships with children: "Cory, when I was a kid, I was denied not only a childhood, but I was denied love. When I reached out to hug my father, he didn't hug me back. When I was scared on an airplane, he didn't put his arm around me and say, 'Michael don't worry. It's gonna be okay.' When I was scared to go on stage, he said, 'Get your ass on that stage.' And not just him, but every other adult around him."

Michael himself, in a speech at the university of Oxford speaks openly and in detail about his relationship with his father.

"He had great difficulty showing affection. He never really told me he loved me, and he never really complimented me either. If I did a great show, he would tell me it was a good show. If I did an okay show, he would say nothing. He seemed intent, above all else, on making us a commercial success. At that he was more than adept. My father was a managerial genius and my brothers and I owe our professional success, in no small measure, to the forceful way that he pushed us."

And Michael continues: "Is it any mystery that he hardened his heart, that he raised the emotional ramparts? And most of all, is it any wonder why he pushed his sons so hard to succeed as performers, so that they could be saved from what he knew to be a life of indignity and poverty? I have begun to see that even my father's harshness was a kind of love, an imperfect love, to be sure, but love nonetheless. He pushed me because he loved me. Because he wanted no man to ever look down at his offspring. And now, with time, rather than bitterness, I feel blessing. In the place of anger I have found absolution. And in the place of revenge I have found reconciliation. And my initial fury has slowly given way to forgiveness.

Almost a decade ago, I founded a children's charity called Heal the World. The title was something I felt inside me. Little did I know...that those two words form the cornerstone of Old Testament prophecy. Do I really believe that we can heal this world, that is riddled with war and greed and genocide even today? And do I really think that we can heal our children, the same children who...can walk into their high school...and shoot down two students just at the beginning of their lives?...Or children who can beat a defenseless toddler to death?...

Of course I do, or I wouldn't be here tonight. But it all begins with forgiveness, because to heal the world, we first have to heal ourselves. And to heal the kids, we first have to heal the child within, each and every one of us. As an adult and as a parent I realize that I cannot be a whole human being, nor a parent capable of unconditional love, until I put to rest the ghosts of my own childhood. "

And that's what I'm asking all of us to do tonight. Live up to the fifth of the Ten Commandments. honor your parents by not judging them. Give them the benefit of the doubt. That is why I want to forgive my father and to stop judging him. I want to forgive my father, because I want a father, and this is the only one that I've got. I want the weight of my past lifted from my shoulders and I want to be free to step into a new relationship with my father, for the rest of my life, unhindered by the goblins of the past."

Also when at the beginning Michael Jackson – as is the case by all who have experienced a difficult childhood – was filled with resentments and anger against his father, so he worked hard on reconciliation and has known the power of forgiveness and non-judgment. Nobody can take the burden from our shoulders, only we ourselves by the power of love. Cory continues: "So he said to me, 'Cory, I will never deny a child love. And if it means that I have to be crucified or put in jail for it, then that's just what they're gonna have to do.' And so when it was time for him to stand trial, the first time he went through it, his advisors told him, 'Michael, this is not good. Pay this kid off and let's keep moving. The second time he said, 'You know what? All that did was make me look guilty like I was hiding something, so this time there won't be any payoffs. I'm gonna fight this in court, and you'll see, I'll be innocent.'" (http://thesportsinterview.com)

Michael has been one of the greatest philanthropists of our time. A philanthropist knows about the goodness in men. He is a friend of humanity from the depth of his heart, somebody who directs his attention not to the tiny black spot in a white blanket, but who sees and honors the whiteness (or the wisdom) (wordplay in German: Weißheit = whiteness; Weisheit = wisdom) of the blanket. He is somebody to whom the benefit of men – all men – is near and dear, one hundred percent Michael Jackson.

By doing my research and having my own experiences I often asked myself: What sort of world is that which turns everything upside down? Man creates himself the ugliest creatures, which then strike terror into people's hearts, after being brought to life. Every single thought you send out into the world creates the respective creature. Did you ever think about what is happening to the thought that wanders permanently through your mind? Do you really want the creatures that you are producing? How insane is someone who detests his own creatures and tries to get rid of them immediately after finishing them? The wars and fights you are conducting are nothing other than wars and fights against your own creatures.

Why don't we use the same powers with which we create monsters to send a glimmer of light into the world? To create works that the heart enjoys and that elevate the soul – like Michael did his life long? The glimmers of light, that he gave us as presents, have their impact.

The number of tributes to Michael Jackson which are taking place worldwide, and thanks to the internet can be seen by everyone, is growing daily, from Taiwan and South Africa to Greenland. All continents, all races, all classes, all religions, all nations, all cultures – united in commemoration of a "Great Soul" and thus united in the massive flow of awakening from a collective dream of humanity. Here is a part of a common product (YouTube) from The Game, Chris Brown, Polow da Don, Diddy, Usher, Mario Winans, Boys 2 Men, "Better on the other side":

"I remember the first time I have seen you moonwalk. I believed I could do anything. You made the world dance. You made the music come alive....Who is Michael Jackson? You are Michael Jackson. I am Michael Jackson. We all are Michael Jackson....This is the type of song that makes the angels cry. I look up in the sky and I wonder why. Why you had to go, go? I know it's better on the other side. You were chosen from the start."

Even from Bollywood the tributes are coming over. For example on 26th July 2009 the "Seagrams Royal Stag" brought out "Make it Large – A Tribute" with the song, "We lived in His World": "We've lost a part of our history,...thanks for being with us...we love you MJ, your legend will never die...you truly inspired the whole world...You made the music come to life..."

The composer Visha speaks about the background of the song: "The idea was derived with just from the thought of Michael. It's just awesome to see all of us come together out of love for one person and his music. It's magic!...A tribute to MJ is something any musician would give his right hand to do." (www.redchillies.com/atributetomj)

At the BET Awards 2009 singer Ne-Yo, with whom Michael Jackson had planned a common project, which would not be realized, sings Michael's hit, "The Lady in My Life," honoring him. Even sportsmen honor Michael. In September 2009 the Norwegian ski team dances a tribute to "Beat It" in ski clothing high in the mountains in Portillo in Chile. Aksel Lund Svindal, who had won the gold medal on 19th of February 2010 in Super G in Vancouver, is part of it. (YouTube: Original Michael Jackson Tribute by the Norwegian Skiteam).

21. We Had Him

Dr. Maya Angelou composed a Tribute to Michael Jackson, "We Had Him":

"Beloveds, now we know that we know nothing, now that our bright and shining star can slip away from our fingertips like a puff of summer wind. Without notice, our dear love can escape our doting embrace, can sing our songs among the stars and walk our dances across the face of the moon. In the instant that Michael is gone, we know nothing. No clocks can tell our time. No oceans can rush our tides with the abrupt absence of our treasure.

Though we are many, each of us is achingly alone, piercingly alone. Only when we confess our confusion can we remember that he was a gift to us and we did have him. He came to us from the Creator, trailing creativity in abundance. Despite the anguish, his life was sheathed in mother love, family love, and survived and did more than that. He thrived with passion, compassion, humor and style.

We had him. Whether we know who he was or did not know, he was ours and we were his. We had him beautiful, delighting our eyes. His hat aslant over his brow, he took a pose on his toes for all of us. And we laughed and stomped our feet for him. We were enchanted with his passion because he held back nothing. He gave us all he had been given. Today in Tokyo, beneath the Eiffel Tower, in Ghana's Black Star Square. In Johannesburg and in Pittsburgh, in Birmingham, Alabama, and Birmingham, England, we are missing Michael. But we do know that we had him - and We Are The World."

(YouTube "Michael Jackson Poem Recited by Maya Angelou")

On 21st of June 2010 she recited this poem for Michael the first and only time in public during a meeting with David Ilan, where he placed her dot in the Michael Jackson Portrait. She knows what she is talking about, because a great soul recognized a Great Soul. And she adds: "Michael had no modesty. Modesty is a learned affectation. It's stuck on from without, like decals. What Michael Jackson had was humility....He was everybody's baby brother, or everybody's big brother."

What is happening worldwide since Michael's disappearance from the earthly stage makes us speechless, as everything that he started during lifetime, and blows up any dimensions, borders and imaginations. And that is good as it is, because imaginations are products of the human mind which a priori is only a tiny part of life and the cosmic order. And when the borders of the mind are blown up, in some time the way from the outer layer to the core will open. Michael's short films in HIStory are telling us about this way, which will only be revealed to the one who has lost his belief. All believers must stay outside for the moment. I'm not talking here about devotees of religions, but about the strict believers of concepts.

Even though not Michael Jackson's declared goal, he won all prizes as musician and artist that can be won in general in the music industry. For example, on 15th of November 2006 he received from Beyoncé, at the World Music Awards in London, the "Diamond Award." He holds numerous records in the Guinness Book of World records as well, in relation to the number of singles and albums in the charts and Top Ten, as well as in relation to the numbers of his sold songs.

Compared to awards for the musician and artist Michael Jackson, his awards for his actions as human and humanitarian, for his unparalleled engagement as philanthropist are rare. This side of Michael Jackson, which lay at his heart as well as his being an artist, was perceived by the public only marginally. And Michael wasn't interested in being of service for reasons of public relations, because his caring about children and suffering was born out of love and came from the core of his being.

Twice Michael was suggested for the Nobel Peace Prize, but unfortunately this honor was not granted him. In July 2009 he was posthumously bestowed with the "Save the World Award." This ceremony took place in Zwentendorf in Austria, in a nuclear power plant that never functioned. In the presence of two of his sons, Michael's brother Jermaine sang his favorite song, "Smile," to honor him.

Michael Jackson was at first sight the King of Pop, but at second sight he was the King of Hearts and on third sight even much more. And Michael Jackson was unwaveringly persuaded: The truth runs marathons, while the lie runs only sprints. And at the time of Michael's disappearance from the earthly stage this marathon is not at all finished. That does not only mean, that the truth in long run will defeat the lie and finally win through, but also that the opposite „lie – truth is only an illusion. There is a truth which knows no more an opposite, which reveals itself, when all opposites are transcended.

In the world of phenomena there are two poles, which are like opposites, like a wave in the ocean, which comes and goes. But the ocean itself stays untouched by the wave. The wave is part of the ocean, even feeling separated from the ocean. The ocean doesn't mind. Therefore I always wonder when the question arises, "How can God let this be?," How can it be God's fault when the wave in its phantasies of allmightyness does what it wants. How can it be God's fault when the wave – believing as it is – believes itself to be separated from the ocean? Should God really come and interfere into the human works of insanity, which the human mind in its hubris and ignorance has created itself? Why does man not bethink himself of his Self and cease the production of things he doesn't like? Be careful what you think and wish; it could be fulfilled.

A story hereto: "Once there was a couple who were happily married for fifty years. Then the man got seriously ill. Every day he got worse. They had undertaken everything, consulted the best doctors – without success. The illness unceasingly progressed. The woman prayed to God every day, that he may restore the health of her husband. Nothing helped. The less the doctors could do the more intensive were her prayers, that God may maintain her beloved husband for still a while. And she prayed and prayed. And really his state improved. She continued to pray. Nobody had an explanation, but it really seemed as if he would totally recover from illness. His wife was overly happy, thanked God and continued to pray.

One day he could leave the bed and was considered well. He again could leave the house for a walk. And one day he did not return from this walk. He had got to know another woman and simply stayed with her. His wife was deeply depressed and did not want to live any longer. Again she directed herself to God and complained bitterly, why he had done this to her. And God answered: 'From exactly this experience I wanted to save you, when your husband got deathly ill.'"

22. The World in You

"The sense of 'the world in me' is how I always want to feel. That one in the mirror has his doubts sometimes. So I am tender with him. Every morning I touch the mirror and whisper, 'Oh, friend, I hear a dance. Will you be my partner? Come.'" (That *One* in the Mirror, Dancing the Dream)

As long as there is someone who has wishes, imaginations and longings, the wheel of reincarnation will rotate. What is born is the "i" and what is reborn is again the "i". Everything what "i" has sown, "i" will harvest. And when the "i" has sown something that it could no more harvest as long as it resides in the body, then these "i-forces" will attract the energies after the physical death, until the momentum is reached that again a physical body will be formed to receive this "i".

Awakening means the end of the wheel of reincarnation, to leave the cycle of birth and death. In awakening the "i" dies and thus there is nobody to attract the energies for a new incarnation. What incarnates is only the "i." The one, who I really am does not reincarnate, because I was never born.

On the other side the argument, that there is no incarnation, because you can't remember one, is shortsighted. Do you remember what you have done the 16th of January 1991? And if not, does this lack of remembrance mean that you were not existent on 16th of January 1991? At that time there was an "i" and who remembers or does not remember is this "i". All this happens around this small "i" and this small "i" is responsible that there is "i." When this "i" has melted away in the heat of the sun then only "I" remain, or "IT" or "THAT," or whatever. Before the melting away, the "i" is full of fears, literally the fear of death, and therefore the „i" shuns the closeness of the sun. Therefore the seekers avoid the door with the sign, "Here lives God." Around this search developed a whole industry, the so called esoteric. The joke thereby is that this industry is guaranteed that nothing will never be found. Because in reality it is not about finding, but about the "i" remaining the searcher forever. And thus it inflates under the cover of spirituality even more and gets big and fat.

Spiritual egos are most dangerous because they are the most difficult to see through, especially because they put the words love and light on their flags. Therefore train the capability of discrimination and get in contact with the seer in your heart. "Inside your heart sits a Seer." (Magical Child, part 1, Dancing the Dream)

If anybody wants to make you believe that there is an "either – or," then mistrust him, because he is living in the world of the mind and has not yet found the door behind which the opposites are extinguished. "The power of discrimination enables him (man) to put his life in loving order, that means that what creates disorder will be seen through by insight and overcome." (Mantese, 2009, p. 42)

Pupils and teachers are not different from each other, neither winner nor loser. Everyone is in each instance also the so-called opposite of everything. There is no opposite of black and white. These are only two sides of the same medal. Everyone is pupil and teacher at the same time. Everyone is winner and loser at the same time and everyone is black and white at the same time. If you don't believe that, then simply do the 365 lessons of "A Course in Miracles," every day one to three minutes, for one year, and the illusions which are produced by the human mind and thinking will be dissolved on their own.

Nature named Maya produces a fata morgana, which is thought to be delusively true and genuine. The personality is such a fata morgana, which we think to be true and genuine. In reality it is only a phenomenon in the consciousness like a mirage in the water. All attempts to bring about changes on the level of personality are nothing other than attempts to change the fata morgana or the mirage. What is this good for? Do you want to spend your life changing air? Do you want to exchange one nightmare for another one, or a bad dream for a comfortable one?

A dream is a dream, even when we experience it as very real. Chains are chains, regardless of whether they are rusty or golden. Only when you awaken does the spook end. The grossest illusion in the human dream is the one of victim and perpetrator. Man believes himself to be either a victim or an aggressor; most believe themselves to be victims. If we would take a poll, the result would probably be that the perpetrators are extinct. But where there is a victim there also must be a perpetrator. But where are all these perpetrators? We ourselves are perpetrators who feel as victims, victims of our own products, of the products that we produce ourselves as aggressor. For example when I feel threatened then I myself am threatening someone – without being conscious about it.

When I have the feeling that others are haughtily looking down on me then that is the exact mirror of what I myself am doing – without wanting to know about it. Instead of searching inside for what is shown to us on the outside, we prefer to accuse the mirror and demand that it will change, to get rid of this uncomfortable feeling that creeps up when we confront ourselves with the mirror.

Always when you think that you don't like person XY, because he is doing this or that to you, then simply turn the sentence around and look more thoroughly. Because it is fact that I am doing something with this person and not he or she with me. In the moment where you change, in that moment the other also has changed, because he is always only your own mirror. Admittedly it is difficult to stay consequently at this sight, because it is common practice to only look outside and to search others for the blame for everything. Everyone thinks of himself as the good one and believes the other to be the bad one which should change. Then everything is alright!? "You see the splinter in the other's eye, but not the beam in your own." (The Gospels)

"I'm starting with the man in the mirror...if you wanna make the world a better place, take a look at yourself and - make a change." Changing our glasses and our sight we learn step by step that we have created the world we live in by ourselves. When you live in a world full of problems then this is your own creation. Your neighbor may be confronted with a similar situation on the outside and is indeed living in a joyful world. Why? Because he does not perceive and define the situation as a problem, but as a chance to "get out of the way" and integrate into the natural order. There is no wish to control, no likings and no aversions. What remain are humility and devotion to the source.

Michael Jackson was all embodiment of this humility. Don't try to understand it, because the mind cannot grasp things, which are beyond its capacity. This "getting out of the way" does not happen in the room of mind and therefore this one has first to surrender and realize that it has reached its limits, until the room beyond can be entered. In Zen-Buddhism there exists the Koan, paradoxical questions with the goal to bring the mind to surrender itself, to get insight that it has reached its limits. For example: How does the clapping of one hand sound? This question will be moved in the mind for so long until the thinker is extinguished.

23. Planet Joy

Here comes the short form of a story for adults:

"Somewhere in a very distant galaxy there is a planet named Joy. The Joyans were always filled with bliss, full of love and compassion. Joy is a blue shimmering planet, very similar to the Earth, with a tiny difference that three suns are shining on it. So there is only day, no night. The light is ever present.

Joyans embrace each other regularly when meeting and give one another a huge hug. Every Joyan wears a rucksack which is filled with fluffies — colored smooth, puffy little balls. Every time Joyans meet they give each other a fluffy as a present and put it in their rucksack. That is a signal to the counterpart that they are something special. One can feel how cuddly and warm it feels to the touch, when such a fluffy meets your face.

When a Joyan gets a fluffy as a present it is clear that he will give one himself. "As it belongs to the essence of man to explore the outer worlds, they one day discovered with their telescopes the planet Joy and they succeeded after many years in landing there. When the first human met a Joyan this one gave him immediately an especially soft fluffy as present; but man didn't want to accept the gift and warned him: "Be careful with your fluffies, because if you give them so generously, you yourself will be short of them soon."

Confused, the Joyan returned home and was so irritated that he did not even reflect about how illogical the advice of the human was, as everyone who gave a fluffy also got one. And therefore the store of fluffies was inexhaustible.

For the first time in his life, the Joyan was sad and depressed and felt fear of the future. It wasn't long before a friend came and immediately offered a fluffy to him. But the insecure Joyan denied it: "No no, it's better you keep it yourself. Who knows how quickly otherwise your storage will diminish." He understood nothing at all. But he took the confused thoughts with him and soon everywhere one could hear when Joyans said: "I am sorry I have to take care that I will not go short on fluffies."

All Joyans started to store their fluffies. Now and then a fluffy was given away, but only after thorough reflection – and the initial joy was also gone. Soon there were the first cases of fluffy robbery and a common mistrust had spread. The time of bliss lay behind them, was soon forgotten and erased from memory. But nevertheless the Joyans dreamt at night of the good old times." (www.we-move-people.com)

How will this story continue?

24. Capacity of Discrimination

I hope that all those who enjoy their moth-being will one day be called to account and have to experience firsthand what they did to other innocent souls. The first and only human right, "to be left alone," which was denied Michael Jackson during lifetime, is even denied to him posthumously. These moths are a shame for humanity, as they day and night provide us with so-called news. Do you gradually realize which brainwashing is taking place with you?

James Redfield calls it a "century-long weltanschauungsdream," where we purposefully go through the world with blinders. In a sort of collective obsession, we jumped upon the material illusion and fell into the trap of our own creations" (Redfield, 1998, p. 57f).

Nothing has yet changed about this, as is demonstrated by the disparaging reactions to a private video of Michael, which appeared in 2009. The five minutes show Michael playing with his three children, Prince and Paris in pajamas, and a scene at Paris' birthday. I will not comment on the comments of the moths. Everybody can make sure of this for himself on YouTube.

"Prince, I wish for you to learn about perseverance and confidence and the true meaning of success, which is love. That you know that you can reach any goal that your heart desires,…and I love you, thank you." While Michael, Prince and Paris are sitting on the floor playing, Michael sings: "When you sit there addressing, counting your blessings, biding your time. When you lay me down sleeping and my heart is weeping - Because I'm keeping a place …". The children join in: "… for all the lost children. This one's for all the lost children - This one's for all the lost children, wishing them well - And wishing them home." (The lost Children) Paris with shining eyes: "Daddy, thank you for my birthday cake and I love you so much. I love my Daddy so much. You're the best daddy in the whole world." Michael: "I love you more Paris." Then he turns to Prince: "Why don't you stand next to Paris?" And Prince says: "Okay, Daddy, thank you for giving me ice cream. You're the best daddy in the whole world and I love you" (runs towards his father and kisses him). Michael and the children continue to play, dance and tease each other. Then follows a new scene: Paris blows out the candles of her birthday cake. Michael applauds. Michael: 'Good Paris, what do you want to your birthday, what shall happen? What do you like? What do you wish?" Paris: "I want to do what you do." Michael: "What do I do?" Paris: "Sing and dance." Michael: "Really?" Prince: "Me too." Michael: "I'm talking to Paris right now." Paris to Prince: "It's my birthday, Prince." Then Prince and Paris sing Michael's song "The lost children": "We pray for our fathers, pray for our mothers, wishing our families well. We sing songs for the wishing, of those who are kissing, but not for the missing. So this one's for all the lost children, this one's for all the lost children, this one's for all the lost children, wishing them well and wishing them home."

There follows again a change of scenes with a song of Prince and Paris: "You are my daddy, my only daddy, you make me happy, how much I love you." Michael: "I love you, all you three." (Copyright Slash, Copyright Bild)

This video shows a very normal family live, where all treat each other very lovingly as everybody would wish for himself. Who would not like to have such a loving father, who spends time with his children, plays and sings with them, assures them how much he loves them, embraces and kisses them and fulfills wishes? And which father would not like to have children, who give him back something of what he gave them? I myself cannot remember that my parents ever told me they loved me, and I even can't remember that they ever kissed or embraced me. Perhaps the way that my heart bonds to Michael, who also did not get all this and nevertheless was able to give it examplarily to his own children, has its origin in these experiences.

On 20th of July 2009 another text reaches me, which proves how busy the moths are at work. Deepak Chopra, a friend of Michael, who wrote the foreword to "Dancing the Dream," writes in "Tribute To My Friend Michael Jackson":

"When we first met, around 1988, I was struck by the combination of charisma and woundedness that surrounded Michael. He would be swarmed by crowds at an airport, perform an exhausting show for three hours, and then sit backstage afterward, as we did one night in Bucharest, drinking bottled water, glancing over Sufi poetry as I walked into the room, and wanting to meditate. That person, whom I considered (at the risk of ridicule) very pure, still survived – he was reading the poems of Rabindranath Tagore, when we talked the last time, two weeks ago." "At the risk of ridicule" was translated to German on login.wordpress.com as "until the border of ridiculousness" and thus falsified the whole meaning.

Such dilettante translations are a reason for rumor, slander and misunderstandings. In reality the translator only outs himself in relation to his own projections. When you read things, always use your capacity of discrimination, because only with viveka you are able to separate true and untrue. The power of discrimination is an inherent capability which has atrophied in most people, because the mind with its concepts has taken command. As soon as the mind is mastered, the door to viveka opens again. Viveka is the sine qua non for wisdom and discerns it from cheek (wordplay in German: wisdom = Weisheit; cheek = Naseweisheit = wisdom of the nose). The capacity of discrimination appears naturally when the flute is hollow and empty.

25. Joy

It took seventy days for the stone that was thrown into the water in Stockholm to travel 8880 kilometers and arrive in Los Angeles, Hollywood. A breathtaking velocity for an impulse of the heart. On 25th of July 2009, hundred dancers in Los Angeles performed the same "Dance Tribute for Michael Jackson" to the music of "Beat It" as had 300 dancers in the Swedish capital. On 26th of July 2009 also in Hong Kong, a flashmob was performed to "Beat It", and at the same time in Paris and Montreal. Prior to that, on 26th of June in London on Liverpool Street hundreds had gathered singing and dancing to "Thriller", while in another quarter of London a flashmob to "Moonwalk" took place. In Vienna on the same day, a flashmob was organized to honor Michael on the Karlsplatz. On 27th of June, one day later, hundreds met in Paris for a "mass-Moonwalk." And on 17th of July 2009 on YouTube, a 40-second flashmob to "Beat It" was uploaded from Taipeh in Taiwan.

These are not the only tributes which circle the world. More exactly, these actions are not really flashmobs, but rather smartmobs, but the term flashmob is being used for all types of mobs. A flashmob is initially an action without any sense, whereby only the fun counts. A smartmob on the other hand is an action where an impulse is set, which then centers around. But in any case the internet user will see that in the meantime we have arrived on the planet Joy and started to distribute fluffies ourselves.

Deepak Chopra's "Tribute" for Michael ends with the following words: "When the shock subsides and a thousand public voices recount Michael's brilliant, joyous, embattled, enigmatic, bizarre trajectory, I hope the word 'joyous' is the one that will rise from the ashes and shine as he once did."

Here is the version circulating on the Internet: "... I hope that the term 'happy' is what rises from the ashes and radiates so much as Michael did once." "Joyous" does not mean "cheerful," but "full of joy".

Again and again you can see that the translations of Michael's words tend to make him smaller and ordinary. We have not enough big vessels ourselves to be able to hold his Greatness. Do you have the capacity of discrimination to see the difference of "cheerful" and "joyful"? Joy is a vibration at the level of divinity – even higher than love, because it contains the love energy. Joy is a vibration which embraces and encloses everything, without making a difference, without judgment. Cheerfulness is like a wheelchair in comparison with a moon rocket, and a superficial temporary emotion.

Purify your flute from judgments and prejudices to elevate your capacity of discrimination from the level of a hamster to the level of an eagle. Michael Jackson was sent from the planet Joy to transform the planet Earth into the planet Joy.

"Adults get tangled up in complications over whether to eat the ice cream or not. A child simply enjoys." (Children, Dancing the Dream)

"What delight nature must feel when she makes stars out of swirling gas and empty space. She flings them like spangles from a velvet cape, a billion reasons for us to awaken in pure joy." (Magic, Dancing the Dream)

"When it's allowed to be free, love is what makes life alive, joyful, and new. It's the juice and energy that motivates my music, my dancing, everything. As long as love is in my heart, it's everywhere." (Love, Dancing the Dream)

"I miss you, Ryan White, you showed us to stand and fight. In the rain you were a cloudburst of joy, the sparkle of hope in every girl and boy. In the depth of your anguished sorrow was the dream of another tomorrow." (Ryan White, Dancing the Dream)

"Child of innocence, messenger of joy, you've touched my heart without a ploy. My soul is ablaze with a flagrant fire. To change this world is my deepest desire." (Child of Innocence, Dancing the Dream)

"You can change the world (I can't do it by myself) - You can touch the sky (Gonna take somebody's help) - You're the chosen one (I'm gonna need some kind of sign) - If we all cry at the same time tonight." (Cry).

Michael's dearest wish and his deep longing was to motivate people to act, to come together and collectively save this wonderful planet from destruction by egomania and greed for power. How urgent this call was and how far ahead Michael was in his time, is shown to us quite plainly nowadays day by day. Since his going off the earthly stage Michael's awakening call has won even more actuality.

It was never Michael Jackson's purpose to think of himself as the healer and savior of the world, and never did he elevate himself in such a way, as is indeed still claimed in unison by tanners, shoemakers and moths and what then fills them with indignation. It was Michael's vision to awaken humanity, to encourage them to be warriors of light. Gandhi's salt march to the sea, an act born from non-violence, could serve as a model for us. Such are the visions of Michael, even when his films are riddled with symbols that are similar to war. To decipher the meaning, capacity of discrimination is needed and not narrow concepts. The power of transformation is derived from joy, not from political actions, resistance talking or protest marches.

"That lonely child, still clutching his toy, has made his peace, discovered his joy." (Once we were there, Dancing the Dream)

"Let us celebrate the joy of life, let us dance the dance of creation." (Heaven is Here, Dancing the Dream).

Who did not yet feel the joy in every physical or mental cell when attending a concert or hearing music, and expressing it, simply hearing such sounds as in "Wanna be Starting Something"? „Ma ma se, ma ma sa, ma makossa, ma ma se, ma ma sa, ma makossa, ma ma se, ma ma sa, ma makossa, ma ma se, ma ma sa, ma makossa ....". This chant is initially a riff in a song, which used the saxophonist Manu Dibango from Cameroon; in 1973 he landed the hit "Soul Makossa" in Africa, Europe and America, which is regarded as the first disco hit. Makossa is a traditional dance from Cameroon. Michael did not only produce a hit with this song, but also honored his black ancestors from Africa.

Don't you wonder how many things Michael did or said of which you have had not the slightest idea until now? In reality his work is so enormous that it is impossible to get an overview even in months and years. When I got the following feedback from Roland in 2009 about the first chapters of my book, I got curious. "I also believe that the message of videos like 'Earth Song' or 'Black or White' is awesome. But Michael made to each 'Earth Song' ten songs which do not have a special engagement, where no particular message can be realized. These are Pop/Rock/Soul/Funk/Disco-Hits; they belong to the best of the genre, but the man did not write the Bhagavadgita and not the Matthew-Passion. When I therefore ask myself the question if Michael was an enlightened one, I realize that especially the most famous and 'typical' hits have an aggressive, hectic and frenzied radiation."

But hello, does Roland not recognize that he is outing himself right now and only using Michael as projection screen? Who finds aggressiveness in Michael's work should research more exactly in his own inner self. And besides I cited enough proof that Michael Jackson has written many things that can definitely compete with the wisdom of the Bhagavadgita. And I prefer to read "Dancing the Dream" to the Matthew-Passion. And third, I took all songs – more than hundred – again to heart and did not find any trace of aggressiveness (not even in "Bad" and the "Panther Dance").

The message in Michael's songs, lyrics and films is joy, magic and love – at times provoking and defiantly ranked by "bad energy." Thereby he always portrays a mirror of our society. And even then Michael expresses in some songs his more than justified anger – like in D.S. and Scream - so he never does it in an aggressive way.

Aggression means offender and is directed at destroying an adversary. Anger instead is a very strong emotion, which directs the attention to injustice. Whether a strong emotion is destroying and defeating, or awakening, depends on the state of consciousness of the sender. Michael Jackson as embodiment of love is working with strong emotions – as Jesus drove the dealers out of the temple. "I did not come to bring peace, but the sword." (Matthew 10:34)

26. Power

Michael's poems and reflections in "Dancing the Dream" are an increase of intensity compared to the lyrics of his songs. "The faster I twirl, the more I am still inside. My dance is all motion without, all silence within." (Dance of Life, Dancing the Dream)

Stillness. True stillness has nothing to do with sounds and tones; true stillness is the mind standing still. Stillness is the room one enters when the exit from the room of the mind is found. Besides this awakening call there is the message of the angry black man, who rebels against injustice, discrimination of races and prejudice. The issue is to make conscious the oppression of men, hubris, boastfulness and ignorance of the mighty.

Michael Jackson was always aware of his own roots, he toured in Africa with this consciousness and encouraged others to self confidence and steadiness. I cannot find aggressiveness, hectic or frenzy anywhere. Even in videos like "Bad" and "Scream," the power of a human and man is given expression, who uses the energy of slavery and persecution.

An author of crime books is not a murderer himself. The apparently most "aggressive" film is Michael Jackson's "Panther Dance," which is still misunderstood until today and was even banned for some time. Michael's message is, with full bodily commitment and without words, directed to the terror of destruction and prejudice, especially against the energy of Nazism, which since then has lost power, but the rest of which is still circulating the globe. Michael arises in the video from "Black Panther Power" and destroys, with immense power and anger, the swastika and the discrimination indicated by nazistic "KKK" phrases (Klu Klux Klan or kitchen, children, church = in

German: Küche, Kinder, Kirche). The film ends with the statement, "Prejudice is Ignorance." And with this Michael Jackson gets to the core of the problem of humanity.

In 1984, Michael had already spoken about ignorance in an interview with Ebony: "The main thing that I hate most is ignorance, like the prejudice problems of America. I know it is worse in some other countries. But I wish I could borrow, like from Venezuela or Trinidad, the real love of color-blind people and bring it to America. I'm prejudiced against ignorance. That's what I'm mainly prejudiced against. It's only ignorance and it's taught because it's not genetic at all. The little children in those countries aren't prejudiced....I'm really not a prejudiced person at all. I believe that people should think about God more and creation....Look at the many wonders in the human body – the different colors of organs, colors of blood – and all the different colors to do a different thing in the human body. It's the most incredible system in the world; it makes an incredible building, the human being. And when this can happen with the human body, why can't we do it as people? And that's how I feel. And that's why I wish the world could do more. That's the only thing I hate. I really do."

One who looks carefully at the Panther dance and feels the energy, instead of projecting his own prejudices onto it, can see very clearly the difference between "power" and "force." Power is the innate inner energy, which lets every seed sprout, which lets every flower blossom and brings every tree to fully unfold its beauty. This power which can even be used for wrongdoing must not be mistaken as force of evil, where blocked aggressions are discharged and thereby others are destroyed. Power is a constructive energy, which is needed to break the old and to construct the new.

Most people suppress the courage to use this power, because men are not yet ready to confront wrongdoing. The concepts of mind to "behave well" or wishing to be a "good person," or "you may not do that" or "you may not say something like that," function like filters before authentic sensing. They are one reason that we go through life with brakes on, instead of full steam ahead.

"Force" is an energy which is directed against something and tries in hubristic assertiveness to destroy and extinguish. It is not at all interested in constructive things. I always wonder when prisoners are untimely set free due to "good conduct." "Good conduct" says nothing about whether someone has defeated his inner demons and will be able to control his monsters in the future, affects and impulses, but solely says that the inner child of someone is well adapted and not so uncomfortable for therapists and keepers.

Nelson Mandela was not set free due to good conduct; he did not adapt himself. John Brown was "bad." Martin Luther King was "bad." Malcolm X was "bad." Gandhi was "bad." We should look more carefully at which motives stand behind resistance and not confound the resistance of a criminal with the resistance of a freedom fighter and visionary.

But when people use their power to debunk injustice and prejudices, we should support instead of ridicule them.

The one who is empowered is connected to the power of the highest self, to whom everything is possible, who creates works and art works, which blow all dimensions, which touch people in their deepest places and awaken lost remembrances of what we really are. Only the veil of oblivion and forgottenness has to be put aside.

On 5th of August 2009 Karin writes: "With your wonderful words I can understand what I am feeling deep inside." And that's exactly the point. Through "my" flute nothing new comes into the world, but the words only remind you of that which you have known long before, what you are carrying inside and until now have forgotten to water. As soon as you start to water it, it will start to blossom. Step by step the petals will open, until they will only sing in all their majesty and fullness the song of the Elevated.

In his autobiography, "Moonwalk," we get to know that Michael Jackson, when just a little boy, said that he will only sing what he means. Also the songs and lyrics that come not out of his own pen – in the majority early songs – express his matters of the heart. I have noticed that there are many good songs that I like to hear for a time again and again, but at some point I grow weary of them. This never happened to me with Michael Jackson's songs. I can even hear the old songs day in and day out and I have no feeling of saturation. Michael himself has said that he "binds his soul to his music." Perhaps it is the power and greatness of this soul which is the reason that we don't get tired of Michael's music and that makes it immortal. To the question of how he expressed his opinion when not performing or speaking in public he answered:

"I try to write, put it in song. Put it in dance. Put it in my art to teach the world. If politicians can't do it, I want to do it. We have to do it. Artists put it in paintings. Poets put it in poems, novels. That's what we have to do. And I think it's so important to save the world....And that's the best way to bring about the truth, through song. And that's what I love about it." (Ebony, 1984, 2009) "I know I'm an imperfect person. I'm not making myself an angel because I'm not an angel and I'm not a devil either. I try to be the best I can and I try to do what I think is right. It's that simple. And I do believe in God." (Ebony, 1984)

Michael Jackson has, without being a teacher, taught more than most teachers during a lifetime; he worked through his work and through his being – as an artist, musician, entertainer, humanitarian, benefactor, and especially as a human being.

27. Spiritual Teacher

The psychologist Adele R. McDowell, Ph.D., sums up her recognitions about the spiritual work of Michael in an article: "Michael Jackson was a shining star in the firmament of Zeitgeist. He defined and redefined pop culture for over four decades. He stretched us with his resonant music, bigger-than-life videos, iconic moonwalks, and unique style....For many, Michael's death felt personal. Like a stone thrown into a lake, the reverberations of grief expanded in ever-widening circles across the globe....It is reported that over one billion people across the globe watched his memorial service....This is feeling people deeply about the influence of Michael Jackson and his music....

He was an enigma – at least on the personality level. On the soul level, Michael Jackson might be seen a bit differently. The soul level speaks to the bigger picture. Things are not always as they seem. There is more beyond the 3D world....Essentially, we are one. And ultimately we are all here to develop…unconditional love and acceptance for all." Adele enumerates four spiritual teachings that Michael Jackson left behind as part of his legacy:

The lesson of Oneness: We are all one; we are all connected. The anthem, "We Are The World," expressed this impressively.

The lesson of Responsibility: Michael Jackson felt a sense of responsibility for the homeless, sick, and hungry of this world. Here too the song, "We Are The World," says that to save ourselves we have to support others.

The lesson of Sameness: The video to "Black or White" shows clearly the morph and shift among racial and gender lines. The message says: We all are souls in human "outerwear."

The lesson of Courage and Vision: Michael Jackson thinks big; he had large visions. For all of the discussion about who he was or wasn't he was not afraid to be himself, his full, out-in-the-world, out-of-the-box self. That is a huge lesson for all of us. Give up fear, think above and beyond, and do not be afraid to let your light shine in its fullness. (www.americanchronicle.com)

Spiritual teacher Karen Bishop also sees Michael as a soul of high vibrations, who has completed his soul work here. "When substantial shifts occur, it can create the departure of souls who have been carrying significant amounts of higher level energy....When souls depart who carry significant amounts of energy, their sudden absence can be greatly felt, and what they leave behind creates a ripple effect as it migrates and dissipates out for the entire planet to embrace and now embody in a more evenly distributed way.

Michael Jackson, perhaps the most talented performer of all time, embodied a massive amount of higher level energy. He was extremely connected to a higher level and to 'the other side.' He was unmistakably a bridge, bringing this higher level energy into form and then giving it out to the masses. Remembering so well what the 'other side' was like, he...found it extremely difficult to exist within and understand the strange and many times darker energies that were on the planet while he was here....

He embodied massive amounts of energy relating to the other side and bringing it here. In this way, he suddenly departed precisely around the time we experienced the solstice of June 21, because it was now time to dissipate that energy to the planet. He has now given us this energy to embody ourselves. He no longer needed to hold so much of it himself, as the shift of the solstice created this new connection for the planet to now experience on its own." (www.emergingearthangels.com)

And if you belong to the wild side of life and believe in reincarnation, then you perhaps are interested in the claim of Walter Semkiw, a well-known psychiatrist, that Michael Jackson was the reincarnation of Charles Dassoucy, the sovereign of entertainment. (www.johnadams.com) Or the speculation that Michael Jackson was the embodiment of Mozart or on a five-level scale with seven different levels had reached scale four, level six – mature soul.

But instead of digging in the past of the "i," I prefer to stay with both feet on the ground, because knowing about earlier lives does not serve for anything and didn't support me in no way in bearing the ignorant dull and destructive energies, which are still to be felt in some corners of this world. Or may it be different? The information helped me a little bit that I have had a certain fool's license in a former life, when I lived as court jester and delighted people with my little jokes.

Unfortunately in this life as scientist and academic I don't enjoy this privilege of fool's license, and that's why I have been more life artist and bounce-backer than concentrating on climbing the ladder of a career.

Also Adele Ryan McDowell is persuaded that in the end it does not matter what we believe about Michael or don't. What is certain is "that Michael Jackson left the world behind as a place with more soul." When more than a billion people, almost every seventh inhabitant of the Earth, assemble at the same place at the same time, as with the worldwide broadcasting of the memorial in the Staples Center in Los Angeles in July 2009, then immense power fields emerge which circle around the whole globe.

"Great fields of power are the future of healing, of awakening and an elevation of the level of human evolution. Superconscious fields can be made available as flow of energy for everyone concerned....We can imagine this as a download from the internet...Thus innumerable people get it, which we would perhaps have named a blessing at the time of Jesus Christ. This process is comparable with the advent of the Holy Spirit." (Hübl, p. 306)

Everyone who was lucky enough to have met Michael Jackson, or experienced one of his concerts, or who may have attend one less intensively on television, internet or DVD can feel the blessing of these power fields.

Rupert Sheldrake has extensively explored these morphogenetic fields and described their effects and meaning in "Die Wiedergeburt der Natur." (2nd edition, 1992)

After every Michael Jackson concert, where there were never any excesses, not even with more than 100,000 attendees, one could feel how the people were inspired, fulfilled and enthusiastic, even hours after the event. In-spired, that means filled with Holy Spirit. Filled, that means full of energy. At Michael Jackson concerts there was no aggression nor negativity, as is quite common at mass events. Michael's light radiated so intensely that nobody could escape it. He attracted all – young and old, black and white, man and woman, large and small, poor and rich, big and little, fat and thin, beautiful and ugly – and fascinated them with his magic and made them all equal.

28. Black Soul

Contrary to the claims of the media Michael's soul was black. On 5th of January 1994 he appeared as a surprise at the NAACP Awards in Pasadena, to bestow an award himself. When he started to speak he was applauded frenetically for nearly one minute until he succeeded to get a chance to speak:

"Thank you for your warm and generous support, I love you very much. For decades the NAACP has stood at the forefront of the struggle for equal justice under the law for all people in our land. They have fought...for justice, equality and the very dignity of all mankind. Members of the NAACP have been jailed and even killed in the noble pursuit of those ideals upon which our country was founded. None of these goals is more meaningful to me at this time of my life, than that everyone is presumed to be innocent (frenetic applause) and totally innocent, until they are charged with a crime and been convicted by a jury of peers. I never really took the time to understand the importance of that ideal until now, until I became the victim of false allegations, and the willingness of others to believe and exploit the worst before they have had the chance to hear the truth. Because not only am I presumed to be innocent, I am innocent!

And I know the truth will be my salvation. I have been strengthened in my fight to prove my innocence by my faith in God and by my knowledge that I am not fighting this battle alone. Together we will see this thing through." (www.mjcafe.net)

It's strange how negligent and careless professional translators transfer Michael's words into German. Last time I noticed this with the subtitles to the film, "This Is It." Therein Michael says at one point to Kenny Ortega: "I trust in you" and the subtitle says, "I count on you." "I count on you" is much more superficial than to trust in someone. Trust has a high frequency vibration, which only mature souls can hold. "I count on you" is as banal as counting apples.

It shows one more time that our mode of expression tells more about ourselves than about the object we are talking about. I myself have had the experience that even publishing companies are not always interested in the truth of the author when translating a book, but that their own imaginations come out on top. As translator of two books of Chuck Spezzano, my transcript of "win-win-situation" as "Gewinn-Gewinn-Situation" to German was changed by the editor to "win-situation" without my knowing – an amendment for the worse, because the initial meaning was completely lost. The term "win-win" indicates that both sides are the winner. The term "win-situation" is senseless.

The mind needs separation and therefore is unhappy with a double "win-win." In a "win-win-situation," the usual "either – or" is replaced by "as well – as." The mind disgusts in leaving things as they are. It needs a difference and a judgment. In sporting competition is may be delightful to match each other, but for what do we need a range of artists and creativity? Why is a doctor better than a mason or a white better than a black or a Christian better than a Muslim or vice versa? Why are such things measured? Who decides which benchmark is used? Does God's sun shine less on a mason than on a housewife or more on a prisoner than on a holy man or woman? When we all stood forwardmost in the same line, what would then happen? Couldn't we march on like as one man and master the challenges together?

Joyans give everyone they meet a fluffy. They don't first ask if the other one won the competition. They don't use a mental scale and measure who deserves a fluffy. For them everyone is unique and special. Look for the video "Free Hugs" on YouTube, which thus opens our hearts. Instead of writing a book about Michael Jackson and Sathya Sai Baba I also could have written a book about Michael and Campino from "Die Toten Hosen" or about Bushido and the Dalai Lama. They are not different, besides their progress in peeling onions. When all layers are removed with all those nothing remains. I chose two who are dear to me. But is there really a difference between humans, just because one is peeling the fourth layer and the other has reached the sixth?

Let's once again give Michael Jackson his say with his Black Man speech, also called "Angry Black Man" or "Warrior." On 9th of July 2001 he spoke at a summit of the music industry in Harlem at the Headquarters of the "National Action Network," which had been organized by Rev. Al Sharpton, Johnny Cochran and Michael Jackson. On this occasion Michael made some "unprejudiced, open and straight-lined statements about the historic racism and economic inequality which prevail in the music industry."

The summit was meant to direct attention to the historically corrupt, exploitative and one-sided business which was perpetuated in the music industry. Besides it was about strategies to put an end to the injustice. As I found no transcript, what follows here is most of it:

"I remember a long time ago in Indiana, I wasn't more than like six, seven years old, I had a dream that I wanted to be a performer, you know, an entertainer."

Michael stresses that it has been black artists above all who brought much joy to the world, and are later penniless.

"It is not like they always say, they built a big house, they spent a lot of money, they bought a lot of cars....That's stupid. That's nothing compared to what artists make....I'm tired, I'm really really tired of the manipulation, I am tired of how the press is manipulating everything.... They do not tell the truth, they're lying. They manipulate our history books. The history books are not true. It's a lie. The history books are lying. You need to know that, you must know that. All the forms of popular music from jazz, to hip hop, to bebop, to Soul,...the different dances, from the cakewalk, to the jitterbug, the Charleston, break dancing, all these are forms of black dancing. What's more important than giving people a sense of escapism, escapism meaning entertainment? What would we be like without a song? What would we be like without a dance, joy, laughter and music? These things are very important. But if you go to the bookstore down the corner, you won't see one black person on the cover. You'll see Elvis Presley. You'll see the Rolling Stones....Otis Blackwell was a prolific, phenomenal writer. He wrote some of the greatest Elvis Presley songs. This was a black man."

Michael encourages us vigorously to put an end to the injustice and to honor those who deserve to be honored.

"You gotta remember something. The minute I started breaking the all-time record in record sales – I broke Elvis's records, I broke Beatles' records – the minute I became the all-time best-selling albums in history,...overnight they called me a freak, they called me a homosexual, they called me a child molester, they said I bleached my skin. They made everything to turn the public against me....you have to learn that. I just look in the mirror, I know I'm black....It's time for a change. Let's not leave this building and forget what has been said. Put it into your heart, put it into your subconscious mind, and let's do something about it. We have to. We have to....A change has got to come. Let's hold our torches high and get the respect that we deserve. I love you, (sings) I love you. Please don't put this in your heart today and forget it tomorrow. We will not accomplish our purpose if that that happens. This has got to stop, it has got to stop....I love you folks. We're all brothers and sisters, no matter what color we are."

Such words were ignored by the moths' press. It wanted scandals, sensations, in its ever insatiable greed for more stuff for destruction. The corrupt world, where reign ego and force, is a dangerous place for true humanity. True humans are the ideal victims for blood suckers and vampires. The rare exemplars of the species human with big, pure and innocent hearts are not prepared to brace themselves.

"Leave me alone – stop doggin' me around." (Leave Me Alone)

This human right was not conceded to Michael Jackson. Michael was a proud black man, who transcended the difference between black and white. His unique mark was the "Jheri lock", even when it was no longer popular, which is named after its inventor Jheri Redding. It was a symbol for belonging to African American society and culture. Michael was always conscious about his black African American roots and proud of it.

29. Addiction Reigns the World

L.O.V.E, the stuff of which the world is built, was spelled by the creations of the ego. In economy, politics and working life, it is rather suspicious when someone lives love. Instead various addictions hold control, which at first sight come along masked and are not immediately recognized as such, like greed, envy, curiosity, possessiveness, addiction to sex, jealousy, craving for recognition, the thirst for revenge. At the front line marches the greed for money.

"Lie for it, spy for it, kill for it, die for it. - So you call it trust, but I say it's just in the devil's game of greed and lust. - They don't care, they do me for the money. They don't care, they use me for the money. - So you go to church, read the Holy Word. In the scheme of life, it's all absurd. - They don't care, they kill for the money, do or dare, the thrill for the money. ... - You would do anything for money....Even sell my soul to the devil." (Money)

Michael Jackson uses himself as an example to direct attention to common bad state of affairs, not to underscore himself. It is not about his person or his personality, but about awakening consciousness and looking more closely at things. We all are actually experiencing first hand more and more chaotic states, whereto addictions and greed have led us.

Our societal system is nearly collapsing – even when some who forever are living in the past don't want to realize this. Everything we thought to be normal, right and true for a long time, because unexplored imaginations and assumptions were handed down from generation to generation, turns out to be built on sand.

The German, Anne T., a former market trader at a renowned investment bank in Frankfort blows the whistle about her insider information in her book: "Die Gier war Grenzenlos". She describes in all details the bizarre world of unscrupulousness, aggression, decadence and cynicism, which was and is determined by greed and addiction – including addiction to sex. Our world was and is ruined by our actions. Addictive behavior is not rational and cannot be changed by reasoning.

A change will only be possible when there is no more escape, when we have reached an impasse, look into the bottomless abyss and have lost everything. The actual analyses of the reasons for the state of our society and the world, which are made by critics of society and researchers, are mostly limited to one limb of the chain; the insights never reach back to the beginning of the chain – to the motives that determine our actions.

The American psychiatrist Professor Hare has during decades of research drawn a profile of properties of psychopaths. At first sight we believe the myth that the prisons and psychiatric hospitals are filled with psychopaths. Naturally we will also find some of this type there. But the most dangerous psychopaths are living directly among us and are working in the most respected professions, and are highly remunerated specialists and leaders, as for example Richard S. Fuld Jr., one of the CEOs of the Lehmann Brothers Bank, whose insolvency was the trigger – I say trigger, not cause – for the actual crisis. Whoever sees and hears Fuld's speeches and uses the capacity of discrimination can clearly realize that such forces can only lead to abysm. His eyes emit sparkles of the will to destroy and defeat anything and everyone in all cardinal directions. The last cause of the world crisis is the addictive behavior of egos as well as greed, greed and greed again, which lusts after permanent self-satisfaction.

Michael Jackson included for a long time hints to the causes of the dilemma of mankind in his songs and lyrics. But instead of listening to the wisdom of a pop star we prefer to gather in front of televisions, and millions listen when politicians again tell us nothing with many words – and then press, broadcasting and television will analyze this nothing in articles, documentaries, comments, talk shows and interviews, until one has reached the mutual back slapping or come to a duel. And thus the world shall be moved?

There are only a few people who become loud – not loud by screaming out aggressively, but loud by speaking out against this. Isn't it amazing how loud the shy, gentle Michael could be and how bad he was at times - or not? Was something ever created that was groundbreaking, breathtaking, mysterious, or fascinating magic by someone who dutifully reads day by day the newspaper and fulfills his duties as citizen, goes to church on Sundays and makes a good impression, who never hits anything, is always only friendly and polite and smiles with clenched teeth? Someone who always wants to do everything right?

For years allegations have been circling that Michael Jackson was heavily indebted. It may be that he had debts; but we only call it heavily indebted when the debts exceed the wealth. The nations and states all are really heavily indebted, because there is no wealth to balance the debts. They even praise it as a success when the new debts in a year are smaller than the year before. In a private household it would then be a great success when in 2012 the credit of 90,000 Dollars is only raised about 10,000 dollars compared to 15,000 in the year 2011. Such madness is praised as progress.

It is a fact that Michael Jackson's wealth was immense. He owned the Sly-and-the-family-Stone catalogue and the Northern Song catalogue with the rights to 251 songs of the Beatles, which in the year 1985 was valued at nearly 47.5 million dollars. After the purchase he noted that the Little Richard catalogue was also contained in it, and so Michael contacted Little Richard and devolved the rights. The value of the Beatles catalogue is today estimated at 1.5 billion Dollars.

Later Michael bought Sony-ATV, so that the rights to the Beatles catalogue were divided 50/50. In return, Michael Jackson owned half of the whole publishing rights of Sony (for example, more than 900 country songs, all songs written by Babyface, Latin songs from Selena and Enrique Iglesias, Roberta Flack songs, Mariah Carey songs, Destiny's Child songs, Tupac, Biggie Smalls and Fleetwood Mac songs, songs from Bob Dylan and Leonard Cohen, to mention only a few, in total nearly half a million). Moreover Michael Jackson owned the rights to the Elvis Presley catalogue.

Each time Michael published a new song, he gained "under his own steam" about 500 million dollars. Nevertheless people did not shy away from expanding the announcement that "Michael has gone crazy." It was said to be another bizarre "publicity stunt" to "call attention to himself." The media used Michael as a puppet however they liked, to satisfy their egos.

On the cited site we find the following comment: "The larger media outlets have always been fond of attacking him at random. Michael was in Harlem just seven weeks ago alongside the likes of former president Bill Clinton as a fundraiser for the Democratic National Committee and the larger media outlets called him an ICON then. Why is he now Wacko Jacko for bringing up some very real issues that directly impact people's lives?...

Please don't believe the false hype and media propaganda tactics deployed by the larger communications outlets. They are only presenting distorted facts in an effort to discredit what is credible. They are trying to put the emphasis on a few people...to fool you into believing that this issue is irrelevant and inconsequential to the lives of the everyday person....

It is really the tip of the iceberg of a long overdue need to reform how big business operates in America and globally....It is time for this generation to pick up the torch and continue to build on what our ancestors have accomplished so far. As Dr. Martin Luther King Jr. So eloquently stated: 'Injustice anywhere is a threat to justice everywhere.' Thank you for reading and Blessed Love!" (Dick Gregory, Rev. Al Sharpton, www.hiphopandpolitics.wordpress.com)

It also is always again stated that Michael Jackson was angry that his last album "Invincible" was a flop and sold only two million copies, and that he had desperately tried to save his career. In reality the album "Invincible" sold ten million copies worldwide - and how many will be sold in the future is written in the stars. When other artists sell ten million albums they are praised to the skies, but with Michael it is called a flop, an indication that we have lost every measure and sense of proportion.

30. Michael Jackson and Sathya Sai Baba

There is no doubt that Michael Jackson was always proud to belong to the black community and never denied his roots. Nevertheless his skin got whiter and lighter with the years. He got the diagnosis vitiligo from the doctors, a slowly progressing pigmentation disease, where the skin loses its pigment. Michael himself believed in this disease too. But perhaps it was quite different.

There are things between heaven and earth which we are unable to explain and which are a fact indeed. I could write books about my own experiences with "miracles." We always use the term miracle when the mind does not find an explanation. No more no less. Why do we arrogate to ourselves to prescribe what life has to do or not to do? And why do we deny the existence of things only because our limited mind is not able to grasp it? Shall life adapt to our little mind, or would it be better for the limited mind to exercise humility and adapt to the much-larger life?

For example, is it a fact that the heart of Master M. is no longer beating and nevertheless he is living happily? His heart does not beat but breathes. And the doctors are clueless and don't have any explanation for this (personal information). That Sathya Sai Baba deactivated the laws of physics is widely known. But it is idle to stay on such a minor matter, because it has no relevance. From time to time I was asked in relation to "Das Mysterium" if Michael and Sathya Sai Baba met personally. For me this question is totally irrelevant, and therefore I did not mention it in the book. When I find two pure flutes at opposite sides of the world, through which flows the One Breath, why should these two flutes have met each other?

For all who are hungry for personal issues, your curiosity shall be stilled. Lukas from Switzerland had taken my book in October 2000 to the Ashram in Puttaparthi in India hoping that he would have the opportunity to hand it over to Sathya Sai Baba. He wrote me on 5th of November 2000: "Now I have the time to report about my journey (with your book in the luggage). I discovered Sai Baba on the internet and immediately I knew: there is more behind all this. Your book topped my picture off. Therefore the wish to travel to India and see this man on site prospered....When I arrived at the Ashram I participated the first time in Darshan – blessing by a holy man or woman.... I sat in the second row....The book is lying in front of me on the floor. Suddenly behind me a man taps on my shoulder and asks me if he could have a look at the book. He got curious because of the illustration of Michael Jackson on the cover. He wanted to know....if the author believed Sai Baba and Michael Jackson to be the same. I explained to him that it is about the same MESSAGE.

Then he told me a really unbelievable story. He said that he had a friend who lived in Taiwan, who was in contact with Michael Jackson. And now comes the point. When Michael gave two concerts in India – in New Delhi and Bombay – he had expressed his wish to meet Sai Baba. This man from Taiwan then brought a booklet from Sai Baba and a picture from Sai Baba in the hotel. He could only leave the booklet and the picture with the secretary. What happened then he didn't know."

Thus far Lukas' report. Was something blocked here, as with Michael's angel portrait, that could have endangered the "King of Pop" and brought out the Mahatma? We don't know. And we also don't know what happened afterward. But I know that Sathya Sai Baba once spoke about Michael Jackson, and to my knowledge he never did this with other pop stars. On 4th of October 2001 following news reached me: "Dear Margot, now it happened. Sai Baba has mentioned Michael Jackson in a dialogue with his simultaneous translator Anil Kumar. Quote: 'Then I asked another question: Bhagavan, this morning you spoke about poets and poetry, literates and scholars, whose works are read daily. Swami, is the literature the highest of the fine arts? Swami said: Not literature, but music is the highest. Music is the greatest of the fine arts. To understand literature you need a certain background. You have to be educated and need a certain knowledge to be able to understand. To enjoy music only your ears have to be in order. You don't need to read or write. You don't need education. You need any knowledge. You sway the head in the tact, independent if it is bhajans or Michael Jackson. Music therefore is the greatest of the fine arts.'"

What greater recognition you can get for your musical work than to be put on the same level as traditional bhajans? Bhajan is Sanscrit and means literally, "hymn of praise." It is the ritual praising of the different names and aspects of God, which has been practised in India for ages in temples and at prayer meetings. Thereby a presenter sings one line and the group repeats it, until the sound resounds in unison into the world. Thereby the mind is directed to God and the heart filled with love.

Beethoven once said in this respect: "Music is a higher revelation than all wisdom and philosophy. Whoever opens up for my music will become free from all the misery the other people are carrying with them."

In connection with this statement, Horst Stern's critique of my book, "Das Mysterium," can be seen in a different light. "Strictly one could summarize all in these two lines, which the late poet of personalized joy has tossed to us: 'All man will become brothers where your gentle wing resides.'" (FAZ 13th of June 2000, p. 55)

It seems as if the music of Beethoven has so far not revealed itself for most people; otherwise people would not lament and complain so much. But those who gradually become sick of misery can open up for Michael's music. Or what is the difference between his songs and Beethoven's music, when he says:

"How long will it be before the world hears your song in mine? Oh that is a day I hunger for." (Two Birds, Dancing the Dream)

Critics of my book "Mysterium" claim that I have the opinion that one has to recognize the second bird to realize that one has only one and the second is only an image (www.Perlentaucher.de). I ask myself, what type of weirdo (wordplay in German: weirdo = Vogel = bird) is that, who writes such things? And even more is calling himself "Perlentaucher" = pearl diver? I have never seen pearls at shallow banks. To find pearls you have to dive deep to the bottom of the sea. At times I have thrown pearls before swine. But thank God each swine has also a bird, or maybe two birds? (Wordplay in German: to be batty in the brain = einen Vogel haben = have a bird). Or will eventually change a swine into a bird? The answer to these questions we will probably still experience first hand.

31. Humanness

What was the reason that Michael Jackson was the chosen stuff for the moths? Why was he such an attraction for ignorant people, paparazzi and people with destructive frenzy? Moths due to their nature are attracted by light. When they come too near, they are burnt and destroy themselves.

Michael is light, so that consequently also the moths have to whir around him. Moths have no free will; they follow instinctively the power of attraction of light. Nevertheless many media moths succeeded in staying distant enough that his light was not life-threatening, out of pure instinct of self-preservation. Their moth instinct of self-preservation kept them from melting with the light. From the distance they then tried to extinguish the light. It's indeed logical to try to eradicate something life-threatening, and apparently the media moths did succeed in this. On the other hand they did not consider that light needs no physical body to shine and radiate, and that without a physical body it even shines brighter. Be careful, you moths, that you don't now come unintentionally too near, because nonphysical light is more difficult to avoid than visible light. Perhaps your time has come to be burnt in the light. I'm sorry, but remember that your dharma is not existence as a moth, but as a human being.

On 7th of March 2003 the journalist DeBorah B. Pryor wrote the article, "Will humanity ever visit the media?": "If the documentary 'Living with Michael Jackson' is any indication of what journalism has become, we're in trouble. I have to wonder what the bottom line is on the media's obsession to defile the character of Michael Jackson. For Martin Bashir, it was clearly money and fame. But, for the record, the public should also know that not every journalist shares this view. And if for nothing but balance alone, our stories should be told as well. As journalists, there is something we seem to have forgotten: our 'title' should not replace our 'species.' We are still human beings, but in our work, do we always act as such? While we may certainly recognize the eccentricities and even the naiveté of someone like Michael, these traits in themselves are not crime. We should be careful not to use them as a summation of his character, or as a means to detract from his long-standing career as an entertainer and humanitarian. If journalism were truly unbiased, this would not be the case. Martin Bashir's documentary, 'Living with Michael Jackson,' was lacking integrity. In the opinion of this writer, it should be remembered as nothing more than an exercise in how to gain someone's trust, then manipulate it to tell the story you had written before ever meeting the man or setting foot on his property.

Apparently the need for journalistic excellence has left the building, leaving behind in its place only two prerequisites for getting your story picked up: how low you can go and how much they are willing to pay. Clearly Bashir fulfilled the first requirement, and with several airings of his documentary on ABC and VH1, the second. By all accounts, I'd say the attempts to castrate Michael Jackson are keeping a lot of people in business. The sad part is that the tabloid style of the documentary has become more prevalent over the years.

Jackson has arguably been the only celebrity continuously raked over the proverbial coals. It seems such a shame that all the media choose to grasp from such an illustrious, long-standing career, is material from plastic surgery and unfounded allegations of child abuse. It is the blatant obsession with and subsequent regurgitation of this type of biased material that encourages dehumanization....Celebrities, Jackson in particular, are seen not as people, but as objects. Even so-called 'serious' journalists have stooped to new levels, asking shameless questions like Diane Sawyer did a few years back in an interview with Jackson and former wife Lisa Marie Presley: 'I've spent most of my life being a 'serious' journalist, but do the two of you have sex?.' Excuse me? This line of questioning is more than intrusive; it lacks any association with civility!

Yet, these ridiculous questions keep surfacing for Jackson. No other celebrity has had his or her dignity tested in this way. The type of programming reiterated by Bashir's documentary has contributed to the perception of the media by the more discerning public as a growing joke. If ever there was a sense of trust, it's flying out of the window fast. There was a time you could turn on the television or pick up a newspaper and clearly distinguish serious news from tabloid....Such distinctions have now become much more difficult....Couldn't Bashir have explored how this icon uses the power of his celebrity and wealth as a vehicle to change the state of the world?

Now is the time the public needs to hear such things. With the dawning of a new century, and our society's undeniable state of spiritual awakening, more than ever before, we are learning not to judge. It's insulting that judgment is the exact tool continually used by the media to perpetuate prejudice, and in this case, via Jackson. Because there is such a lack of balance where he is concerned, it's that much more noticeable to discerning eyes. Bashir used the word 'disturbing' several times with regard to Jackson's relationships with children. I'd like to flip the script and offer some disturbing perceptions of my own. With regard to his abuse of Jackson's young friend, Gavin, did he put any forethought into the fact that he had to return to school the next day and face his classmates and friends?...As a mother and grandmother, I know that life is hard enough for young boys entering into manhood without having their faces plastered on television and adding insult to injury – as Bashir did – with innuendos of reference to sexual impropriety. As a friend of Gavin's family I am very aware of the effect that Jackson's unrelenting support and compassion have had on them through their lengthy battle with Gavin's illness. Bashir's decision to exploit the relationship as anything more than genuine sickens me. ...

In the media, as in society, we work to create these larger-than-life figures and then seem to revel in the dismantling of our own creation. It's a very sick cycle. If humanity ever decided to pay a visit to the media, I hope it will consider staying a while. I hope it will pull up a chair and have a sit-down conversation on how we can implement it in our work without the threat of our stories having any less substance. I hope it will show us how to bring respect back to the media, so that we can respect the public enough to trust they will come to their own conclusions, based on the presentation of unbiased material. If humanity ever decides to pay a visit to the media, I hope it has the opportunity to get a two-hour interview, on television, in primetime." (www.mjfriendship.de).

At least also the New York Times calls Bashir's work "blunted self-interest disguised as sympathy." (www.wikipedia.org) Matt Semino calls it a PR nightmare for Michael: "Examining these interviews, it becomes clear that Michael Jackson is one of the most misunderstood figures in modern day popular culture." (http://elitestv.com)

Bashir accomplished his goal. After the documentary he made a career jump and was hired by the American Broadcasting Network ABC; in 2010 he changed to NBC News. Aphrodite Jones reveals in her book "Conspiracy" the exact details of how Bashir succeeded in luring Michael and how he with a sweet voice hid his shrewdness. When the film was shown to the jury in court everyone witnessed how Bashir succeeded in deceiving Michael Jackson. The twelve jury members were wide awake and ready to discover the truth unprejudiced. Therefore they saw things which the prejudiced press in its keenness for incrimination had overseen. "Prejudice is ignorance."

Bashir heaped Michael with compliments, pretended to be enthusiastic about his great talent. "With each compliment and promise, the journalist was able to get the King of Pop to open up about everything in his world. Somehow Bashir had won so much trust, that *nothing* about Jackson was deemed off-limits. In the end, Bashir had used Michael Jackson to pull off a great media stunt." (Jones, p. 29)

Chris Apostle, vice-president of "Special Recording Projects" at Sony Entertainment at the time, describes his impression of the Bashir work as such: "When I watched the Bashir thing last night, I just wanted to see what it was all about and reflect on that. When Martin asked him about the first incident where he paid off these accusers, I found it very ironic and it looked unbelievably sincere and honest the way he said, 'I just decided I wanted it to go away.' And he made it go away, which by the way, again, not the first person to do this in the history of our business. He wanted to make it go away. The second time he fought....As for his bit with the second thing, I believe a thousand percent, I'll go to my grave with it, that he was innocent completely. He was being blackmailed by that gentleman that wanted to be a screenwriter or write books or do movies." (http://the sportsinterview.com)

Although later Michael's own footage from the Bashir film shooting was aired, which showed point-blank which distortions and misrepresentations Bashir had undertaken, only the Bashir version was etched in the memories of the viewers. Most people think poorly about correcting a thing because that would be highly uncomfortable for themselves. They would have to admit their prejudices and their ignorance. Better to close their eyes and pretend to be clueless. Cory comments on the topic: "He was smart enough to video camera it and it clearly showed that the guy just twisted everything and made it, he turned everything into like a false or a lie. You know, they asked Michael a question: 'Are you gay?' And Michael said, 'I don't want to answer that question.' Now that was the one that he said. So then they quickly edited to Bashir going: 'Obviously he didn't want to answer for obvious reasons.' So then when Michael showed his version, he said, 'Are you gay?' Michael said, 'I don't want to answer that question.' Then he paused and said, 'But if you turn your camera off, I will answer your question.' And then the guy said okay, turn the camera off. He turned the camera off, and Michael said, 'No, absolutely not. I am not gay, but I have millions of gay fans and if they want to believe I'm gay, then let them believe I'm gay.' He said, 'I don't care. I don't want to offend anybody.' You know?"

Chris adds: "I gotta say something here. I can't believe at this point that these are even issues that are being discussed." And Cory adds: "Yeah, I mean this is crazy." (http://thesportsinterview.com)

Perhaps there is, in some place in the world, one or another journalist who shares the opinion of DeBorah B. Pryor and Charles Thompson. But the mass of the media – therefore it is called mass media – behaves like a herd of sheep. They trot behind the one they have always trotted behind without knowing where to, how long and why. Sheep are called sheep because they are sheep.

Michael's brother Jermaine talks in the Big Brother house open about Michael: "The world is ugly. It's not so much the world, certain people, and it's sad, very sad....He was a human being....He was hurt during that time. We have someone who, every song they write just about is message to make the world a better place, and then to be treated that way is like, what do you do? What do you say?...They build you up to tear you down, to destroy you." To the question of whether Michael was bankrupt Jermaine answers: "No, that's what they want the public to believe." And the questions for Michael's identity he answers: "He is a hundred percent pure black." (YouTube: Jermaine talks about Michael Jackson Celeb BB 2007) Great souls know that a long wind is necessary: "First they ignore you, then they laugh at you, then they fight against you, then you win." (Gandhi, cited on www.mjam.com)

At the end of the 1990's, Carol Mecca presented the book "Michael Jackson – American Master" to the American public, where she elaborated the master qualities of Michael Jackson. She shows that Michael can keep pace with great masters, from Leonardo da Vinci to Michelangelo. At that time I translated the whole book, as the publication of a German edition was planned. Unfortunately Carol was not able to find enough readers in America for this costly designed and therefore expensive book and therefore the German edition was cancelled too.

The book is out of print. On 2nd of August 2010 one example was offered on www.amazon.de for 2.150 €. America at that time was not ready for a Master Michael Jackson – and he is still now used with the same greed as ever. As long as humanity stays in the phase of kindergarten or defiance, Mahatmas that don't fit into its concepts have to be ignored and fought against or used to earn money. A Mahatma in the business of pop stars is absolutely unthinkable for an immature mind. But victory is sure when the time has come, when the civilization of humanity enters the phase of humanness, not only that of looking like a human.

In an interview with Ebony in May 1992, which was conducted during a visit in Africa, Gabon, Ivory Coast, Tanzania and Egypt, Michael answers the question: "Do you have special feeling about this return to the continent of Africa?"

"For me it's like the 'dawn of civilization.' It's the first place where society existed. It's seen a lot of love. I guess there's that connection because it is the root of all rhythm. Everything. It's home." Ebony: "You visited Africa in 1974. Can you compare and contrast the two visits?" Michael: "I'm more aware of things this time: the people and how they live and their government. But for me, I'm more aware of the rhythms and the music and the people. That's what I'm really noticing more than anything. The rhythms are incredible. You can tell especially the way the children move. Even the little babies, when they hear the drums, they start to move. The rhythm, the way it affects their soul and they start to move. The same thing that Blacks have in America..." Ebony: "How does it feel to be a real King?" Michael: "I never try to think hard about it because I don't want it to go to my head. But, it's a great honour...."

32. Dangerous

Then the talk shifts to Michael's music when Ebony asks: "Speaking of music and rhythm, how did you put together the gospel songs on your last album?"

Michael: "I wrote 'Will You Be There?' at my house, 'Neverland,' in California.... I didn't think about it hard. That's why it's hard to take credit for the songs that I write, because I just always feel that it's done from above. I feel fortunate for being that instrument through which music flows. I'm just the source through which it comes. I can't take credit for it because it's God's work. He's just using me as the messenger...."

Ebony: "What was the concept for the 'Dangerous' album?"

Michael: "I wanted do do an album that was like Tschaikovsky's 'Nutcracker Suite.' So that in a thousand years from now, people would still be listening to it. Something that would live forever. I would like to see children and teenagers and parents and all races all over the world, hundreds and hundreds of years from now, still pulling out songs from that album and dissecting it. I want it to live."

"Dangerous" is still regarded today as the most creative album of Michael, as Joe Vogel states in his work, "Man in the Music – The creative Life and Work of Michael Jackson." The cover of the album is also an outstanding work of pop art which was designed in six months by the artist Mark Ryden from symbols and experienced images that Michael had discussed. Mark Ryden has also worked for Stephen King, Leonardo DiCaprio, Robert de Niro and others.

Michael trusted that he had the mentality and capacity to transmit the images in the way Michael imagined it. Mark said that Michael wanted the design to be mysterious, that people could interpret it in their own way. And indeed it is riddled with sufficient symbolism that it offers enough stuff for everyone and all levels of understanding and consciousness. Similar to an onion you can be satisfied with the surface – a circus world – or decipher the symbols, which come from different traditions, some of which are thousands of years old. Michael wears the album cover like a mask, where only his eyes are visible. He is wearing a crown which itself is decorated with the crowned monkey God Hanuman from the Vedic teachings. In the center we find various animals including a peacock, representing the glitter and glamour of the show world. We recognize Ganesha, the elephant God with the number nine, a rhinoceros, a walrus etc. Two clown faces, one with a laughing eye and the other with a crying eye, represent the circus and the world theatre. Two cherubs appear besides a Lucky Star with sound and music. On a ghost train we see Michael's monkey Bubbles and the rat Ben.

On the left side the half-opened hand of Michael, which can be identified by the three fingertips that are wrapped with tape – thumb and middle finger were not bandaged. On the palm of his hand stands a black child with the skeleton of the elephant man. In the palm is painted a map of the world, which indicates that there is only one world and that We Are The World. At the wrist we can see the number seven, which besides the number nine has a special meaning in numerology.

In my book, "Das Mysterium," the sevenship is described in a chapter. In the inside of the cave with the inscription "Dangerous," we can see a world upside down. The upper body in front is a picture of Barnum, the founder of the world famous circus. When the ghost train appears again everything has changed. Bubbles has disappeared and Michael as a child is sitting in his stead, after that a skeleton, and after that Michael's good friend Macaulay Culkin. The

One (Greek) eye is watching above the exit, a symbol of protection, which says that the eye of God sees everything. The cover of "Dangerous" belongs beside the cover of the Beatles' "Sergeant Pepper" undoubtedly to the most significant in music history. (http://webproactive.wordpress.com/2009/11/08/)

As of today, I have still seen not one documentation in the media about this artistic master work – understandable, because the limited media reasoning is insufficient for a profound analysis. In the above Ebony interview Michael's charity activities are mentioned: "I notice on this trip that you made a special effort to visit children." Michael: "I love children, as you can see. And babies." Ebony: "And animals."

How deep was Michael's love even for the tiniest living beings we could see at a concert of HIStory Tour in Leipzig. While performing Michael discovered a small insect on the floor and asked security, who wanted to remove it: "Don't kill it, don't kill it." This incident was copied in the video of the concert in Munich from July 1997 in the Olympic stadium, that I was lucky to be part of and where I was able to stand in the arena near the stage.

On this day Michael made his Munich fans happy and said goodbye in German with the gesture of Namaste and a deep bow: "This bow is for you - 'Ich liebe dich mehr.'" (YouTube: Michael Jackson speaks German – Ich liebe dich mehr)

In the same article in Ebony Michael says: "Well, there's a certain sense that animals and children have that gives me a certain creative juice, a certain force that later on in adulthood is kind of lost because of the conditioning that happens in the world. A great poet said once: 'When I see children, I see that God has not yet given up on man.' An Indian Poet from India said that, and his name is Tagore.

The innocence of children represents to me the source of infinite creativity. That is the potential of every human being. But by the time you are an adult, you're conditioned; you're so conditioned by the things about you – and it goes. Love. Children are loving, they don't gossip, they don't complain, they're just openhearted. They're ready for you. They don't judge. They don't see things by way of color. They're very child-like.

That's the problem with adults: they lose that child-like quality. And that's the level of inspiration that's so needed and is so important for creating and writing songs and for a sculptor, a poet or a novelist. It's that same kind of innocence, that same level of consciousness, that you create from. And kids have it. I feel it right away from animals and children and nature. Of course. And when I'm on stage. I can't perform if I don't have this kind of ping pong with the crowd. You know the kind of cause and effect action, reaction. Because I play off of them. They're really feeding me and I'm just acting from their energy."

And at another time Michael said: "Jesus said, continue to love...People think sex...I see the face of God...that's not where my heart is. That is not Michael Jackson, that's someone else." (see also: Larry Nimmer)

In the Ebony interview the question follows: "Where does all this come from?" Michael: "I really believe that God chooses people to do certain things, the way Michelangelo or Leonardo da Vinci or Mozart or Muhammad Ali or Martin Luther King is chosen. And that is their mission to do that thing. And I think that I haven't scratched the surface yet of what my real purpose is for being here.

I'm committed to my art. I believe that all art has as its ultimate goal the union between the material and the spiritual, the human and the divine. And I believe that that is the very reason for the existence of art and what I do. And I feel fortunate in being that instrument through which music flows....Deep inside I feel that this world we live in is really a big, huge, monumental symphonic orchestra. I believe that in its primordial form all of creation is sound and that it's not just random sound, that it's music. You've heard the expression, music of the spheres? Well that's a very literal phrase.

In the Gospels we read: 'And the Lord God made man from the dust of the earth and breathed into his nostrils the breath of life and man became a living soul.' That breath of life to me is the music of life and it permeates every fiber of creation. In one of the pieces of the Dangerous album I say: 'Life songs of ages, throbbing in my blood, have danced the rhythm of the tide and flood.' This is a very literal statement, because the same new miracle intervals and biological rhythms that sound out the architecture of my DNA also govern the movement of the stars. The same music governs the rhythm of the seasons, the pulse of our heartbeats, the migration of birds, the ebb and flow of ocean tides, the cycles of growth, evolution and dissolution. It's music, it's rhythm. And my goal in life is to give to the world what I was lucky to receive: the ecstasy of divine union through my music and my dance. It's like, my purpose, it's what I'm here for." (Ebony, 1992, 2007)

33. King of Hearts

Michael Jackson was not only the "King of Pop," but was also declared a real prince in the kingdom Sanwi in the southeast of the Ivory Coast. After his death, this Kingdom celebrated their prince for three days and claimed the delivery of the mortal remains, as members of the Sanwi royal house, according to their tradition, have to be buried at home.

Michael was declared prince on 13th of February 1992 during a journey to Africa in Krindjabo, the capital of Sanwi. At the crowning ceremony he wore a golden crown and a black/red velvet gown as well as held a sceptre. It was a journey to his African roots, as his ancestors had come from the Ivory Coast.

Bob Jones, who accompanied Michael on the journey, describes the impressive event: "We came to a village and approximately 125,000 people were waiting for us. And this joy was simply overwhelming – such a thing we had never seen before....He was considered with the highest honors, which normally only are bestowed to heads of states. Michael was made King in Africa, he was gifted with gold and all such things." (Tagesschau).

In the race for humanness the supposedly lesser civilized regions of the world are much ahead of the USA and the Western world. Too much reason and mind is the trap into which the most progressive once fell, and now it is difficult for them to feel their hearts. Besides royal honors Michael also received scientific awards. Already in the year 1988 – with thirty years – he was awarded an honorary degree for literature from the president Dr. Henry Ponder of Fisk University (Ebony, 2009).

Unimpressed by worldly honors, Michael followed his vision to hold the energy of love, and despite gleefulness and derision he stayed true to himself.

Michael's commitment becomes clear not only in his music, but also in every word in "Dancing the Dream." Michael's dear connection to animals shows in "So the Elephants March," "Enough for Today" and "Look Again,

Baby Seal." Thereby especially the poem of the Elephants is a witness of the devotion which Michael himself lived. "Not to fall down is their mission."

He tells about the decision of the elephants to teach the ignorant human beings the consideration for life. "'Let us show them our reverence for life', they said. And from that day on, elephants have been silent, patient, peaceful creatures....But the elephants' most important message is in their movement. For they know that to live is to move....Innocent animals, they do not suspect that after all this time, they will fall from a bullet by the thousands....'We do not hate you. Don't you see at last? We were willing to fall, so that you, dear small ones, will never fall again.'"

In "Enough for today," we feel Michael's limitless compassion for all beings, especially the suffering of dolphins, which are caught in the nets of the fishermen. "Dolphins love to dance – of all the creatures in the sea, that's their mark....So there I was, in the middle of the rehearsal, and I thought, 'They're killing a dance.' And then it seemed only right to stop."

These reflections on consciousness and creation are about transcendence of duality. "I keep on dancing and then, it is the eternal dance of creation."

Not only Michael talks about the whole creation being a dance: "The power of creation dances through all of us. We all will find different expressions for it, individually and collectively....In the end all people want to dance on earth, they want to let Shakti, the Goddess, the flow of things flow through them. Let's orient after this flow, and then our life is in the flow, we are happy and follow our life purpose. We no longer will ask, what is the sense of all this, because we find it in each and every moment. When Shakti is allowed to dance, then the world is healed and in order." (Hübl, p. 88)

Michael Jackson has clearly emphasized that he finds his music – he does not invent it - by stepping into the flow. "Momentarily only a few people are really dancing wholeheartedly on earth. But only when we all dance the whole art work can be performed." (Hübl, p. 89)

That ever more people join the dance we can observe in the internet, as due to the immensity of the internet the control and one-sided selection of news is no longer possible, and we have access to all events in the world firsthand. The heartbreaking messages which Michael threw like a stone into the world ocean continue to circle concentrically. Michael's "Earth Song" has such an impressiveness that nobody who has not a heart of stone can escape its effects. Those who look at the video will no longer live on unreflecting as perhaps they did before. Once we have been touched by the heart energy, we are changed forever, and the lip service which we used for centuries from the powerful and the rulers are simply deflected by us.

In "Dancing the Dream" we find love songs to mother Earth: "Planet Earth" and "Mother Earth." "Planet Earth, gentle and blue, with all my heart, I love you...." (Planet Earth) "I felt sad to think how carelessly we treat our home. The earth is...a living, nurturing being. She cares for us; she deserves our care in return....We've...just trashed it and move on....We must begin to clean her up, and that means cleaning up our own hearts and minds first, because they led us to poison our dear planet." (Mother Earth)

In "Wings Without Me," Michael describes his ideas of love, freedom and ecstasy. "I was the falcon and the child and the saint. In my eyes their lives became sacred, and the truth came home: When all life is seen as divine, everyone is growing wings."

With "Dance of Life" Michael left behind for us a love song to the cosmic music and cosmic dance. "Silence is my real dance, though it never moves."

The symbol of cosmic dance we find in Indian mythology in the figure of the dancing Shiva, whose destruction and ignorance is considered a blessing. Also known as Nataraj, the Lord of the dance destroys all worldliness and cannot be disturbed by anything in his unwavering calmness. The encouragement of the little Fox in "The Little Prince" to see with the heart we find again in "But the Heart Said No":

"The years rolled by and they got old....'We've had a good life,' they said, 'and we did the right thing.' Their children looked down and asked why poverty, pollution and war were still unsolved. 'You'll find out soon enough,' they replied. 'Human beings are weak and selfish. Despite our best efforts, these problems will never really end.' The head said yes, but the children looked into their hearts and whispered: 'No!'"

"The Boy and the Pillow" shows how the son becomes the teacher to his father, when he sells a valuable pillow not for gold, but for a penny, which was given with devotion. Devotion is even more powerful than love.

"'When is a penny worth more than a piece of silver?' 'When it's offered out of devotion....Poorer than the poorest, she still had time for God.'"

The deeper meaning of Rabinadrath Tagore's statement, "A good wanderer leaves no traces," is revealed in Michael's story, "Mark of the Ancients"

"'Where are the Ancient Ones buried?' Without reply, he poked his stick into the fire. A bright flame shot up, licked the air, and disappeared. My teacher gave me a glance to ask if I understood this lesson. I sat very still, and my silence told him I did."

The poem "Heal the World" in "Dancing the Dream" we all know as a love song to the world:

"There's a place in your heart and I know that it is love.... There are ways to get there, if you care enough for the living."

Its video and many performances at concerts are the proof that nobody remains untouched by the innocence of children. The message in "The Fish That Was thirsty" says that we search for God in the wrong places.

"How strange," the little fish said, "to miss what is everywhere." One could argue which of the following two sentences is true: "God is nowhere," or "God is now here." Independent of which version we prefer, we will surely not find him because God was never lost.

What we lost is trust. Michael Jackson talks about this topic: "In accepting yourself completely, trust becomes complete. There is no longer any separation between people, because there is no longer any separation inside." (Trust, Dancing the Dream)

One who has realized the Self has also found God.

34. Cutting the Ties

The outer and the inner is only a mirage in consciousness. And whoever wants to create clarity in his life cannot avoid this fact, even when the mind is reluctant against it. My motto is, "Be clear and the rest will follow." When the mind is cleared, that means freed all conditionings, life is easy and effortless. The way to this state Michael describes in "Courage."

"It's curious what takes courage and what doesn't. When I step out on stage in front of thousands of people, I don't feel that I'm being brave. It can take much more courage to express true feelings to one person.... That takes real courage, the courage to be intimate. Expressing your feelings is not the same as falling apart in front of someone else – it's being accepting and true to your heart....In spite of the risks, the courage to be honest and intimate opens the way to self-discovery. It offers what we all want, the promise of love."

In "Love", Michael concretizes his message: "When it's allowed to be free, love is what makes life alive, joyful, and new. It's the juice and energy that motivates my music, my dancing, everything."

Freedom requires breaking the powerful mental conditionings and cutting the ties that bind us.

"Many a time I tried to break, This shadow following me I could not shake. Many a time in the noisy crowd, In the hustle and bustle of the din so loud, I peered behind to see its trace. I could not lose it in any place. It was only when I broke all ties,...I suddenly stared in your fiery eyes. All at once I found my goal. The elusive shadow was my soul." (The Elusive Shadow, Dancing the Dream)

"Your words stabbed my heart, and I cried tears of pain....How strange that all these tears could not wash away the hurt! Then one thought of love pierced my bitterness....'Why have you come?' I whispered. 'To wipe away your last tear,' you replied. 'It was the one you saved for me.'" (The Last Tear, Dancing the Dream).

When the last ties of mental conditioning are cut, one will be able to look through the games of the ego and realize immortality and bliss.

"I was born to never die, To live in bliss, to never cry, To speak the truth and never lie, To share my love without a sigh....This is my dance, this is my high. It's not a secret, can't you see, Why can't we all live in ecstasy." (Ecstasy, Dancing the Dream)

"The wise little girl" warns us before ignorance and judgment. She was wheelchair-bound.

"She made no judgments about herself. That was her wisdom. I have seen the same wise look in other children, 'poor' children as society sees them....The way that adults look at their lives...they begin to believe they should feel bad about themselves...But this wise little girl...All I saw was light and love....It smiles to be alive, waiting patiently for ages of ignorance and sorrow to pass away like a mirage...her prophecy must come true." (Wise Little Girl, Dancing the Dream)

"What we need to learn from children isn't childish. Being with them connects us to the deep wisdom of life,..." (Children, Dancing the Dream)

"The truth is that you and I would have given up long ago, but We won't let us. It is too wise. 'Look into your hearts,' it says. 'What do you see? Not you and I, but only We.'" (I You We, Dancing the Dream)

Michael reports how he searched for his star in the sky during childhood and could not decide which he should take because then he would have destroyed the wonderful constellation-picture.

"I'm going to search for my star until I find it. It's hidden in the drawer of innocence, wrapped in a scarf of wonder." (I Searched For My Star, Dancing the Dream)

When Michael sings "Will You Be There?," we feel physically how important it is to have the certainty that people are there for one another. When critics use the killer argument, "kitsch," for the video to this song and Michael's stage performance, they out themselves in their own harshness and lack of heartfulness. Each time I hear this song and see the film, my heart is warmed and I cry tears of joy. "Breaking Free" is dealing with the wish to get rid of the corset of time and space. We cannot succeed by breaking out because then we would be outside instead of inside, but still not free.

Being free means free of outside and of inside. Don't try to understand, because that is impossible. When you let yourself into the issue, the meaning will reveal itself to you. Master M states respectively: "That which you believe you understand is nothing than a delusion. What can you yet understand, as the awakening state, where the mind is active, does not at all exist? The understanding one as well as the understood exists only as mirages in consciousness." (Mantese, 2008)

"All this hysteria, all this commotion, Time, space, energy are just a notion. What we have conceptualized we have created, All those loved, all those hated. Where is the beginning, where's the end, Time's arrow, so difficult to bend." (Breaking Free, Dancing the Dream)

World, time and space are only constructs of our mental activity, only imaginations in the mind. The drama – consisting of imaginations – is our work. We are the author of the spectacle that brings us pain and joy. Why are we still playing a role in the piece even when we don't like it? In "Look Again, Baby Seal," Michael picks up the topic of trust in life itself.

"I realized that nothing would finally save life on earth but trust in life itself, in its power to heal, in its ability to survive our mistakes and welcome us back when we learn to correct those mistakes....'I am life and life can never be killed. It is the power that brought me forth from the emptiness of space....I am safe because I am that power."

That led to the gate of timelessness, whose mystery Michael reveals in „Once we were there". "Where time is not, immortality's clear, Where love abounds, there is no fear,...He (the child) is now, ready to share, Ready to love, ready to care, Unfold his heart, with nothing to spare. Join him now, if you dare."

And when we have passed through this gate we recognize: "Heaven is here." Then the "Quantum Leap" is mastered:

"Only now, by letting go, I can bask in your glow. No matter where I stray or flow, I see the splendor of your show. In every drama I'm the actor, In every experience the timeless factor. In every dealing, every deed, you are there as the seed."

And we realize what Plato already expressed two thousand years ago in the saga of the cave and what Michael tells us in "That One In The Mirror":

"What if that one in the mirror isn't me? He feels separate. He sees problems 'out there' to be solved. Maybe they will be, maybe they won't. He'll get along. But I don't feel that way – those problems aren't 'out there,' not really. I feel them inside me....The pain of life touches me, but the joy of life is so much stronger. And it alone will heal. Life is the healer of life, and the most I can do for the earth is to be its loving child....Seeing 'problems' was much easier, because love means complete self-honesty. Ouch....One thing I know: I never feel alone when I am earth's child. I do not have to cling to my personal survival as long as I realize...that all of life is in me. The children and their pain; the children and their joy....This sense of 'the world in me' is how I always want to feel. That one in the mirror has his doubts sometimes. So I am tender with him. Every morning I touch the mirror and whisper, 'Oh, friend, I hear a dance. Will you be my partner? Come.'"

Most people dream of a better world and are not really happy with their actual life. Thereby many tried sincerely and full of hope to change something for the better. Why then are there still hunger, poverty, surfeit, violence and suffering in the world? Because we don't care enough about the roots of the misery, about the mental conditionings and the resulting entanglements, which have been lined up for centuries like a chain and are passed along from generation to generation. Instead we are busy with superficialities.

Michael Jackson really spells this out in his poems and short stories, which most have overlooked until now. We have the chance to break this inauspicious chain instead of pointing the finger at others.

Master Jesus once said, "He who is without mistake may throw the first stone." After two thousand years these words have not yet found entrance in our hearts, but are still only lip service. Why have adults so much trouble dealing with the realization that wisdom is coming from the lips of children? Why don't they really listen? When children make some noise then adults hear it very well, but they are not willing to really listen. "'Human beings are weak and selfish. Despite our best efforts these problems will never really end.' The head said yes, but the children looked into their hearts and whispered: 'No!.'" (But The Heart said No, Dancing the Dream)

The real noise which fills the whole universe and reaches to the farthest corners of the cosmos is the noise in our heads and thoughts, this eternally rattling, ridiculous chatter of the mind, which is okay with nothing and is permanently grumbling. Michael Jackson has always looked in his heart, followed it and was true to himself until self-abandonment.

The mass of people instead listen to conditionings and never question the endless gibberish in the head, but mistake it to be words of wisdom. Uneasy truths will be quenched into the mind bed of Prokrustes to make them fitting. That's pressing and squashing and twisting and lying like a trooper. Whoever gets one will feels like a winner. When the heart is of stone so what. When somebody with a soft heart raises his voice, then this is just what the moths, parasites and the wise guys with their deadly arguments are waiting for: "Sentimental" and "kitsch." Alone the stamp "kitsch" is sufficient that many people are afraid to look closely. Kitsch is seen to have lesser value and is looked at with disdain. The so-called literate are truly illiterate, the wise guys know truly nothing, and the aesthetics are also really not aesthetic. From their limited perspective they look down disdainfully on a "less valuable yearning emotional expression," as kitsch is defined in Wikipedia (German). Michael's "Earth Song" was for example labeled like this. The songs "Heal the World," "You Are Not Alone," "The Lost Children" and "Speechless" were put in the same drawer. As soon as something disappears in a drawer we are becalmed, because everything is in order again, an elusive order, which keeps us trapped for centuries in self-delusion. Such a message which comes directly from the soul filled with unconditional love, compassion and caring is killed from an arrogant, hubristic and boastful mind.

There are many versions of murder which our society is not ready to see. While the physical body and consequently the flesh of butchers and slaughterers is totally overvalued, the soul is trampled all over. We urgently need soulguards.

In jurisprudence there is no statutory offense of psychic violation, only physical violation. The offense of insult also does not hit the essential, because only the ego can be insulted, while the soul can be hurt deeply and be traumatized and thereby nonviable. The body can be completely healed from injuries in some weeks or months.

Psychic pain instead can it take years, at time decades for healing. In the case of physical injury we can claim injury award, but with psychic injury there is no such indemnity or redemption. Our society is slave of the body, physical and gross, and neglects culpably the soul and the subtle. What man does not want to hear and see does not exist for him. Thereby it is indeed possible to perceive the subtle, yet the respective receiver organs must consequently be used. Erich Frohmann has explored the geomantic perception of space and found amazing possibilities of the capacity of perception and discrimination. Also other scientists have discovered since long how limited the usual modes of seeing and theories are and used this as an opportunity to take new ways.

Charles O. Scharmer from Massachusetts Institute of Technology (MIT) and founder of the Presencing Institute in Cambridge has with the development of the "Theory U" overcome the limits of the old thinking. Thereby the concept of "presencing" plays an important role, a combination from "presence" and "sensing." It stresses the necessity of "presence" and "capacity of discrimination" to grasp the truth and deeper reality. The physical body, feelings, thoughts and intuition are only different energetically due to their lesser density. The physical body is gross and the most dense, feelings and thoughts are more subtle and less dense, and the intuition is extremely subtle, nearly etheric.

Unfortunately the media are crowded by coarse persons who lack the sensibility to recognize that their perception is limited to the area which corresponds to their own energy density. From their limited view they generalize to everything else. That would be the same as if a camel would conclude due to its experiences what a butterfly is like. Only a few highly sensible and intuitive people have looked through the veil.

In Michael's song, "Speechless," psychologist and educator M. Assheuer-Steiger discovered in the year 2002 a deepness that was hardly bearable: "I had to hear 'Speechless' about fifty times before I was able to hold steadily the high emotional level on which he had already been the whole time. Many people will not understand this at all." (http://freenet-homepage.de(AspieLolita))

Michael Jackson was never a camel, but already a butterfly as a child. At the end he became so subtle that the physical body could no longer hold his great soul.

On the same website we find the witnessing of Don Pedro von Hellmann, a spiritual teacher and author, who stated in 2003: "His voice I heard for the first time in the auto radio. It electrified me immediately: That is an angel, an angel. I nearly screamed it. This unbelievable powerful vibration – that was a real highly developed soul!...Unfortunately most people cannot see the spiritual light of people – but whoever was able to see Michael Jackson's light would fall down on his knees."

When now slowly but steadily the light of Michael enters the hearts of people, then this is not a mystification, as scientists and reviews want to make us believe (for example a bachelor work of 49 pages or "Connection"- the magazine for the essential. Seldom I read something so unqualified about Michael, which misses the real thing), but the inevitable and unavoidable result of a light that is radiating incessantly. The sun can be obscured by the clouds, but its light will not thereby be extinguished.

One who never in his life transcended the mind will naturally not be able to follow. And as the mind will not admit that it is unable to cope and will never surrender and forfeit, but always having prepared a new declaration when the old one is no longer sufficient – that's the dharma of the mind - it will continue to care for its self-satisfaction and self-gratification. Defense mechanisms and suppression are not only found with neurotics and mentally ill people, but these are our "normality." People are afraid of the abyss, which could gape, when they take a look at themselves and direct their view to the inside. They are afraid to lose control of their arduously constructed image. "These thoughts and everything they bring about and construct are the activities of a dream I, which lives in its own dream world....The human mind undertakes to act as referee of truth due to personal experience and thus is creating separation. Countless misunderstandings are thus generated which then are seen and understood as real, even if they are not. The mind takes such a big role in your life only because you never have transcended it and you are afraid to not be able to function without mind." (Mantese, 2008, p. 146)

Out of fear of its own end the mind fights everything that could be dangerous for its survival. Michael's messages are admittedly an immense threat for this mind. Why is the world as it is today? Why doesn't man want to grasp that he has created the world himself with his mind? And why does he continue to try to change it with the same mind? Why does he use again and again an instrument that has already proven in the past to be totally inappropriate? Why has nobody the idea to look for the root of all evil?

Because we are believers. Nobody wants to be considered a nonbeliever. By the way, this is not for me; for what shall I stay an eternity in heaven? Year in, year out circle around God's throne with wings and a candle in the hands singing pious songs?

Oh my God, I prefer to sweat in hell. By the way, as a child it was beaten into me that I am a monster and will make everyone who has anything to do with me unhappy. And thus the daylights were beaten out of me to expel this monster, that in those days was talked into my believing – until I ran away from home at seventeen. Finally at age thirty the excellent American transactional analyst Fanita English discovered this mental conditioning and supported me to free myself step by step. Nevertheless two marriage projects failed. An actor must be able to overtake every role and to play it well. But after the drama he goes home as himself and leaves the role behind him in the theatre.

Most people indeed are so identified with their roles, that they even don't notice – roles like child and parent, mother and father, man and woman, teacher and pupil, virtuous child and rebellious child, the role of petit bourgeois, of interrogator, of the poor victim or of a criminal. All these are only roles in the big cosmic sports or drama.

Everything that happens in this piece truly has nothing to do with who you are. The mind suggests that you are the respective role, as well as it suggests, that a fata morgana is real. Even looking very closely and having sharpened all senses, you are not able to see through the delusion; the mind needs the capacity of discrimination to do so - viveka. You have to come so near the delusion that it dissolves. But that you don't want, or better, your mind doesn't want, because then it has to surrender and admit that it is inept. Clearly the mind is adept to add one and two or to see if the lights are green or red or to remind yourself to take an umbrella with you while it's raining. If it would restrict itself to these areas there would not be a problem, but it chooses as its domain the creation of wrong tracks and errors. It is convinced that man should fly to the moon and mars, but is not able to hold the hunger in the world at bay. It provides billions of dollars to make war, but does not have a thousand dollars to help a sick child. It produces ever new instruments to satisfy the greed of man for more, further, higher, and propagates growth of the economy. Due to its blindness it is not capable of seeing that eternal growth is unnatural and perverse. When in nature something is growing eternally than we call it a tumor, cancer or proliferation, which has to be removed immediately. A sane mind would strictly combat permanent growing. In the so-called health system – which should better be called illness system – billions of Euros and Dollars are spent to combat proliferation. And at the same time in the economic system billions are spent to support proliferation. For many years I have asked myself – I was politically active for some time - what else has to happen before man realizes that he is barking up the wrong tree, that he is lost in an impasse which was created by the mind, produced by thoughts. "The head says yes, but the heart says no."
The head says it will go on like before, but the heart says no, it won't go on like before.

In the actual crisis of the system we can observe how media, politicians and experts try to whitewash everything. It is getting better. Better to where? To the clouds or the sky? Didn't we get the lesson thousands of years before of what happens when we permanently search for more, higher, further? We are again constructing a tower as at the times of Babel. "The whole world had one language...Now they spoke: 'Let us construct a tower whose top reaches to the sky.'...Then God spoke: 'See, they are one folk and they all have one language and now they start to do this....Let's descend and confuse their language, that one cannot hear the language of the other one." (Genesis 11:5–7)

This confused language is the language of the head. Originally the earth had only one language, the language of the heart. And the only reason, why we are on earth, is to find our language again, they language we once have lost.

Michael has been the embodiment of this one lost language, and has confused the world thereby. That's why he had to be defeated, because he shocked the world to its derailment. Devotion and dedication are the first steps towards realization of what you really are. Devotion means to break the all-might of the mind. Devotion means to entrust to something higher. With devotion in the heart people would sing and dance instead of march and protest – joy and life energy would circle around the globe. This joy would destroy all the dark clouds of the mind like a black hole. Then the vision would become real which people with heart have phrased: "What if they had a war and nobody came?"

Why do people go to war? Due to the conditioning of mind. Becoming an adult means losing innocence. No child ever would have the idea to go to war. Adults think for example: "You have to serve your fatherland." What is my fatherland? This body was born in Germany, but why should Germany be my fatherland? I am not the body and not bound to the limits of the body and of a land. My fatherland is the whole world and the universe – I am cosmopolitan, a citizen of the cosmos - and when I want to serve someone or something, then I will serve the world, but not a single land. Such craziness only the head can invent. Michael was not a head man, and even his fame never went to his head. When he met people he always greeted and said goodbye with a Namaste – with hands folded. "Namas te" is Sanscrit and means: "I bow to you." Symbolically the ego is laid down at the feet of the Lord; this gesture is an act of devotion to the divine.

35. Innocent

Michael Jackson has always stayed a child with a very big heart. He succeeded in keeping his innocence all his life long and this made him extremely hurtable. While other people acquire a heart of stone due to fear of hurt, his heart was like an open book. Therefore he represented a great danger for those people who were interested in worshiping the ego to establish their own power.

"Don't stop this child, he's the father of man," (Magical Child, part 1, Dancing the Dream) says Michael – and perhaps this child is also the salvation of humanity. Since the construction of the tower of Babel humanity has never again found a common language. And many are still totally speechless. They use their creative powers to invent such madness as Esperanto instead of looking once into their hearts. Every child is able to do this – but unfortunately not every adult. But how is said so beautifully: the last to die is hope, Esperanto, the eternally hoping ones.

Michael was Master of the one language – which does not need words - and as such he was able to touch and inspire people all over the world. Despite of massive opposing wind he did not bow to the pressure of the hair splitter and secured his integrity. "The most loving thing to do is to share your bed with someone."

These words born from innocence have caused a storm of indignation. They have brought the disgust into the arena to start a dirty campaign. What the disgusted did not consider is that they are like an open book for people with a hollow flute. "Everyone who is indignant has the energy of an offender. It is a murderous energy," Bert Hellinger puts it in a nutshell. Who is able to sense the movements of the soul recognizes that the indignant ones see themselves as something better and think of themselves as the good ones, while the other is wrong.

In reality the "good ones" have the most skeletonnes in their closet, but learned perfectly to deny their own shadow. Conditionings like "What might the neighbors think?" force them to do everything to hide their shadow side, so that the neighbors may have a good impression of them. Until self-abandonment and self-denial – the main thing – the semblance is maintained. They kid themselves to stand there as "honest" guys. When for some reason the shadow makes its presence felt we are flabbergasted that these are the blameless exemplary family fathers or mothers. The gates of the dark dungeons can no longer stand the pressure and burst. "When somebody is indignant he seems to stand at the side of the good ones and against the evil, on the side of justice and against injustice. He steps between perpetrator and victim to prevent something worse. But he also could step between with love, which would clearly be better", states Bert Hellinger (www.der-innere-weg.de/bert.htm).

Exactly that Michael Jackson did. He was not indignant, did not judge. He steps with decisiveness and love between opponents, where you see in them that they are not persons to be trifled with and who will fight to the finish, as we see it in "Beat It." The video was shot in the most dangerous neighborhoods in downtown Los Angeles, directed by Bob Giraldi, not with actors, but with members of infamous gangs that were fighting each other. At the shoot they felt taken seriously, respected and seen by Michael and his crew, so that there were no incidents. Love gets deathly enemies to join the dance of life instead of fighting mercilessly.

This short film was inspired by "West Side Story" and the production costs were about 150,000 US Dollars. How Michael triggered the creativity of people is also visible in a video from "Cat from Japan," that was inspired by "Bad" and "Beat It" (Michael Jackson + West Side Story, YouTube). And it is this "Beat It," which means "go away instead of getting involved", which circles the whole world as tribute since Michael left the stage.

Have we finally reached the point where we are tired of throwing stones and facilitate our lives by dancing? "The indignant behaves like a victim, without being it himself. He reserves for himself the right to demand justice from the perpetrators, whereby he himself did not suffer injustice. He makes himself into the advocate of the victims, as if they had retained him to represent them....And then he takes the liberty of humiliating the perpetrators." (Hellinger, 2008)

Such an attitude makes mischief under the pretense of helping and hinders a settlement between perpetrator and victim, which is only possible by approaching each other, but never by avoidance and separation. An indignant one is not satisfied until the perpetrator is humiliated and destroyed. The indignant one is the executioner, the hangman. "Therefore he knows contrary to the one who loves no compassion and no measure." (Hellinger, 2008, p. 51f)

How far the indignant went with Michael Jackson is known sufficiently. The "good" have robbed his home and broken the peace of "Neverland," the only place on earth where he could just be himself, and raged like the vandals. "My room is a complete wreck. My workers told me.... They were crying on the phone.... The room is totally trashed. They had eighty policemen in this room, eighty policemen in one bedroom. That's really overdoing it. They took knives and cut open my mattresses with knives, just cut everything open."(Bradley interview 2003)

Unfortunately these executioners will never be charged for their home invasion. Moths have a carte blanche to destroy. Due to Aphrodite Jones the complete film material of this invasion was shown to the jury during the trial in 2005. All private rooms and cupboards of Michael were searched and his complete personal belongings inspected down to the last detail. "What a nightmare for Jackson." (Jones, p. 50)

The documentary by Larry Nimmer, which also was shown during the trial so that the jury could see for itself what the Neverland Ranch was, is entitled "Michael Jackson: The Untold Story of Neverland," and shows, besides pictures from the premises, the whole terrain, the zoo, arcades, the amusement park and the theatre also the inner rooms (except Michael's bedroom and the children's rooms). Thomas Mesereau had his say and Aphrodite Jones too. In addition, fans added messages by video, for example, "Neverland will forever be the heart of my soul." Michael himself said in a talk with Ed Bradley, "I've been back there, but not in my bedroom. I won't live there ever again....It's a house now. It's not a home anymore." (Bradley interview, 2003)

This dramatic incident is dated November 2003. Since then Michael Jackson was homeless and has traveled around the world, has sometimes lived here, sometimes lived there, in Bahrain, in Ireland, in Las Vegas and in Los Angeles. Since then he had no more come to rest. Michael answered Ed Bradley to his question, "Tell me why you developed Neverland," what this place really meant to him:

"Because I wanted to have a place that I could create everything that I never had as a child.... I can't go into a park, I can't go to Disneyland, as myself. I can't go out and walk down the street....And so I create my world behind my gates. Everything that I love is behind those gates. We have elephants and giraffes and crocodiles, and every kind of – tigers and lions. And – we have busloads of kids who don't get to see those things. They come up, sick children, and enjoy it. They enjoy it in a pure, loving, fun way. It's people with a dirty mind that think like that. I don't think that way. That's not me."

Ed Bradley: "And do you think people look at you and think that way today?"

Michael: "If they have a sick mind, yeah. And if they believe the trash they read in newspapers....Just because it's in print doesn't mean it's the gospel. People write negative things 'cause they feel that's what sells. Good news to them doesn't sell."

In Nimmer's film, it becomes clear for everyone what a place Neverland really was and what was done to the place during the invasion. It also becomes clear what the media until now have withheld to prevent the picture of the freak and monster that was drawn by them for years from being cracked. ("The Untold Story of Neverland")

Larry Nimmer, a producer of multimedia since the late 1970's, was able to impart to the jury a picture of who Michael really was and to debunk the shameless lies which were brought into the world by the "Santa Barbara Sheriff's department." "I Think it was wonderful how Michael Jackson created Neverland as a refuge for thousands of kids and as well his own inner kid." (www.forumromanum.de)

The documentary also covered parts of the shoot, which Martin Bashir did not want us to see, for example the devastation of all private areas by the sheriffs, the Arvizo family's own video with recordings of the praise of Michael and their talk about what it was like to stay at Neverland. Nimmer also shows parts of Michael's career and discusses, in an interview with the MJJ Community that was made before Michael's death, the question of how the trial has changed his own opinion about Michael: "I'm more sympathetic to him now. I am upset to see how the media will try to sensationalize a story to get higher ratings and make more money. I learned firsthand how people go to great lengths to take advantage of celebrities like Jackson. I have more respect for him when I hear how he uses his childlike nature for creative purposes. I have great sympathy for him seeing how he wanted to do good for the Arvizo family and how they put him through hell....I am more impressed with his multidimensional creativity. He is outstanding as a singer, dancer, composer, choreographer, music video filmmaker and children's humanitarian....As a performer there is no one better. I love how he performs from his gut and from his soul. How he is totally uninhibited when he performs, as opposed to how he is in everyday life. As a person, he seems to be a wonderful guy, although he has not surrounded himself with the best advisors, and maybe because of this, he has shown poor judgment in how the world will react to him....My sons, ages 22 and 25, have new respect for me having worked for Michael Jackson."

In an article in the Huffington Post, the award-winning journalist Charles Thomson took up the topic in 2010 and describes in ten pages how the media in unison, in 2005, tried to bring Michael Jackson to jail and chipped away at the truth systematically. The world – represented by the covering media – had judged Michael long before the trial had started at all.

At last another journalist has the courage to admit how low the media went in their ignorance. Desk criminals are still tolerated in our society, even when they kick up the shiftiest murder. The perfect murder exists, which is difficult to be identified as such. It starts initially with character assassination and then kills step by step, unnoticeably, the soul. This murder in installments is legal in our society. It is not a crime, but usual practice in our corrupt world. In his article, "One of the Most Shameful Episodes in Journalistic History," Charles Thomson describes in details how the sheriffs, with Thomas Sneddon in the lead – I say Sneddon obsessed by the devil – violated on 18th of November 2003 Michael Jackson's Ranch Neverland during his absence and robbed from him his home and only refuge on this earth. From then on Michael was homeless, refugee and expelled.

Thomson further proves that even after the acquittal of all charges, the hounding of the moths media continued, when Diane Sawyer the next day explained the verdict on American television in "Good Morning America" with Michael's status as celebrity. Diane saw herself as the best informed reporter about Michael Jackson and had taken up the cause of hounding for more than ten years. The same horn was blown in the comments in the "Washington Post," in the "New York Post," in the "New York Daily News" and in Britain's, "The Sun." "The Hollywood Reporter" reported that hastily composed specials with Michael's acquittal had less audience than a repetition of "Nanny 911." In Charles Thomson's blog we are informed that the FBI files support Michael Jackson's innocence.
(http://charlesthompsonjournalist.blogspot.com).

Already, beginning in 2001, the American attorney Gloria Allred tried in the name of child protective services to deny custody of his children to Michael Jackson. And when she failed in one court she filed another application in the next court. When will we finally recognize that these persecutors wanted to see

Michael hung at the cross like the masses once screamed to Pilate, "Crucify him, crucify him"?

And exactly that was foreseen by Michael. The answer of the jury to doubters after the acquittal was, "They did not see what we have seen." Thomson comes to the conclusion: "They're right. We didn't. But we should have done. And those who refused to tell us remain in their jobs unchecked, unpunished and free to do exactly the same thing to anybody they desire. Now that's what I call injustice." (www.huffingtonpost.com).

Michael has tried without success to escape paranoia of the insane minds. He did not die in a traffic accident like Princess Diana, who was chased by a horde of moths. But he also lost his life by being chased like her, because he has been a persecute, a hunted one in an unprotected game. Chased by indignant and good people, by greedy and lustful ones, by power-obsessed people and sanctimonious ones.

Michael yet spoke about the immense pressure he experienced his whole life in to Ebony in December 1984.

Ebony: "You have to cope with a lot of stress and pressure in the entertainment business....How do you cope with these stresses and pressures?"

Michael: "I cope with it in a way and I'm not calling myself Jesus because I would never even look at myself on the same level, but I'm comparing it to Jesus because what God gave to him was for a reason and he preached and people came about him and he didn't get angry and push them aside and say leave me alone, I ain't got time." (Ebony, 1984, 2009)

People adore their idols and at the same time declare open season on them. Rosi Mittermaier also talks about it after her triumph at the Olympics in Innsbruck in 1976: "I could no longer live a normal life. I felt like an animal that is chased everywhere it appears." (Mittermaier, 1976)

Who can wonder that Michael created a refuge for himself – his Neverland. He was not chased and besieged by fans and curious people only one summer long as Rosi, but his whole life "shot" by paparazzi as soon he was spotted. Michael was robbed his human rights on earth: "The only true human right is the right to be left alone – by everyone who is not invited or who is not welcome." (Baader, 2008)

When Michael walked the street he was no longer left alone. His pleading cry of SOS, "Leave me alone...stop doggin' me around," (Moonwalker O.S.T.) faded away unheard. Humanity has idly let drown one of its own, an innocent one, who was in need, cried for help and screamed for his life. But nobody will be charged for failure to render assistance. Michael was not chased by a few paparazzi or surrounded by twenty fans, but by hordes of people who pestered him, jumped on him, monopolized him, devoured him completely. More than once, his life and physical integrity were seriously in danger. "Leave me alone...stop doggin' me around." The number of people who violated the human right, "the dignity of man is sacrosanct," cannot be stated.

The wisdom of our founding fathers is still trampled underfoot. Instead of being courageous and showing audacity, even the arm of the law is looking away. Michael has told us that once there were even cameras installed under the toilet in his private rooms. The peak of humiliation was when Michael was presented to the world in handcuffs and frogmarched off. There was no reason that could justify the use of handcuffs, because there was no danger of escaping and no other danger for life or limb.

Michael clearly stated: "They did it to try and belittle me, to try to take away my pride....They manhandled me very roughly. My shoulder is dislocated, literally. It's hurting me very badly. I'm in pain all the time. See this arm? This is as far as I can reach it. Same with this side over here."

Ed Bradley asked "Because of what happened at the police station?"

Michael: "...If you saw what they did to my arms – it was very bad, what they did. It's very swollen....The handcuffs, the way they tied them too tight behind my back...and putting it, they put it in a certain position, knowing that it's going to hurt, and affect my back. Now I can't move. It keeps me from sleeping at night. I can't sleep at night....One time I asked to use the restroom....Once I went in the restroom, they locked me in there for like 45 minutes. There was doo-doo, feces thrown all over the walls, the floor, the ceiling, and it stunk so bad. Then one of the policemen came by the window and he made a sarcastic remark. He said: 'Does it smell good enough for you in there? How do you like the smell? Is it good?'...And then one cop would come by and say: "Oh you'll be out in a second. You'll be out in a second.'...Then there would be another ten minutes added on, then another 15 minutes added on. They did this on purpose."

Dick Gregory, activist, health guru, ex-comedian and friend of Michael comments on the issue: "Whether it is damaging to Michael Jackson or not, he insisted that truth is the most important aspect of the issue." Dick says that he does not believe in his guilt..." He asked why it was necessary for 40 police officers and 20 FBI agents to raid Michael's property. More specifically, why were FBI agents present, especially since the allegations against Michael Jackson are not a federal offense?" Rev. Al Sharpton, who came to the defense of Michael Jackson in this time, was soon overwhelmed by media coverage of a videotape which showed individuals attempting to frame him in a drug deal....Dick Gregory states that the showing of Michael in handcuffs was symbolic and when they handcuffed him, they handcuffed them all (the Black community).

The fact is they allowed Michael to board his private plane in Las Vegas and fly back to California. And then they handcuffed him, then immediately took them off when inside the police station, that is, beyond reach of cameras and photographers. According to Mr. Gregory, law enforcement had not judged him an extreme flight risk if they let him fly in, and obviously not a danger, if they immediately uncuffed him once inside, so why the posturing?" (www.hiphopandpolitics.wordpress.com/2009/06/30/).

If Michael Jackson ever was a danger to anybody, or to order and security, then I will need ten bodyguards from now on in the village near the Alps with 3900 souls where I am living. There it is crawling with people who are certainly more dangerous than Michael.

The interview with Ed Bradley ended with the question: "Michael, what would you say to your fans who have supported you through all of this...?"

Michael: "Well, I would tell them I love them very much. They've learned about me and know about me from a distance. But if you really want to know about me, there is a song I wrote which is the most honest song I've ever written. It is the most autobiographical song I've ever written. It's called 'Childhood.' They should listen to it. That's the one they really should listen to. And thank you for your support, the fans around the world. I love you with all my heart. I don't take any of it for granted. Any of it. And I love them dearly, all over the world."

36. Touring

Michael Jackson was a giver all his life. With the Jackson Five he went on tour for the first time at the age of 12, at 13 on his second USA tour through fifty cities, at 14 when others had not even finished college on the third tour, the first international, to France, Great Britain and Germany. At 15 followed the fourth – this time as "The Jacksons" - in the USA, Japan, Australia and New Zealand. When Michael was 16, the fifth tour led him to Africa, South America, the Far East and the USA. In 1975 the Jacksons toured for the sixth time, to the West Indies, Great Britain and New York. When Michael was 19 the seventh tour followed, to Europe. One year later this Europe tour was expanded to the United States. In 1979 followed the "Destiny Tour" of The Jacksons through Europe and the USA. The "Triumph Tour," which started on 9July 1981 in

Memphis, led once more through 39 cities of the USA. The eleventh tour, where Michael had his 26th birthday, was the "Victory Tour," from 6 July until 9 December 1984, which led the Jacksons through USA and Canada with 55 concerts and two million visitors.

At 29 years of age, Michael started on his twelfth tour, the "Bad Tour," his first solo world tour. It lasted more than 16 months, from 12 September 1987 until 24January 1989. Michael gave 123 concerts for 4.4 million attendees, among those seven sold-out concerts in Wembley Stadium in London with 504,000 attendees, which was Guinness Book World Record.

You have to take one moment of time, pause with the lecture, and shut your eyes, and imagine in your mind's eye what it means that someone who is not even 30 goes on tour twelve times. What did you do with 30 years and what have you done until that time and seen and heard and reached? I don't want you to feel bad or insufficient now, but I only want that you at least develop the minimum feeling of what Michael's life was like. That is absolutely crazy and unique among the more than seven billion inhabitants on earth and also unique among all world- and superstars. And I think it is a wonder that Michael survived it at least 50 years.

At age 34 in 1992, Michael started his thirteenth tour, which also lasted more than 16 months, the "Dangerous Tour" from 27 June 1992 to 11November 1993, with 67 concerts and 3.5 million attendees. The proceeds of this tour were given to charity organizations. On 29 August, his 35th birthday, Michael performed in front of a crowd of 47,000.

Five days before the allegations in the Chandler case had reached the public, three days after the police search at Neverland. Just as Michael in Bangkok was preparing to perform "Jam," he was informed about the shocking news. He started to take painkillers to cope with the stress. He was dehydrated, had eating disorders and lost much weight. Nevertheless Michael gave more concerts, in September and October 1993. On 11 November he gave the last in Mexico City and then cancelled the tour due to health problems. The burden of the allegations of abuse had got the tribute. At the same time he had to withstand a charge in Mexico of plagiarism for "The Girl is Mine," "Thriller" and "We Are The World" against himself, Lionel Ritchie, Quincy Jones, Rod Temperton and his father Joseph. A jury of nine members acquitted all charges. Michael collapsed at the end of the process and went to London for a drug rehab of some months. He again gained weight and regained his strength. In 1994 the settlement between Chandler and Jackson was signed.

Two years later with 38 the fourteenth tour followed, which lasted longer than 13 months. This "HIStory Tour" led him through 58 cities with 4.5 million listeners in five continents and 35 countries from 7 September 1996 to 15 October 1997. That would be his last world tour. I was lucky to buy a ticket for one of the two concerts in Munich as a gift for my 50th birthday.

In the year 1999 followed another two concerts, "Michael Jackson & Friends," one in Seoul in South Korea and one in Munich, and in September 2001 he gave two more concerts for his 30th birthday on stage as solo artist in New York in the Madison Square Garden.

Michael himself often repeated: "I go through hell touring." The stress of touring was painful for him, the time changes, the permanent traveling, no home, all the changes, a life in a fishbowl. When you sum up the time which he spent traveling, then Michael Jackson spent more than ten years of his life in hell.

Nevertheless there was the other side, the dimension of fulfillment, when he was on stage. "It's a spiritual thing also…I realized I have got family all over the world". (YouTube, Private Home Movies)

When you realize the above dates you get dizzy when reading them. Can you imagine such a life for yourself? Would you come through such a life unscathed and immaculate? And the touring? And that was not all – much more serious things happened: The allegations of child abuse in 1993 and again the allegations in 2003 and the trial lasting five months in 2005. Then came countless charges where people tried to milk him, which he nearly without exception could win. But the stress was there.

The one who believes he is able to survive such hell without damage may take the first stone and throw it. And after all that, Michael was capable and ready to give even more. Instead of the originally planned ten concerts of the "This Is It" tour in 2009, which were planned for London, 50 concerts were burdened upon his shoulders. Instead of saying no Michael said yes. I can well imagine that the super big father "i" had his effect with the instilled belief, "Never disappoint your fans." Such conditionings are deep like a thorn in the side and not easy to eradicate.

This deep belief contributed also to the fact that Michael left this plane so early. The drugs are perhaps the drop in the bucket, or the trigger, but the cause and root is to be found in the past and lies deeper. The drugs are the consequence of Michael's attempts to survive with this sentence in mind, to cope with the allegations made up out of thin air, the humiliations and degradations. Such conditionings are the first link in a chain of causes which force us internally to do certain things or to refrain from others. The tampering with the consequences is purposeless and senseless, as long as the roots are not debunked and erased – in this case the prohibition or demand of the critical parent "i" state. Otherwise the inner belief is hanging above us like the sword of Damocles.

We all are overloaded with conditioning of this type and try all our lives to weaken, change or come to grips with its consequences, an impossible task which equals the work of Sisyphus. Matt Semino, a New York attorney and legal commentator writes: "Michael Jackson was a modern Sisyphus, the loin clothed man condemned to repeatedly pushing a rock up a mountain only to see it roll back down. Sadly though, our Sisyphus collapsed under the weight of his struggle." (http://elitestv.com)

Michael all his life until his last minute gave everything and was even willing to give more, until he was dead on his feet: "What more can I give?"

Life finally delivered him by death. I remember the last concert in the Olympic stadium in Munich, about which Karen Faye, Michael's hair and make-up artist, reported. At the time Michael gave two charity concerts for the International Red Cross, the Nelson Mandela Children's Fund and UNESCO. Besides himself many artists participated and flew from Seoul, South Korea, where the first concert was given, with a chartered airplane to Munich, where two days later on 27 June 1999 the second concert was held with the title, "Adventure Humanity."

At 2:00 p. m. the spectacle started and lasted nine hours. I had secured a ticket for the arena and was waiting since 11:00 in front of the gates of the Olympic stadium. It was a hot sunny day. I carried a bottle of 1.5 litres of water. That had to be enough until midnight because that was when the concert was scheduled.

It was a mammoth event with thirty top stars and 4000 artists like the old rockers of Status Quo, the group Boyzone from Great Britain and the American Luther Vandros, Udo Jürgens from Austria, the Italian Andrea Bocelli, the exceptional guitarist Slash from Guns N' Roses, the Kelly Family from Ireland, Zucchero from Italy, Patricia Kaas from France, the Scorpions from Germany and many more.

There were collected one million Pounds for charity purposes. The presentation of the whole event was made by Thomas Gottschalk and Michelle Hunziker and aired live in ZDF. The stadium rocked the whole day. I was lucky to stand quite near the stage and was concerned about dosing my water so that it would not be necessary to leave the place. This was not so easy, but I succeeded.

Finally it dawned and everyone was chomping at the bit to see Michael performing, who was announced to be the last one, at 23:00 ready at last. Michael started with a medley, followed by "Beat It" and "Black or White" with Slash and then "Earth Song." The stadium was boiling.

A bridge was lifted over which wandered the forgotten ones. And then Michael ran above the bridge, the intensity of the song rose, Michael stamped his feet, smoke and explosions intensified the effect. The bridge was rising higher and higher – 18 metres as I learned later - and suddenly it dashed down and nearly disappeared in the orchestra pit. Michael could no longer be seen, but continued to sing.

What a crazy performance, I thought, that does not look good. The audience was screaming. Was this really scheduled or was something wrong? And then Michael's arm appeared and he climbed from the orchestra pit on stage and finished the song. A tank drives in, and a soldier with a machine gun at the ready launches threats a Michael. Michael is standing firmly, withstands with unerring eyes the threatening soldier and parries off the offense by pure presence. A child enters the stage with a sunflower and gives it to the soldier, who sinks on his knees shamefully....Devotion....The stage is cleaned and again Michael appears to the audience of more than 60,000 fans and says goodbye with "You are not alone."

And then shortly before midnight, the day I had longed for so long is finished. And will still be remembered for a long time. Slowly the stadium empties, this time very slowly, as if people guess this has been the last time to see Michael in all his glory. People are discussing what happened with the bridge. Something must have happened; that looked very dangerous. Rumors are circling that Michael was brought to the hospital.

And here again the whole incident as viewed from backstage by Karen Faye: "The sun was setting. The darkness changed the entire feeling of the arena. It was a hot summer evening. The crowd had been enjoying performances of other artists all day...but it seemed the audience was waiting for Michael....I could feel the energy of anticipation the crowd directed towards us....He would peek out at the audience from behind the curtains. The band came up the back stairs. Michael met them for the traditional prayer joining their hands. The show began with all the frenzy and excitement that they all did....Everything was going perfectly....Earth Song began...then the bridge appeared, just as it had done in Korea.... Michael flies up the bridge and gyrates and pounds his feet, twirls as the bridge lifts away from its braces.

Smoke, explosions, bombard our eyes and ears...the bridge continues higher and higher, but unlike rehearsals, and the last show....it didn't pause at its pinnacle. INSTEAD it came careening down gaining speed with Michael tightly grasping the railings...still singing. I started screaming....I started running out from behind the stage...as the bridge (was)...slamming down on the concrete floor....Backstage, there was crying and screaming, only the crew and performers knew there was something desperately wrong....Even though the show continued for everyone else, time stood still for me, as I could not imagine how Michael could have survived such a fall.

But slowly,...I saw one arm reach for the floor of the stage...he was up...finishing the end of Earth Song! My mouth dropped open in relieved amazement. Looking dazed, he made his way to our side of our stage....'Security...please get him to the hospital!' I was begging. 'NO!' He grabbed the microphone and ran out to finish performing "You Are Not Alone."...He...took his final bow and returned once again to his stage dressing room and then...collapsed.

Security whisked him off to a hospital in Munich....I got the reports that nothing was broken, but he was badly bruised, and his back was very badly strained....The next day...I asked him...why did you continue? I cannot believe you were able to do that. 'You know Turkle, the only thing that I heard in my head, was my father's voice saying to me, 'MICHAEL, DON'T DISAPPOINT THE AUDIENCE.'" (http://karenfayeblog.com/)

"My father was a genius when it comes to the way he taught us, staging, how to work an audience, anticipating what to do next, or never let the audience know if you are suffering, or if something's going wrong. He was amazing like that." (Ebony, 2007)

37. Conditioning

The purpose of the human being is to follow his dharma, to be what the human, due to his essence, is. That is the task for which he came into the world. Most people have no idea what their dharma is and live lives that are the product of unconscious conditionings. Dharma, a term from Sanscrit, which is also familiar in the ancient Vedas and in Buddhism, describes that which makes someone or something into that which it is.

Even when we don't want to realize it, from the innocence and pureness of our early childhood we change systematically into a guilty and corrupt adult. When growing we are filled with concepts and mental constructs which shape in our life and our decisions and which determine our ways. At some point our socialization comes to an end and we have been successfully made into the product of our parents and other social influences, which reach back many generations. It is of little importance if these are genetic roots or verbal and nonverbal conditioning.

But as most people firstly don't want to be like their parents, there starts an interesting mechanism. One fancies not to be like his parents and makes his decisions accordingly to prove to himself and others that one has succeeded in being different. The result is rebellion. Rebels naturally don't have an easy life; they rub the wrong way, spoil things with the parents, teachers and authorities and have a hard time with their bosses.

Besides the rebels there is the type who make their lives apparently easier and prefer to adapt to others. Those are the exemplary students, the teacher's pets and the well-behaved ones. It is interesting that the psychodynamics beneath the two behavioral types is the same. The behavior of both is always predictable and exactly predetermined. The adapted one follows the conditioning and the rebel behaves exactly the opposite. That means that one acts according to pattern A and the other one according to pattern minus A. Mathematically predictive, without any degree of freedom. The rebel believes to be free because he does not follow his parents, and is in reality as adapted as his well-behaved brother.

You are only really free when you look through the conditionings you are following or are following oppositely, and identify these and free yourself of them. Until then you don't live a self-determined life, but like a puppet on strings. Transactional Analysis has described these connections in an easily understandable, pragmatic model which can help us to look through these mechanisms of conditioning. Models are always simplifications, but concentrate on the essential. Transactional Analysis, called TA, differentiates between three principal ego states which are the source for actions: The state of the parent, of the adult and of the Child. These states of the "i" are patterns of thinking and feeling, which lead to a certain predictable behavior in a certain situation. The state of the child is separated in the adapted and the free child. One who fulfills the expectations of parents (and authorities) is adapted and not free, even if he is telling himself a thousand times he is free and believes it. Many people act and react most time of their life from the state of the child. Thus the adapted ones have extreme difficulties in dealing with the rare people who live in their free child state. While Michael acted from the adapted child in relation to his obligations and his fans and the public, he was in his artistic and personal expression most of the time unconventional and free, so that the adapted ones had a difficult life in relation to him. Acting from the free child is spontaneous, unpredictable, crazy and therefore creative. While the adapted child is having a hard time in the office or the fabric and the rebellious child is marching and organizing protests, the free child has fun in the circus or is riding a rollercoaster. Logically the adapted one is envious, because secretly he would like to do exactly the same what the free child is allowing himself, but the conditioning does not permit it. He would have a bad conscience and feel guilty, and thus even rollercoasting wouldn't be a pleasure.

The conditioning functions like an invisible tie. In extreme cases it equals a gordic knot which nobody will unwind – except by sword. Did you ever notice that Michael had always a sword on him? Did you ever notice that Jesus had a sword on him? And to calm down all religious sects' advisors, I did not say that Michael is like Jesus, but I said that both brought the sword. "I did not come to bring peace but the sword." (Matthew 10:34)

It is not easy to accommodate this statement of a messenger of God who came to the world to pray love for the conditioned mind when he feels the gordic knot in the region of the umbilicus. Jesus taught and brought us exactly what could unwind the knot for ever, the sword of the capacity of discrimination. And Michael Jackson, where did he bring the sword? He once founded "Kingdom Entertainment," whose logo was a sword, Excalibur, the sword of discrimination. On YouTube we find pictures of prison inmates who are dancing to Michael's songs and show discipline and cooperation to study the performance. It is said that they adore him "like a God."

What does this mean in plain terms? Nothing other than that they believe in him, trust him and attribute superhuman powers to him. And that he had them is without doubt. Michael succeeded with his work and actions such that millions look at a prison and observe thousands of detained lawbreakers, without passing judgments about their crimes and supposed contemptibility, but allow themselves to be touched by these people at the edge of our society. I don't believe that the ones who click on the video on YouTube feel indignation and disgust, but that simply the joy which the confined radiate leaps to them. Delinquents bringing joy to the world. Isn't this genius? Michael Jackson was free to venture on issues that are absolutely taboo for the adapted ones. In "Dancing the Dream" he let himself portray with armor and sword. Shouldn't all of us be better armored instead of being indignant? What sort of sword is this? The sword of revenge as little minds are claiming? I think it to be the sword of capacity of discrimination - viveka. Only with viveka can you look through skin and shell, through the surface to the ground. "The emanating light of the natural source enables people to perceive intuitively, to recognize clearly and to discriminate. The power of discrimination enables them to lovingly put their lives in order, that means that they by insight look through that which creates disorder and overcomes it. When that happens the coexistence of all living beings comes into order, as nothing can exist separate from the all-order. Then man lives in harmony with the whole world events and discovers therein his universal being." (Mantese, 2009, p. 42)

Without the power of discrimination you are rotating in your own mental universe, like a fan (in German =Ventilator). You are searching desperately for explanations to satisfy your mind, nothing more, nothing less. You are searching for killer arguments to be proved right. This wish is the most important distinctive marking of ignorant people. A knowing one would never think about discussing an issue. He remains still and in silence. The goal of discussions is always only to be proved right. It's always about persuading the other one that he is wrong. Always. When somebody looks deeper, then he knows that the other is not able to do the same and therefore he does not hit on the idea to try to persuade him. And when the response is shallow nonsense then he leaves it there where it belongs, at shallow banks. One who talks has nothing to say. One who has something to say will not talk. When you now think why I am talking so much – writing is also a form of talking - then look more closely. I don't talk much, but say always again and again the same, yet with different words.

The "Course in Miracles" – a work of more than 1000 pages – is built after the same principle. The exercise part contains 365 lessons, one for every day of the year. And each lesson has the same goal and the same "learning content" – to sharpen the sword. The sword of discrimination, for which Jesus has come, not for love, peace and harmony, as some smart alecks make us believe (wordplay in German: "Naseweis" = smart aleck; "weismachen" = make believe). Transactional Analysis provides us with some further interesting knowledge. Each person has one of four basis attitudes towards himself and the world. "I am OK – You are OK"; "I am OK – You are not OK"; "I am not OK – You are OK"; or "I am not OK – You are not OK." (Harris, English, Berne) These attitudes develop unconsciously in the first years of life due to parent messages that the child is confronted with, especially from mother's side.

With the attitude, "I am OK – You are not OK," one thinks they are the good one and has much to criticize about others. Someone with the basic attitude "I am not OK – You are OK" has only a low self-confidence, orients himself by others and tries to do it right for them. The attitude, "I am not OK – You are not OK" is marked by negativity and is not life-affirming. These people tend to be depressive or at times violent. They feel as victims and turn rapidly to be perpetrator, when their aggressions are directed to the outside. The prisons and psychiatric hospitals are filled with people of this basis feeling pattern. In the attitude, "I am OK – You are OK," one is born and then adopts due to the conditioning one of the three other attitudes.

To recover this attitude in its ripe form, awareness and conscious work are necessary to unbind the emotional and mental ties. Michael Jackson has preserved the fourth attitude since childhood: "I am OK – You are OK." Michael's unwavering believe in the goodness of men made him the target of envy, hate, derision and gleefulness. Envious people claim that "I love you, I love you more," is only a lip service and a cheap PR line.

With an ice-cold heart made of stone one really cannot imagine something else. A warm heart and compassion are suspect for the poor in spirit. How shall someone who never left prison know how someone feels in outer space? Media and press project their little minds on someone who is greater than life. A cosmic joke. It's their film and their truth – but not the truth. Only when you are willing to search for the things you perceive outside in yourself can the conditionings be looked through. Only then is one capable of seeing without projecting. With the basic attitude, "I am OK – You are OK," there is no more fertile soil for condemnation, judgment and prejudice. There is no "either – or," but only "as well – as." "Prejudice is ignorance," Michael has said.

Prejudice, as well as thinking in races and classes, belong to a backward level of consciousness. The Vedas, the ageless wisdom teachings, know three basic marks of all existing. In Sanscrit: tamas - darkness, rajas – dust and sattva - being. Tamas describes the dull, inactive powers in nature, which manifest itself as inertia, darkness and ignorance. Rajas, the second of the gunas, describes the active powers of nature, which can overcome inertia. They manifest themselves as striving, greed, passion, restlessness and also as audacity. The third mark, sattva, has the same meaning as life and existence. It is the quality of balance, pureness and clarity.

A consciousness dominated by tamas is related to material and not able to recognize reality. It tends to misunderstand things and to think the false to be true. Rajas is the power which helps to overcome inertia and ignorance. The essence of rajas is development and change. The development ends on the level of sattva, balance and serenity.

During the process of change all these three qualities are present in various degrees in every human. People with much sattva don't have any more egotistical desires and are free from passions. For them self-realization is natural, because this is the only way to joy and happiness. While in nature all three qualities are balanced, the human mind develops from tamas and rajas to sattva. From ignorance to aspiration and being. In Sanscrit the awakened level of consciousness is called "sat – cit – ananda."

Michael has written about this level of bliss." "From bliss I came, In bliss I am sustained. To bliss I return." (Are You Listening? Dancing the Dream)

38. Selected

From the year 2003 is the following channeled message, which tells us something about background, about why things happen as they happen.

"There indeed are those who come in – how to say – in a sense, give themselves in sacrifice – in this particular case with this dear one known as Michael, who indeed does carry the Michael energy – to achieve a high status, a high profile in order to expose other problems because of their status. They expose things like child abuse, even though they weren't necessarily directly involved ... wrongly accused, you could say, in this case, in particular. But, this soul has agreed to do this to bring attention to a problem, to an abuse that is taking place.

This one indeed is also celebrating life in his own way by integrating the masculine and feminine by allowing himself to express. He is very burdened right now with critical energy being directed his way. It has been directed at his way for quite a while. This is taking a toll on his health, on his own stamina. But, he has many angels from our side, from the family of Michael, working with him. This was his passion to come into the world to draw focus on imbalances....So, dear friends, when you come from a place of compassion, you get out of judgment. You understand what is truly happening, how these dear souls are bringing enlightenment to Earth." (Crimson Circle, shoud 5 Q&A, Tobias, 13 Dec. 2003).

This information, which reached us one month before the infamous press conference from prosecutor Sneddon, has a prophetic character. What happened to Michael at that time was only the beginning of what he had to bear during the next one and a half years until the acquittal. On 13th of June 2005 he was acquitted of all ten charges. Who gets back to business as usual after such a horror process, where the whole world was assisting and witnessing the most intimate and private parts of one's life? Michael Jackson has tried since the end of the eighties to bring some normality into his life by creating Neverland, beginning a family and having children. But the world did not want to grant him what everybody has a right to have. I don't know how much insight Michael himself had into this deeper context. I believe that he primarily followed his distinct intuition and let himself be led. He himself stressed various times that he did not know where certain things came from and that he would not claim to be the originator. And with humility he added as explanation that it was coming from God. He was a free and willing instrument. The Australian guitarist Orianthi once said that Michael Jackson did not have an ego. An ego is never a willing instrument, but is resisting the leadership of God or some higher force. An ego never says, "Thy will be done," but only, "My will be done." Ergo ego.

That Michael was longing for normality was witnessed by his long-time friend Frank Cascio. Both knew each other since Frank was 4 years old and their friendship survived all highs and lows. Frank worked as Michael's assistant and often traveled with him around the world. On 7th of July 2009 he said on "Good Morning America" that now and then Michael would sneak to his home in New Jersey hoping to get hold of some normality. "And he came without security and without a nanny. So he was himself." Michael would have much fun with the simple pleasures of life. "He even helped my mother vacuum cleaning. He loved to help at the housecleaning. He was simply a real man." He would even go to the local shops or unnoticed to dinner, disguised and without security. "You know, everybody can cross the street or go shopping. And we take this for granted. But he never could do this."

Frank praises Michael in this interview also as a perfect father. "He was the greatest father of the world for these children." And from this father Gloria Allred was trying to take custody. When will this world which is upside-down stand again with its feet on the ground? Frank also talks about Michael's close relationship with his mother Katherine, who, as we know, obtained custody for his three children after his death, Prince Michael 1, born 1997, Paris, born 1998, and Prince Michael 2, known as Blanket, born 2002.

Michael always appreciated the doing and being of his fellow humans. Michael Jackson's sight was big and profound. He took things as they were, unconditionally, and he was able to see things in a greater cosmic context.

"Eons of time I've been gestating - To take a form been hesitating - From the unmanifest this cosmic conception - On this earth a fantastic reception - And then one fateful August morn - From your being I was born. - With tender love you nurtured a seed - To your own distress you paid no heed - Unmindful of any risk or danger - You decided upon this lonely stranger.... - No matter where I go from here - You're in my heart, my mother dear." (Mother, Dancing the Dream)

This is only a small part of Michael's song of praise for his mother. On reading it I get pure goose bumps. Who can be greater than someone who is able to bow before his mother, the source of life? Only a mahatma! At this point I want mention a killer argument that the moths when criticizing my book will surely knock out: "That is esoteric."

Ouch, that struck home. Quick, hands off. Otherwise my neighbor might think something about me I don't want him to think. Esoteric is ugh. Do you actually know what the word esoteric means? The term is old Greek and means "inner" in contrast to "exoteric," which means outer. Do you cotton to it? Does it click? Or do you still have no clue? What is wrong with dealing with inwardness instead of outwardness? The Duden defines "inwardness" as "profoundness of mind." Mind describes a pattern of thinking and feeling. Thus it means "profound thinking and feeling," or deep compassion, thus the opposite of shallow thinking and feeling. The world is struck by so much brainwashing that deepest compassion has turned into cuss word. Perhaps we should instead look more closely at the word "exoteric" to debunk all those who are standing at the shallow banks with hammer and mace and are belaboring those who are diving to the bottom of the ocean.

Yes, this book is very esoteric. Esoteric also means secret knowledge, the knowledge that is only determined for an inner circle. By the way, Plato was one of the greatest esoterics. What is the secret in this? Who is the inner circle? All those with the capacity of discrimination, who are able to discern between right and wrong. When someone has adjusted his radio to the wrong frequency, then he is himself responsible when he cannot receive certain things. When your instrument is not tuned correctly, don't hand someone else the blame, but start instead to tune your own instrument. A heart full of compassion, a heart so big that the whole world would fit in, is not a bed of roses. With such a big heart it can happen at times that you feel you cannot survive.

In an interview with Barbara Walters on 12th of September 1997 Michael spoke about the death of Lady Diana. Barbara: "How did you hear about her death?"

Michael (thoughtful): "I woke up and my doctor gave me the news, and I fell back down in grief, and I started to cry. The pain, I felt inner pain, pain in my stomach and in my chest. So I said, 'I cannot not handle this, it's too much,' just the message and the fact that I knew her personally." (www.mjfriendship.de).

Bert Hellinger realized the meaning of the psychic weight of various ways of life and destinations. Research shows that the big changes in the world are caused by grave things. One who lives year in, year out, the same routine, does year in year out the same job, lives his life with working, eating, drinking, sleeping and in between some or sometimes more sex, will not move many things. Maybe he is a good citizen but psychologically he is a lightweight who cannot move much in the world. His work will be limited to the immediate nearest environment.

Michael Jackson on the other hand has moved and touched the whole world; he has literally turned the world upside-down. And after he left his body, the whole energy which he himself had held during his physical life was released.

How much was moved and what was moved everybody can research and witness in the various forums and websites which were initiated to honor him. The partially unbelievable experiences of people from all over the world cannot be explained reasonably. Nevertheless we can state that Michael functioned more than ever before as catalyst and transformer. This especially hits and affects people who never have been Michael Jackson fans in the narrow sense of the word. We are not informed about these amazing things in the news, from the press or in radio and television, where the same crazy things are ruminated, same as before, like a prayer mill. But the internet kills off the subventioned lies so that the marathon of truth can reach its goal, as Roland Baader calls it in "Freiheitsfunken" (Baader, 2008)

Yet without the power of discrimination you will not get far there, because fifty percent of the information in the internet is right and fifty percent is not. In the manifested world everything will balance itself; every minus creates a plus and every plus creates a minus. Only viveka – the capacity of discrimination – is suitable as the leader through the jungle of mental creations. Only with it you realize whether tamas is the mother of certain claims, or sattva, clarity. Clarity only flows through a hollow flute, which is free from conditionings.

If you have problems with discrimination then turn first esoteric, before you believe or expand things you heard somewhere. Go inward and purify your flute. Purifying flutes is not always fun, especially as long you don't want to admit that your flute is clogged. Who has the courage to admit that it looks like a pigsty inside him? Cubbies are there to store something, not to take something out.

Michael did it another way. *"I'm starting with the man in the mirror. I'm asking him to change his ways."*

Change in the world starts with self-change. When even one body or mental cell is renewed then the whole is already different than before. But when one cell tries to change the whole, but excludes itself, then this work of Sisyphus must fail. Inesita from Chile tells it point-blank: "Michael was not only the 'Man in the Mirror.' HE WAS THE MIRROR. You cannot see the light in Michael if you don't see it in yourself. You cannot decipher the message before you know what you are searching for and what you are looking for. You have to vibrate in the same way. You don't get Michael's invitation before you understand that 'We Are The World' and 'you are the chosen one.'" (www.michaeljacksontributeportrait.com).

Michael Jackson was given the Award for the "Best R&B/Urban Contemporary Music Video" for "Man in the Mirror," which was seen as a substantial social critique contribution, during the Soul Train Music Awards in April 1989. It portrays a mixture of stirrings and warrings of humanity – from the Ku Klux Klan to Hitler and Chernobyl - and the contribution of great souls with their blessings and consecrations – from John Lennon, John F. Kennedy, Martin Luther King, Desmond Tutu, Gandhi to Mother Teresa, to name only a few. Michael Jackson's message is that everyone is elected to take responsibility for the world and its healing. You are not elected by a third person, but you elect yourself.

Day by day I see the world is changing and indeed so quickly as never before, especially when researching about Michael Jackson. Thus naturally I find exotic things such as a discussion of Michael's reincarnations. Hape Kerkeling already stirred up the media in 2007 with a short report of one and a half pages about a former life in his book, "Ich bin dann mal weg". On 20th of July Bild wrote, "Has Jacko lived already in the 17th century?" And now we find even on Japanese and Chinese websites reports about Michael's similarity with a young man of the 17th century. "'The Portrait of A Young Man' from Barent Fabritius, painted in 1650, at the Städel-Museum in Frankfort, shows astonishing similarities to Michael Jackson. The experts have been puzzling ever since over the question of who the baroque artist from Delft wanted to represent, and are astonished about the 'unconventional and wayward iconography of the painting. The 'very eccentric male earring' for example is not usual for painters from the Netherlands in the 17th century, according to the art and fashion historic Marieke de Winkel from Amsterdam." According to Wikipedia it is assumed that it could be a self-portrait.

Is it possible that Michael was at that time just as cool as today? His answer to the question of why he is always only wearing one silver glove, is simple: "Because it is cooler than two." Armband at the right upper arm, right lower arm bandaged, fingers bandaged, only one glove, white socks to black trousers, golden or black gaiters which reach above the knee, gangster hat aslant over his brow, riveted jacket and trousers, self-portrait as King Lewis the II, as knight with armor, helmet and sword, as knave. Self-portrait on three-doored altar, as Napoleon, self-portrait with angle at the third eye, self-portrait with radiant halo made of children or with sun at the crown chakra. With all these things he made the world "crazy." Hasn't the time come that the world has to move?

Michael gave the world enigmas which it will still be cracking in a hundred years. As of today the enigma around Egypt's Child King Tut, also called Tutankhamun, has not been solved. According to Wikipedia Tut was nine years old when he was enthroned and became pharaoh of Egypt. His kingdom lasted eight to ten years. He died at the age of nineteen. Tutankhamun was extremely popular during his time. Although very young, he was given great responsibility and he died much too soon. "Gone too soon."

As of today the cause of the death of King Tut is not clarified and there are publications which claim that he was murdered. (Patterson, 2009) It is said to be "a real criminal story made of intrigues, betrayal and tussling for power, which forcefully suggests that the death of King Tut was all else but not natural."

Is it a coincidence that the book was published in 2009? And is it a coincidence that on 10th of August the following message was circling around the world? "A bust from Egypt which is 3000 years old (1550 to 1050 before Christ) is attracting hordes of Michael Jackson fans to the Field Museum in

Chicago in Illinois, where the bust made of chalkstone can be looked at since 1988. The bust has astonishing similarities to Michael as he looked shortly before his death. It comes from the Tut epoch."

King Tut by the way was also a black man. It is known that Michael Jackson bought a copy of the tomb of Tutankhamun with a golden sarcophagus. On www.associatedcontent.com on 1st of July 2009 was published, "King Tut and the King of Pop Michael Jackson," which describes in detail the similarities in the lives of both.

In the web we also find speculations that Michael is the reincarnation of Mozart, whereby there are also listed astonishing similarities. My impression is that the human mind likes to create enigmas with its creative forces and then tries to find the solution for an eternity, a good idea for occupational therapy. All these rumors and speculations satisfy curiosity, that means the rajas forces in us, but beside that they don't have much force of expression. It is for certain that our present body mental system is only one link in an endless chain, as a garland of flowers, which reaches back countless generations until long before the beginning of the computation of time and the writing down of history. Life does not align itself according to the mind. Life is larger than the mind. Elizabeth Taylor said about Michael: "He is larger than life." Michael was a beacon for millions of people all over the globe. And his presence was perceptible even at the memorial in July 2009. As Usher intoned Michael's song, which was written for Ryan White, it created pure goose bumps: "Gone too soon."

39. Trappers

Even months later, the news and notices about Michael Jackson, his death and his life followed in quick succession, and daily new rumors involving the King of Pop. Journalists are responsible for news. The definition of journalist is, "someone who reports for a magazine, television or radio."

Okay so far, but what is a report? Referring to Wikipedia a report is "a text, which describes a fact or an action, without containing judgments by the author." I see, and now may someone explain to me, who is the one who on 12th of August 2009 during a press conference of Michael Schuhmacher said literally: "Speculations are part of our business"? A journalist certainly not. There someone has formulated point-blank his "professional ethic" and admitted that we are not provided with news, but with speculations.

What is the difference to our economic, financial and social system that is beginning to totter? Our mental and information system is also led by speculator. Do you slowly realize how the wind blows? Before you swallow only one word or one sentence which is presented to you in the media, it's better to ask yourself first which profession the author has – journalist or speculator.

There are situations where one may indeed speculate, for example, when betting or playing poker, but in that case I know from the beginning that I am speculating and don't sell the products of an insane mind as facts. People love enigmas and mysteries. They need the kick, the arousal of the senses and occupations for the mind. First we need problems so that something happens in our life, else it would be boring as shit. In reality there are no problems. There are situations which require solutions, or creativity is in demand to find a way out of an impasse or to make a decision. But why should this be a problem? The statement, "my problem is," says that I am adopting things which are then "mine" and I don't want to lose. People don't realize that they are setting traps day by day, putting stones in their way, and are leading themselves around by the nose.

Michael was, by the way, a genius trapper. He loved to test the capacity of discrimination. The critique of the album "HIStory" proves the inadequate power of discrimination of the critics combined with arrogance.

Long before Michael's death, Joseph Vogel published in "Man in the Music: An Album Guide to Michael Jackson" his elaborate and excellent explorations about the artist Michael Jackson. For him the HIStory album is the most underestimated of all. One who interprets "Childhood" and "Tabloid Junkie" as a sign for paranoia or self-absorption has missed the essential. "Jackson, in this rather ambitious track, is singing truth to the power in an issue with relevance far beyond his personal life… 'Truth' simply doesn't matter (for the media). What matters is entertainment, ratings, and a drug-like addiction to endless spectacle." (www.huffingtonpost.com)

"Speculate to break the one you hate, circulate the lie you confiscate, assassinate and mutilate the hounding media in hysteria. Who's the next for you to resurrect?" (Tabloid Junkie)

According to Joe, "many people don't realize that Jackson, in this track and others, specifically uses the vehicle of hip-hop to deliver a political message."

"You say it's not a sword, but with your pen you torture men, you'd crucify the Lord." (Tabloid Junkie)

In an interview with James Montgomery in 1996 Michael says, "If people hear a lie long enough, people believe it. People have lied about me." (www.mvt.com)

In my times as a student in the seventeenth I experienced that people swallow everything that they are fed. My professor was the co-author of a "scientific" publication whose results were in later years again and again cited and expanded. In reality they had written a joke book with pure inventions – camouflaged as research project - and we have at the time laughed in our sleeves. The challenge for the reader was to discern the right from the wrong and that is only possible with viveka. Viveka is not a function of the mind, but it comes when thinking has stopped.

As mankind has enthroned the mind and not the real ruler, it stands today at the edge of the complete breakdown of all systems – social system, economic system, financial system, money system, health system, scientific system, education system, culture system, work system, tax system, income system, political system, system of parties etc. The only system which is freshly flowering is that of the fine arts – literature, painting, sculpture, theater, dance and music.

Art is the only thing that transcends borders, languages and cultures and is understood worldwide by anyone – and art is not ruled by speculators. By dance and music one world is created. By mind and thinking many worlds are created, as many as there are brains. Language is superfluous for communication and understanding, because with the first word the seed of separation and misunderstanding is laid. "In the beginning was the word." (John 1:1)

In the moment where there is a word there is a beginning, and when there is a beginning there is also an end. But life has neither a beginning nor an end. And there are also people with a life without beginning and without end. The gate to this endless life is the death of mind. Everything you have thought out throughout your lifetime you will take with you when you leave the body, as seed which will again search and find its way into manifestation. And so "you" will reincarnate some time, so that the seed can reap harvest.

The only way to finish this cycle consists in dying before you are dead. When during a lifetime there are no more seeds produced, then there will no longer be fruits. "A good wanderer does not leave marks." (Rabinath Tagore)

But there is still a little problem in writing books. In the moment I am putting a word, I have laid the seed for misunderstandings. But as any word is nothing but a projection surface, a screen where you project your film, you always only look at your own films. With my word I have no influence on your film. Therefore everything I have written is completely superfluous and senseless. Superfluous because I cannot add anything to what you know, and senseless because sense cannot be transmitted by words. "Be still and know." (Das unpersönliche Leben, p. 11)

Being still does not mean to say or write nothing, but to be without mind. Without mind life gains a new quality and reveals the True, the Beautiful and the Good. Let's follow the traces of Michael Jackson as trapper. His fifth solo album is named "HIStory – Past, Present & Future, Book 1." Did you ever ask yourself why it is named "HIStory"? And why "Book 1," when there was never a "Book 2"? And why did he call it "Book 1" and not "Part 1"?

Alone in the word HIStory there are three hidden meanings: "His story," - the story of Michael Jackson, "History" – the story of mankind or humanity, and "HIS story" – the story of the One. HIS story is the knowledge of the absolute that is described, for example, in the Ashtavakragita. Ingenious, isn't it?

In Michael's songs various levels of consciousness are always addressed. You can look at the texts superficially by paying attention to the first layer. At that point most critics are stuck. Or you peel away more layers and look deeper.

Let's take as example, "Teaser," from HIStory. The term has various meanings, "scriber," "lead feature," "braintwister," "difficult issue," "ribbing." In the interview from June 1995 Diane Sawyer confronted Michael with the argument that his film equals the Nazi film "Triumph of the Will" from Leni Riefenstahl.

Michael: "It's not true. None of that's true. None of those things are true....It has nothing to do with politics or communism or fascism at all." Diane confronts him: "Well the critics have said that it's the 'most boldy vainglorious self-deification a pop singer ever undertook with a straight face.'"

Michael: "Good! That's what I wanted." Diane insists: "For the controversy?"

Michael: "Yeah!...They fell into my trap....I wanted everybody's attention....The symbols have nothing to do with that. It's not political, it's not fascist, it's not dogma, it's not ideology and all this stuff. It's pure, simple love. You don't see any tanks. You don't see any cannons. It's about love. It's people coming together....It's art. It's art." Diane is not satisfied: "In a song you say, 'Jew me, sue me.' And some people are saying that that is antisemitic." Michael explains: "It's not antisemitic, because I'm not a racist person. I could never be a racist. I love all races of people from Arabs to Jewish people, like I said before, to Blacks. When I say 'jew me, sue me, everybody do me, kick me, kike me, don't you black or white me,' I'm talking about myself as the victim, you know? My accountants and lawyers are Jewish, my three best friends are Jewish....How does that make sense?"

Denny Lyon has presented a spiritual analysis of the background of Michael's message, where he states that healing leads to anointing. Michael could not express his spirituality in full measure due to some unsolved post-traumatic experiences. "A proof for Michael Jackson's anointing was this new energy, which connected races, to love the same music, to think better about the other, the decision to live a better way....Michael has changed all this for his generation and the next. In this area his anointing was very successful....in the short time he was here be brought the races in America closer to each other. We may not allow this dream to be lost with time." (http://thesocialpoet.blogspot.com).

One who has read "Dancing the Dream," and really listened to the content Michael's songs and interviews are transmitting, would never think to ascribe racial prejudices to him. Speculators, though, hear a sentence and – without really listening – start to associate. Usually only children and mentally retarded will do this. Without consideration of the frame and the total work they deduce wild conclusions from some parts of the puzzle and sell them to a stupid public at expensive prices. Free associating during adulthood is a disease and seen as pathological in psychology.

Never before has ignorance blossomed so wildly in the media than in the reports about Michael Jackson. And according to the law of balance, also, wisdom – which chose the direct medium of the internet – has never blossomed as recently. An amplitude to below will be followed by an amplitude to above. Giving is followed by taking and vice versa. When there are individuals or groups which take more, then there are individuals or groups at other places who give more. Energy never gets lost; it cannot lessen or grow – it only changes its form of manifestation.

And to not fall into the trap of ignorance, armor yourself with wisdom. When Diane Sawyer confronted Michael, thinking he overvalued his appearance, she only looked into her own mirror and should have grasped her own nose. For decades there were reported speculations about Michael's skin color. Perhaps Michael Jackson turned white only because he embodied more wisdom than all the media together (Wordplay in German: white = weiß; wisdom = Weisheit). Little joke.

To the repeated questions of Diane Sawyer in regard to his look Michael answered: "I think it creates itself, nature. I'm an artist, I'm a performer. I might want to put a red dot right there one day (forehead), or two eyes right here (cheeks)." Diane continues: "Do you wish you were the color you were again?" Michael: "You have to ask nature that. I love black. I love black."

In an interview in 1996 Michael is confronted with the suspicion of abuse of children. One can see that Michael is speechless hearing this question. His body language says everything there is to say. He denies it with his head, puts the hands in front of his face, is really bewildered. Then they give him hand-written notes which seemingly served to prepare the interview. When Michael is asked by Diane, what this is, Michael answers:

„Crazy stories that people have created, things I want to set straight in an interview ... I want to set the record straight. That when people hear lies long enough, people believe it. People have lied on me. I am a black American, I am proud of it, I am honored by it. The bleached skin rumor, which is a rumor. I don't bleach my skin. I am not gay. Don't judge a person unless you have spoken to them one on one. Jesus said to love the children and to be like children, be...innocent, be pure, be honorable. He was talking to his apostles, who is the greatest among them? Whoever is humbled like this child is the greatest among us. He always surrounded himself with children. I was raised to believe and to be like that and to imitate that." (YouTube: Unseen footage: Michael Jackson interview)

Michael's statement is confirmed by Margot O. Strebel after Michael's death in all details. The transformation from black to white happened, and in some way Michael had a clue about the fact that nature does what it wants and not what we want. The arrogate mind then comes with its measuring stick and benchmark, its explanations and theories - and interferes in life. Then things get complicated and life is no longer joyful. Who was ever harmed when Michael Jackson turned white? Nobody. Why then has it been for more than twenty years a constant topic in the media? Aren't there more important things to report? Yes there are. Some time ago we were informed that cucumber is again allowed to be crooked.

Look once at "Teaser." The way Michael is greeting the crowd, his radiant smile, all embodiment of joy, it opens the heart. Where is there energy of the Nazis? It's not the first time in history that the embodiment of pure love was crucified. It is about coming together of the world, to unite all races, cultures and religions: "We Are The World." Michael indeed came closer to this goal during his lifetime and even closer after his death. Never before have so many people in so many places in the world come together at the same time, to give tribute to Michael and to honor him. These people don't protest, they don't fight against anything, and they are not against anything. They dance and sing. Change happens by setting an impulse. When one is free from every idea that will be the result of this impulse, then it expands free in the universe. This purposeful acting releases much effective power. How the initiated energy works is decided by life or nature, without any inflated ego to interfere.

40. Fall of the Wall

This chapter I am writing on 13th of August 2009. As of today, 48 years ago the Wall of Berlin was built and Berlin was transformed into a prison. Michael Jackson came the first time to Berlin on 19th of June 1988 at age thirty, and gave a concert in front of the Reichstag and the Brandenburger Tor. Thereby he was targeted by the "Stasi" (State Security of the GDR), as the main department 20 noted on 4th of May 1988: "Young people will try by all means to assist this concert in the region of the Brandenburger Tor," and with this expectation they were quite right.

But they erred in assuming that it would only be young people, because Michael has always addressed and reached all ages. The original plan of the Regime of the GDR to arrange a "side track concert" was finally not realized. Instead the State Security chased Michael fans in East Berlin. According to Bild from 30th of July 2009 the documents of the Birthler office prove these facts. Not only in the former GDR were unwelcome people spied upon and persecuted, but also in the West this was and is common practise.

I myself have had a traumatic experience on a Sunday morning on 1978. I was just dressing myself when the doorbell rang. I quickly put on a pullover, which I later noticed was inside out, and pushed the door opener for the house door and opened the apartment door on the ground floor to look for the visitor. Directly pointed to me were three machine guns at the ready. I had only one thought: Assault, and threw myself instinctively against the door to slam it. There already three men in civilian clothing had entered my flat and stormed in all directions. With my back leant at the wall I slumped to the ground. I was in shock. I was dispirited. I had the feeling that I was breaking up. In the long distance I heard 'Police.' Only peripherally I registered that they were invading all rooms. Nobody was interested in me as I was squatted there on the ground. After three or four minutes, which seemed to me like an eternity, the scare then ended, at least seen from the outside.

In between I had again pulled myself together. The policemen in civilian clothing stammered something like false alarm, an anonymous phone call. Later I got to know that somebody had informed the police that the RAF terrorist Frederike Krabbe was living there under my name. Why were they bringing the big guns in instead of talking to me beforehand? Danger was at hand and they were not allowed to waste time. And then they withdrew, with not a word of excuse. And they also gave none the following day when I, together with my at-the-time separated husband, was asking for more explanations at the police station. At that time all Babbitt in Germany were hysterical. And when one is yet moving to a bourgeois estate none has to bear the consequences. What was my crime?

I had moved there some time ago into a flat with three rooms on the ground floor and had painted the walls of the sitting room in black – which looked really cool with the light rack wall. And I got now and then visits from friends and colleagues from the campus in Münster, at times only one, at times various friends. And we were sitting and discussing the whole night long about God and the world. By the way Friederike Krabbe has a small frame, is slim with black hair. I am 1 meter 70 tall, well built and blond. Zero similarity with the photo on the wanted poster, which was stuck for weeks on all advertising columns. Frederike Krabbe by the way has still not been found as of today. Eventually it's me after all?

But back to Michael and Berlin.

"They hated the Wall...They feared the Wall...They distrusted the Wall... The Wall laughed grimly. 'I'm teaching you a good lesson,' it boasted. 'If you want to build for eternity, don't bother with stones. Hatred, fear, and distrust are so much stronger.' They knew the Wall was right, and they almost gave up. Only one thing stopped them. They remembered who was on the other side....Beloved faces that yearned to be seen. 'What's happening?,' the Wall asked, trembling. Without knowing what they did, they were looking through the Wall, trying to find their dear ones. Silently...love kept up its invisible work. 'Stop it,' the Wall shrieked. 'I'm falling apart.' But it was too late. A million hearts had found each other. The Wall had fallen before it came down." (Berlin 1989, Dancing the Dream)

After 28 years of separation work the wall was no longer able to stand the power of love.

In November 2009, exactly twenty years after the fall of the Berlin Wall, another wall of remaining silence falls. Teresa Enke, spouse of the football player Robert, who made suicide due to depression, a woman of small frame, breaks the silence with her admirable courage to reveal intimate things, softening stoned hearts of men, when she reported about the soul pain and fears of her beloved husband Robert to the public in a press conference.

Theo Zwanziger, President of the DFB (German football league) later confesses also publicly that also sports should pause at times for a moment and that issues of humanness and prejudice should be focused on. Oliver Bierhoff, a powerful man, shows at a press conference the greatest power of all powers, tears in public. Hardened hearts turned soft like butter, triggered by the fact that again a human being was sacrificed, this time a wonderful sportsman. Broken by the hardness and coldness of those which are tied and imprisoned by the force of century old I forces.

"This is my dream," to install humanness among humanity, that was and is the dream of Michael Jackson, Martin Luther King, Princess Diana and many more unknown souls in all corners and edges of the world. If the advent of humanness to the media is approaching, as DeBorah B. Pryor wishes, I can't judge precisely, but at least it has knocked already at the gates of sport. Usher acknowledges Michael Jackson's merits in the area of music when stating, "He has brought humanness to the music industry." (Usher, N-TV, 27th of June 2010)

Even when many are blinded at these eyes, Michael's work is undoubtedly soaked by the energy of love, independent of the respective form. The presence of soldiers does not mean that we are dealing with war. Soldiers are members of an army. Armies are not only found in wars; we also know the army of ants and the Salvation Army. In "Teaser" we have clearly to do with an army of lovers – with soldiers of light. And Michael has always surrounded himself with armies of children, pure embodiments of love.

"Children of the world, we'll do it, With song and dance and innocent bliss, And the soft caress of loving kiss, We'll do it." (Children of the World, from Dancing the Dream)

Michael embodied a softness, which constituted a strong contrast in our loud gross world. "The eye of man turns soft, when he sees the world with soft eyesight. He sees the softness and vulnerability of all living beings and the divine spirit in every corner of the earth. Whoever lives in harmony with the mysterious course of the world, will never purposefully harm a living being." (Mantese, 2009, p. 48)

"I want my work to help people rediscover the child that's hiding in them." (On Children of the World, Dancing the Dream)

Psychotherapists confirm that the access to feelings and the inner child is an essential factor for healing trauma and psychic suffering.

Diane Sawyer asked Michael even in 1995 questions in regard to the allegations two years before: "You have said that you would never harm a child....Did you ever, as this young boy (Jordan Chandler), said you did,...sexually engage, fondle, have sexual contact with this child or any other child?" Michael answers patiently: "Never ever. I could never harm a child or anyone. It's not in my heart. It's not who I am and it's not what I – I'm not even interested in that." Diane persists: "And what do you think should be done to someone who does that?" Michael still patiently: "To someone who does that? What I think should be done? I think they need help, in some kind of way, you know."

While Diane's questions are directed to hear a judgment of Michael, Michael is neither thinking about judgment nor penalty, but instead sees the deeds as a cry for help. So he is able to look deeper even in the case of perpetrators, where the masses have only judgment and punishment in mind. The mainstream of our society is not yet ready to look at criminal acts as an emergency call, and then to find ways to turn the distress into healing, but their focus is lying on punishment and atonement, at times even vindictiveness and vengeance – like thousands of years before in the Old Testament.

After for example Armin Meiwes, who had a life sentence, the so-called cannibal of Rotenburg, recognized how insane his longings and wishes were, which had turned him into a murderer, had applied for a psychotherapy, this help was denied to him. In our (German) judicial system there is no possibility for therapy when the forensic experts have judged someone as fully criminally guilty. Thus it depends on the judgment of the expert if someone gets help or not. Why does someone who is guilty not have the right to get therapy? His soul is as insane as that of someone not able of guilt. Lack of money? There is no lack of money in the world. There is only a faulty distribution of money. What type of social system is one that rejects people who call for help and does not care about them? Where are the human rights and more than ever the humanness? Our judicial as well as our health system are two class systems. The statement - by law everyone is equal – is only lip service. Where is, by the way, the difference to the much criticized Indian system of castes?

It is not blasphemy when Jürgen Klinsmann is crucified in a caricature, but it is blasphemy when someone places oneself as judge over others and thus is concurring with God. I'm not saying that criminals should not be punished justly. But with this our right to judge ends. From this point all have the same rights. But unfortunately our social system is still far off justice. When someone is denied help he will feel like the scum of the earth. And one who feels like the scum of the earth will someday again coldcock. These are the roots of persons running amok. Often they come from parental homes which represent a whole family to the outside and where the abysms of the psyche are swept under the carpet. And when suddenly the abysm gapes, neighbors, acquaintances and friends are flabbergasted. Why? Because they are not here – I really mean Here - but in cloud cuckoo land.

Some time ago I had to give expertise of a young drug addict in relation to traffic, who had consumed cannabis with a bong for eight years and daily smoked 25 bowls. With such a quantity you are nothing but stoned all the time. When after six years he finally realized his addiction, he needed another one and a half years to free himself from the addiction, even being full of good intentions.

One who hears such a case is quickly ready to judge and condemn. I myself am more interested why someone is as he is and why someone does what he does or why someone does not what he wants to do. This young man gave me insight into the background of his life. His father was very capable in his profession and even at night brought work home, but he drank too much alcohol and often the whole family had to take the rap for his frustration. Looking from the outside it was an ideal family. This young man was as a child awakened from his sleep by his father to wipe away what he had vomited. Freely spoken, if this had happened to me I also would scarf down 25 bowls of marijuana each day. Does this young man know what love is? Unconditional love? At least he got positive expertise.

41. Love is spreading out

Michael Jackson's whole work is soaked with love. After the stone was thrown into the water he no longer cared if and when and how it was spreading out. Michael also never gave bigger explanations to his work, possibly in wise foresight that explanations always only satisfy the mind, and apart from that distract from the essential things. When we are present with open heart no explanations are necessary. "It is love, it is about love, it is about coming together."

Michael was a trapper and a hide-and-seeker. Who of us did not like such things during childhood? Easter eggs which have to be searched for taste naturally ten times better than those which are lying in the middle of the street.

"In infinite expressions I come and go, Playing hide-and-seek, In the twinkling of an eye. But immortality's my game....Deep inside I remain ever the same." (Are You Listening? Dancing the Dream)

Michael played hide and seek on the day of his birth and again on the day of his death. Even today it is not exactly clear at which time he was born. There are two times in discussion, 12:44 p.m. or 7:44 p.m. additionally are circling two other times 4:45 a.m. and 11:45 p.m. According to Michael's statement in his autobiography "Moonwalk," to be born in a night during late summer, is 4:45 a.m. the most probable time, which is yet used rarely in astrological analysis.

When exactly he entered the earthly world will stay unresolved and mysterious. Perhaps also for the reason that he was never only a part of this world but transcended all dimensions and wandered between the dimensions hither and yon. In the same way, the official time of his death 2:26 p.m. is probably not the time when Michael took his last breath, but that was possibly about 10:52 a.m.

An astrological analysis is from Holly Coleman who sees her task connecting people with their spirit, their self and nature, in "Michael Jackson and the Chiron Return." (www.globalwisdom.com)

At the time of his death Michael stood at one of three return points, the Chiron return point, which happens between the ages of 48 and 50. At these points powerful initiations happen. Chiron is a centaur and seen as archetype of the "wounded healer" on the physical plane and functions at the same time as profound mentor and teacher for others. It is said that at this age the chi energy in the body lessens and an awakening to new shores is due to happen. This new shore for Michael Jackson is the land without a name. Experiences in childhood are the clue to reveal the wound and to solve the trauma. A developed soul will then succeed in supporting others due to its own experiences and transform the "wound" into a gift. According to the results of the autopsy Michael Jackson was at the time of his death in good health condition and fit for a 50-year-old man. Orianthi says, "The last couple of nights we rehearsed with him, he was just in great spirits, and he was so happy with the way everything was coming together. And you could just tell he was so excited with this vision." (www.examiner.com).

The evaluation of the autopsy report is naturally related only to his organic health and capability of functioning. The quality of the life energy, which is known to us as chi, is not measurable with instruments. It is a subtle energy, the cause of our liveliness and sensibility. This already had started to withdraw from his physical body weeks before. June Gatlin, one of Michael's spiritual counsels, reports that Michael saw her in March 2009 and had asked her to "scan" his body. Thereby she noticed that his life energy was slowly fading away. And in the conversation about it she told Michael, "We both know something they don't not yet know."

Thus it will remain unclarified which purpose in relation to the 50 concerts in London Michael really had. His words, "This Is It," will remain a projection screen for the human mind to find an explanation for what happened in the following months. Michael was his life not from this world and in his death also not from this world, but he is and was always from a world that most people even in their wildest dreams don't dare to dream of and due to their bonding to the personality and individuality cannot reach. He was in this world but not of this world. And now he has finished the journey through time and entered another realm. "In pure awareness the long journey of the soul through time ends, it enters a powerful light and becomes that which she has entered." (Mantese, 2008, p. 146)

"The harmonies of the angelic choir are incredibly complex...but the rhythm is simple. 'It's mostly march time,' one eavesdropper affirmed. For some reason, that fact is almost the best I have learned so far." (Angel of Light, Dancing the Dream)

Do you now understand why there are soldiers marching in "Teaser," in a simple rhythm? Not with guns and cannons, but simply marching in step. The pictures and symbols which Michael used in his films and texts are derived from various traditions and sources. He absorbed like a sponge everything he met wherever, however, whenever. He occupied himself with culture and education, art, artists, poetry, and studied wisdom teachings and let the essence of everything slip into his work, starting with Michelangelo, Leonardo da Vinci, Tchaikovsky, Debussy, Beethoven, Tagore, Gandhi, to Mother Teresa, Martin Luther King, through the teachings of the Kabbalah and Sufism.

Whoever claims to know his work without knowing all these sources only knows fragments. My study of Michael's message takes up until now 21 years and the mentioned sources are accompanying me for more than thirty years, and yet I really grasped until now only a small part of it. To cut through a century of work one needs at least several decades. Here is noted in the margin a little warning: This book also contains many traps. Traps are necessary to finesse the mind and develop the power of discrimination. For what does survival training in the jungle serve, when we find at every lane a sign with "Attention: Danger"? You can only survive when you sense the danger already from a distance – and not if you are running through the world like "Johnny Head in the Air" and not only when you have already fallen into the hole.

In Brazil I got to know the phone gesture connected with the verbal hint, "Se ligue," (connect yourself) serves as a warning. What is the tone I shall connect to? With the higher wisdom, the intuition, the power of discrimination. This level of perception is not at home in the head, but in every cell of the body. What is the reason that the Brazilians are such good and enthusiastic football players, even when their playing is bad? Because they play football with the foot and not with the head as many in the West do.

Andre Agassi speaks in his autobiography, "Open," about his experiences at the French Open in 2000. In the second round when he met Kucera, his right foot was taped because it was covered with blisters. In a play pause his foot was retaped. "But the real blister is on my brain. I don't win another game from that point on. I look up at my box. Stefanie has her head down. She's never seen me lose like this. Later I tell her that I don't understand why I sometimes come apart – still. She gives me insights from her experiences. Stop thinking, she says. Feeling is the thing. Feeling. It's nothing I haven't heard before."

After this game - writes Andre - followed several days of talks on thinking versus feeling. "She says it's one thing not to think, but you cannot then decide to feel. You cannot try to feel. You have to allow yourself to feel." (Agassi, p. 328)

The Ayurveda – a part of the four Indian Vedas, the knowledge of life, knows the fact that intelligence is not only related to capability of thinking and logic, which is measured in the West by the intelligence quotient, the IQ, but that each body cell has its own intelligence. The body cell does not think, it feels. In the meantime also in the Western world the EQ is known, the emotional quotient, which reaches closer to the real intelligence than the traditional IQ. One who has no access to his feelings may become top manager and progress on the highway of daily life and make a carrier, but he will never know what life is really like. Such a carrier has nothing to do with self-realization and does not serve the world, but only the proper ego.

The world is in a desolate state today because we have the wrong traveling guides. "Whatever *is* cannot be reached. There is a way only for the mind." (Mantese, 2008, p. 91)

In the meantime it is the 15th of August 2009, Assumption of Mary, holiday in Bavaria. I ask myself for what do we need an assumption, when heaven is here? "Heaven is here," says Michael and "Heaven is here. There is no other place," we learn in "A Course in Miracles." (Handbook for Teachers, 24, 6, 4-5)

For what serves all striving and searching, when heaven is here? And for what all the religions? During all the frantic trials, to force Michael in a bed of

Prokrustes, it was also tried to press him into the corset of the religion, first in that of Jehovah's witnesses. Later he was exposed to the efforts of good friends who tried to make the Jewish religion tempting for him, like Rabbi Shmuley Boteach. Even brother Jermaine tried to persuade Michael he could find peace with Islam.

Religions are well and good on a certain developmental level, but eventually everyone outgrows the level of religions. They are the kindergarten or the college for humanity. At least when somebody has finished his studies he can leave behind religions. Leave behind does not mean to reject or see as less valuable, but simply leave behind, because one has advanced.

People tend to evaluate phases that they ended some time ago afterward as bad and judge them as senseless. This perception completely ignores the process of growing and development. When I have reached the seventh step of a ladder, than the first step is still a necessary part of the ladder, as during the time when I myself was standing on the first step. It is good to be born in a religion, but not to die in it, says Sathya Sai Baba. I have nothing against religions, as I have nothing against kindergartens. I only ask myself why we are going to kindergarten our whole life long? Until today I also did not understand why every religion claims exclusivity for itself. The Christian church teaches that only "Jesus is the way," the Jewish consider themselves to be "the selected folks," Islam is talking about the "unbelievers," and Jehovah's witnesses hope to be part of the "144,000 chosen ones."

How can someone seriously believe that God has inclinations and aversions? How is it possible that we make God so small, reduce Him on the measly level of man and to imply that he is thinking and feeling like a human being? And God is not only pulled down to the wonderful level of humanness, but to the level of the narrow human mind. From my viewpoint Master Jesus himself has nothing to do with religions, and also Mohammed did not teach what Islamists have made of it. And Buddhism in a strict sense is not a religion, but a teaching about how to calm down the noisy mind.

I myself adore Master Jesus, Buddha, Mohammed and all the Indian and Christian holy people and mystics very much, and I am also a lover of all the other gods in the pantheistic garden. Life itself is larger than all religions together. And when someone is larger than life as Michael was and is, how shall there be a place for him in a small religion?

Michael Jackson often felt lonesome because he had no possibility to meet the rare beings that are incorporated on earth who like himself are larger than life. He was constrained and watched and lived as in an aquarium. When he put one foot outside the door, hordes and mobs were following him; however can one thus find his twin soul? And when you talk about your reality and your visions and always meet lack of understanding, because the capacity of your opposite is too narrow, than you will someday feel like a stranger in this world. Michael often ended a sentence when conversing with someone with the words, "You don't understand."

When looking from the outside it is hard to imagine the forces that were pulling Michael his life long in all directions. One can think about it for a short time and then say, how horrible. But to really feel how he felt one has to take more time and picture to oneself his life situations in all details and let it like a film pass before the inner eye. Only then one senses how he was caught between two stools. Additionally he was not only confronted with various outer pressures, but also with an immense astral pressure, which like meteorites hailed down on him every hour, every minute, every second.

When somebody is thinking of you this thought reaches and influences you in a way that you don't sense, because your antennas are too weak. When somebody is looking at your photo the energetic thought and feeling waves which the observer is sending out are reaching you. The more people think of you the more powerful this energy wave become and the more intense the feeling with which the wave is carried. That means the more fans, adorers and admirers or critics someone has, the more powerful are the forces he is exposed to.

And with every report and the respective readers and viewers, this tremendous energy increases which as pressure wave affects the energy field of the concerned ones. Most celebrities cannot stand this astral pressure. That is the reason for the attempts to compensate it by alcohol, cigarettes, drugs and pills or by excessive sex. They lead an excessive life with parties and binges. Relationships are like a crucial test for the marriage and families break down. In the worst case health is ruined until the physical and psychological break down, burn out.

Many of the superstars can tell you a thing or two about it and even when many someday turn the corner, they always pay tribute to such a life. Only when it clicks do you withdraw and every man is for himself. Or you decay. I doubt if you really have a choice. My experience shows that life takes the decision which way it goes, and the mind only afterward claims the credit for it.

To the ones that made it belong Elton John, George Michael, Campino from the "Tote Hosen," Robbie Williams, Eminem, Britney Spears, Peter Maffei, Konstantin Wecker and some many more. Some didn't make it like Princess Diana, Janis Joplin, Elvis Presley, Freddie Mercury, Falco, Curt Cobain, Heath Ledger, Jimi Hendrix and James Dean. With Amy Winehouse and Whitney Houston we did not know exactly what will be the end, when this book was written in 2009, today we know, they both didn't make it.

And what about Michael Jackson? From childhood he was extremely transparent, had a very thin skin and a huge compassion. He felt the pain of others – especially of children – literally in the own body. Certain feelings were strange to him during all his life, as for example envy, revenge, hate, greed. Many people and especially the media which are driven by greed cannot imagine that this is possible. They are a responsible part in the further nourishment of these destructive emotional forms, so that they can continue to be up to mischief in the world. Reports about perfidy, violence, turmoil and greed for sensation are bringing more quotes and money than reports about reconciliation, acceptance and impartiality.

Michael did not have a thick skin. He was not a wolf in sheep's clothing. His openness and honesty were disarming; he showed himself psychically naked and was thus extremely vulnerable. And thereby the wolves in sheep's clothing, who were always surrounding him, abused this frankness to satisfy their own greed for profit and to be on the take. And thus the gate to exploitation was wide open. Besides the emotional exploitation which Michael was exposed to, he at times had to suffer severe physical pain, for example as a consequence of the burning at the shoot of a Pepsi PR spot in 1984.

Later he was abused by public agents and was for a long time afflicted with the injuries from handcuffs in the year 2003. The huge blue black spots on Michael's arms can clearly be seen in the video, "Michael Jackson – Remembering June 13th." (YouTube) Michael had not a physical stature like a boxer, pimp or doorman. Goons may perhaps remain unscathed when they are led off in handcuffs, but a small-boned, etheric body like Michael's does not survive such an incident without permanent damage. Even when being led off in handcuffs there are two possibilities, one which is compatible with dignity of man, and one where the policemen can wreak their own aggressions at the accused.

There are many policemen and vigilantes who work in this profession because that is their dharma, and who are serving without animosities and personal interest as an instrument for a higher cause. But countless are also the ones who chose the profession to take their anger out on others and to compensate for their own story which they have not yet overcome. Those are the whippers-in, the persecutors, the interrogators, the rewarders, the revengeful, the envious people, the indignant and disgusted. Those are not able to see a human being in the perpetrator, whose dignity is sacrosanct, independently of his doing. In my job I often could witness how policemen were mindlessly calling the other "du" (the familiar "you" in German) or were treating other people disdainfully or only calling them by their last names. But when the same people in return called them "du," they reacted with a complaint to the police due to insult or at least raked them over the coals.

Robert Enke, the exceptional football keeper, who left this world due to its lack of humanness in autumn 2009, often asked, "Robert or Mister Enke please," when someone called "Enke, do you have an autograph for me?" Such seemingly small things can turn into the crucial trigger for the urgent change of the world.

All observers agree that Michael was not led off in handcuffs due to factual necessity, but only because the sheriff wanted to present a trophy to the world and was turned on by the humiliation of Michael.

Producer Cory Rooney confirms that Michael was fighting health problems and pain: "Michael Jackson had other health issues that never were discussed like, he had what's called dancer's feet....Your skin starts to crack and split, almost like paper cuts, and Michael suffered bad with that. What would happen is sometimes it would be so bad that he had to wrap his feet like in a cast....The pain of that was excruciating. And yeah, was he on the painkillers for that? Yeah. I'm sure he was....Now, whatever the autopsy shows, whatever the true fact on how this man has gone from here becomes, it is all still a result of what this business has done to him, period. It's all a result of what the business did to him." (http://thesportsinterview.com/mjackson.html).

42. The Sin Fall of Measurement

Did you ever ponder about which are the most widespread emotions worldwide? Besides greed it is envy. And indeed envy also comes in the form of jealousy or well camouflaged as the feeling for justice or ambition or adulation. Michael Jackson was not familiar with these lower emotions; he preserved his childlike innocence, which was suspect to "spoiled" adults.

On 14th of August 2009 André Stern was a guest on TV-Station "WDR 3" with Bettina Böttinger, where he spoke about his life, his childhood and his book, "Und ich ging nie zur Schule – über eine glückliche Kindheit". André was raised in France and never taught at school, nor in the form of "homeschooling." He also reported that certain emotions and terms are simply strange to him. For example, he has no sense for the term of learning. Learning is equal to playing for him, and the word "working" has no meaning for him. André is not homeless and does not live from Hartz IV, which means alms, but he is a successful working musician, builder of guitars, and author.

Perhaps the time has come to completely put to the test our concepts, which we think to be the ultimate truth. Is it true that we have to go to school to become someone? Is it true that we have to pay high taxes for the functioning of our society? Is it true that everything has to grow constantly and that we have to consume ever more for the economy to function and so there will be enough for everyone? Is it true that man would not work if he were not forced to do so? It is true that all hell would break loose if we had fewer laws? Is it true that we can only guarantee peace when we have armed forces? Is it true that we must measure and grade performance? Is it true that the ones with the most degrees and certificates are the real experts? Is it true that the most important mark of a human being is his profession? Is it true that our quality of life depends on the fact if the DAX or Dow Jones rises or falls?

All these are persuasions and imaginations which were successfully implanted in our minds like brainwashing. We are immensely afraid of the so-called brainwashing sects and at the same time overlook that our own brain was in the washing plant since the beginning. "Starting with pure imagination the thinking in measures became unstoppably lost in the demonic realm of the number, which even coming itself from imagination attached itself to visible matter and practiced there continuously in a disastrous way. From it was derived the measurement of property and with it the whole capitalism, which makes man dependent on the number. Interest and usury are based on calculation....It functions as if the veda had changed to the Jewish Kabbalah, which is ambushing the world secretly with the spiderweb of the number, uncommemorated of the improbability that an eagle will care about a spiderweb, which he could shed off the wall with a soft touch of his wings."..."In reality intuitive thinking is never abstract. All ideas appear like the platonic ones plastically, similarly as artistic figures."...."True love is thinking in tones, as thoughts are standing too distantly,' sings Tieck so beautifully (Ludwig Tieck (1773-1853).."...

"The childish disgust of all adorers of 'mystic' matters thus suddenly denies the natural power, they consider everything as supernatural, which does not add up to plump mechanics, as if the radiation of planets could not proceed equally to x-rays....Since it seems to be a metaphysical law that human reason, as long as it perseveres in the consciousness of mind, without 'inner vision' of the subliminal, is always finding the phenomena of nature as it wants them to be and appears conducive to it." (http://gutenberg.spiegel.de/).

This analysis says basically that everything that the human mind invents is obsolete and meaningless as long it is not soaked by "inner vision." Undoubtedly Michael was a master of "inner vision." The modern theory U knows the concept of "presencing," which wants to stress that we have to consider the source of all perception in science and practice, which can be deduced by "presence" and "sensing."

Everything that people without "inner vision" have said about Michael Jackson is pure flight of fancy. It is idle to cite the whole mess here again. You yourself dispose of the instrument of the power of discrimination. Stop thinking about the meaning of being, but start to live, to think in tones, to enjoy nature, to sing and dance. That is true love. And when you are not able to sing and dance, before you have found the meaning of life, then "eat this." (Black or White)

The meaning of life for me is that I am writing today, 15th of August 2009 page 142 of the first German version of "From King of Pop to Mahatma" at 1:19 p.m. And the meaning of life at 1:22 p.m. is that I will take a break, prepare some coffee, sit in the garden and enjoy the sun (1:25 p.m.). Now at 1: 50 p.m. the meaning of life is that I again am sitting in front of the computer and continue writing and now (1:52 p.m.) am citing Mario Mantese: "The 'I' seeks the meaning of being, that is nonsense. Be aware that that what you *really* are can never be thought or understood. When there is a universal destination for man then it is surely not thinkable, not plannable or graspable." (Mantese, 2008, p. 161)

And now at 1:58 p.m. the meaning of life is that I hear that the washing machine stopped spinning and I will hang out the laundry in the garden. Yes, even being on holiday in Bavaria, bad girl. What might the neighbors think? Now at 2:05 p.m. the meaning of life is that I again am sitting in front of the computer and continue writing. Hanging up the laundry I could have done before writing the citation down, that's a thought in my mind. Oh my goodness, now again I have done something meaningless, is the next thought. Then I can only just laugh about the cosmic joke of thinking and continue to let my fingers run over the buttons. They just know best what shall be part of the book.

Yes that's it. Every second the meaning of life is changing, I'm still getting tousled. Now the meaning of life for you is that you are reading these lines and understand what I am talking about or that you think, it's as clear as mud. .... Do you realize which way the cat jumps? .... Or shall I continue to write about the meaning of life? The problem here is that the moment I start to write about it the meaning already has changed and thus I am always running like the hare and the hedgehog back and forth without arriving anywhere. Every time I think I have finally arrived first at the goal, someone is laughing in my face and says, "I am already here." Thus let's desist to think about the meaning of life and let's have fun.

43. Memorial

In the booklet of the memorial, the mourning and farewell ceremony for Michael Jackson, the last words of people who knew Michael in daily life, have met him as a human being and not as the King of Pop, are collected.

"To the world Michael is an icon. To me Michael is family. He will forever live in all of our hearts. I miss you Mike and I love you. Dunk." Dunk is the nickname of Michael's youngest sister Janet, with whom he had a very close relationship. Janet's farewell words we can find on a beautiful photo, which is from Michael's video to the song "Liberian Girl" (1987) and dedicated to Elizabeth Taylor. "Liberian Girl" belongs to the lesser known pieces and is a parade piece for Michael's humor and joy of life.

He has called together a whole guard of celebrities: Beverley Johnson, Whoopi Goldberg, John Travolta, David Copperfield, Brigitte Nielsen, Paula Abdul, Jackie Collins, Quincy Jones, Amy Irving, Lou Diamond Phillips, Steven Spielberg, Corey Feldman, Lou Ferrigno, Don King and "son," Rick Schroeder, Jasmine Guy, Sherman Hemsley, Olivia Newton-John, Malcolm-Jamal Warner, Carl Weathers, Billy Dee Williams, Debbie Gibson, Weird Al Yankovic, Rosanna

Arquette, Blair Underwood, Suzanne Somers, Mayim Bialik, Virginia Madsen, Richard and Emily Dreyfuss, Danny Glover, Olivia Hussey, Dan Aykroyd, Steve Guttenberg and Bubbles, Michael's ape. All these superstars came for one short film which only lasted a few minutes.

It is not the only music video where Michael employed superstars. In "In The Closet," supermodel Naomi Campbell is his partner; in "Remember the Time," Eddie Murphy and supermodel Iman. For the song, "We Are The World," more than forty "big names" of show business participated.

"Liberian Girl" starts with a scene in an oriental market, and Beverly Johnson sings: "Naku penda piya – naku penda piya – mpenziwe." Head slate. Dancers. The invited actors observe the scene and are waiting for their entry. Some are singing parts of the song, some are rehearsing the lyrics, some are conversing about other issues. John Travolta and Olivia Newton-John are rehearsing a dance scene. Whoopi Goldberg asks, "Who's directing this?" Steven Spielberg on the director's chair grasps the phone, seemingly on edge. To Rosanna Arquette's question of whether she knows what they have to do, Jasmine Guy answers with some pride in her voice: "All I know is that Michael called *me*. I guess when he gets here, he will let me know what we're supposed to do."

Two men are in private discussion, when one of them points to a curly head of hair with the question, "Hey, Mikey?" The one who turns around is Weird Al Yankovic, with the remark, "No, but I think Bubbles is here." Suzanne Somers is sitting at Bubbles' side and points to some people that don't seem to interest Bubbles. Don King is conversing with his "son." Billie Dee Williams says to his discussion partner, Lou Diamond Phillips, "I understand he wears disguises." They look together at a mummy-like figure, and then shake their heads no. Sherman Hemsley practising the moonwalk. Whoopi Goldberg tells her neighbor, "I think we should do a sequel to 'Jumpin Jack Flash'...(both laughing) "Call it what?" "Yes, call it 'Action Jumpin' Jack Jackson.'"

Richard Dreyfuss asks directly, "Exactly which Michael Jackson are we talking about, anyway?" and Weird Al Jankovic is playing accordion. The market operators clear away when two noisy motorbikes ride in. "Hey, where's Michael?" one of the bikers asks as he looks around. Someone points above, saying, "Hey, hey, hey," and all eyes follow.

Now the camera also turns, swings above and there the lost one is sitting in a glaring red shirt behind a camera and is all smiles. With unbelievable wonder the biker utters, "Oh Mike!" Michael says, giggling, "Okay, everybody, that's a wrap." The shoot for the video was finished, before anybody started with his part. Who else besides Michael Jackson would have ideas like that? He was indeed the master of "hide and Seek" and makes us all happy at that.

Michael's sister La Toya, with whom his relationship was not so close, writes in the memorial booklet as the last words for him: "You've lived your dream, you've proved to us all that if you believe, you will achieve....God has now called you for you to come home, collect your wings and to fulfill your demands in Heaven and continue your magic moments amongst the angels."

And from sister Rebbie stems the confession: "I love you so much and I'm looking forward to the time when I'll see you again on Earth (John 5:28-29). I know this is something you not only cherished but talked about with others. Then the world will be a paradise, a place free from corruption and poverty. Then the world will be place of true peace and serenity."

And these are the last words of Michael's elder brother Tito: "My brother has developed a shoe that showed resistance to gravity. What a man!...He gave and he never thought twice. I watched the light in Michael's eyes fade as he faced trials and tribulations for being misunderstood....We will carry the light and make the light shine again for Michael and the world." Tito is relating here to the film "Moonwalker." In this film of 90 minutes Michael invented a dance insert that was not yet copied. Thereby the whole body is bending forward until a point where everyone would normally be flat on his face, but Michael and his co-dancers unbend effortlessly. This passage in "Smooth Criminal" has always evoked storms of enthusiasm and when Michael performed the song on his concerts the stadium clamored. The legendary moonwalk as well as this move were often copied but never equaled.

In the memorial booklet Michael's attorney Thomas Mesereau, who assisted him in his darkest times in the year 2005, also has his say: "I met Michael Jackson during a very dark period. The forces of evil were trying to take him away from us. The man I came to know was a kind, gentle soul who wanted to heal the world through music, art, love and decency. He succeeded. It was an honor and a privilege to defend him. Rest in peace, Michael. Thomas A. Mesereau, Jr."

Michael himself cited Michelangelo in an interview and declared that while composing he always tried "to bind my soul to my work." (Ebony, 2007)

Everyone who gets involved with Michael Jackson's work can feel his presence immediately, his soul in the music and in the lyrics. And this presence will not be changed or influenced by earthly time. This presence is bound to his work and will delight us even in hundred years. Presence is presence.

In the booklet we also find a declaration of love from the Neverland family to their "boss": "Dearest Michael, how do we even begin to tell you what you meant to us? What beautiful journey we had with you. You touched so many lives and we are honored to have been one of them. How blessed are we to have been given the opportunity to see your dream of Neverland grow and flourish. What a lesson we learned in compassion, generosity and love from you.

Because of you, the sound of children's laughter, the whistle of a steam train or the whirl of a carousel will always bring a smile to our hearts. You will forever be felt in the gentle breezes rustling through the trees, in the trickling of the streams and in the stillness of the valley of Neverland. Thank you for allowing us to be a part of your dream. The enormity of what you gave and created leaves us speechless. May you sing with the angels above, our love forever, your Neverland family."

Further moving love declarations stem from Michael's other siblings, from his nephews and nieces, from friends and employees. What sort of man must be someone who gets a declaration of love from his employees?

But not only are Michael's family, his friends, acquaintances and staff mourning a loss, which many did not yet realize even months later. Why even two years after his death are my tears coming, when I read statements about Michael from those who loved him or hear certain songs like "Speechless," "Cry," "The Lost Children," or "Gone too soon," or when I watch his films?

Even at the song of Hip Hopper Derek "Sway" Safo, "The King Full Stop," which he composed as tribute to Michael, tears are coming. The original can be found on YouTube. Sway's phrases and wordplays are brilliant and express his deep concern:

"Jackson, Jackson, the legend Michael Jackson. Forever remember where you were when it happened. Everybody staring their phones, reading their flashes - In hope it was just a rumor and sooner we'll get the facts in. I'll always remember the spot where I was standing - Exact same spot where I felt like collapsing. Our relationship with music he has always been the captain - Even after confirmation is sunk, it never sank in.

The same year I was born Michael brought you ‚Thriller'. - Funny the first ever album that I was brought was Thriller. - Out of this world his moonwalk done brought us all together. - An important figure can't figure a human force that's bigger. - It wasn't right how the media handled Mike - Disgusting how they're always discussing if he was black or white.

His mum was black, his dad was black so it ain't rocket science to say he's black alright. But that didn't matter to him, cause he was not racist. - Self proclaimed „Bad" thus he caught cases - There ain't a smooth criminal without court cases. - Said he was touching, I said he was touching all nations,- Even before ‚Dangerous' he's like a thousand times bigger than the rest. - Rewind his tape like a thousand times Elvis was a great and Lennon was a legend and Michael J. was like both over a thousand time. - They said that his sales declined but after about 750 million what's left to yell about?There ain't a music act that doesn't owe Jacko Jack. - So he's always gonna sell as long as they're about.

Watching his life was an honour and I dont"mean no kinda disrespect to Madonna. But Michael was on a different level, and he adopted all of us in his songs, While he was trying to heal the world like a doctor. - I hope the money goes to the kids, as I hold these two O2 tickets. - For his 50 date tour less then 50 days away so from his death at 50 wish he had 50 days more but never got half, pasted in the 25th of June and we should remember this day as his. I believe he never left and he would never leave, never been a legend that lived that can ever breathe, never been a martyr that fought that can forever bleed, never been a leader, that can forever lead. God will give him to us same God will take him from us. Now he's in his rightful place cause he was so heavenly. All for one and one for all he made a song for all, so I put a copy of his „Off the wall" on the wall. - My town misses him, your town misses him, everybody since Motown misses him. Now when I think of him picture him standing on a stage with his hand up one glove glistening, whole world at a standstill listening anticipating his next move the King is him. From age 5 and the days of J5 he's never took a break, not rest to take 5, there'll never be a next the rest just ain't Mike. - Time to pay our respects and watch the angel stake flight: Under all the pressure he never ever ran, he's the best forever damn, who dressed forever glam. The biggest man on the planet, not just a brother to Janet, our thoughts go out to his family, - He gave his hearts to the fans and he paved the way for the future, still his flame is in you, 'cos he inspired song writers, record labels, producers. - They saying Michael Jackson is the King of Pop.

But I'm saying he was the King Full Stop.
People saying Michael Jackson is the King of Pop.
But I'm saying he was the King Full Stop."

Hiphoppers normally are not so interested in pop stars; on the contrary they are very critical to the commerce. Michael Jackson indeed is honored and respected by all music genres. He does not fit in any drawer and spoke from the soul of young and old, black and white, rich and poor, man and woman.

Michael himself was the embodiment of respect at each encounter with people, privately or in business. He welcomed others most the time with the Namaste gesture, a bow before the divinity in everyone. On the other hand, he was denied the appropriate respect by others. "I don't think people really showed him the love and respect that they should have been showing him at the record company....It was like a kind of lose-lose situation (2002 after the publishing of "Invincible"). And they did that like to dangle a carrot to say okay, we want you to do the full thing. We want you to sell records. We want you to tour. They thought that he was gonna go running after the carrot saying, 'Man, I gotta do all of this so that I can recoup.'" That's the estimation of Cory Rooney. And Chris Apostle adds: "He is probably, arguably the greatest musician we'll ever see in our lifetime. You'll never see anything like this again." (http://thesportsinterview.com)

From Rena Lévano Casas I got the following poem dedicated to Michael: "You were – You were flowing into my heart as you were gone....and it widened – The Earth and all Worlds have now taken a seat therein. And it beats in a rhythm for the angels to dance."

It's amazing how many people are reminded of angels when they try to describe Michael. His influence on the music industry and people worldwide is each time fascinating again. His contribution to expand and dissolve the limits of music is immeasurable. Michael has replaced separation and division by coming together. When you look closely at it, this is a threatening development for all egomaniacs, because the ego is living by separation and defines itself by dissociation. It is absolutely dependent on separation and division; otherwise it would no longer be an ego.

44. Eternal Moonwalk

Today the 16th of August 2009 I discover a genius idea to pay tribute to Michael Jackson, which he deserves. The site www.EternalMoonwalk.com is an endless sequence of scenes with people from all over the world, who are dancing the moonwalk. Even backwards with skis in the snow or with rollerblades, mothers who carry their baby in their arms, people on a trampoline etc. And not only people participate in the eternal moonwalk, but also plushies, comic figures and cars – and even a roach pays tribute to the King of Pop.

Yet the Germans have some difficulty compared to some other nations to change their lifestyle to a moonwalk. While the South Americans are hardly to beat – in first place the Brazilians. I watched more than 10,000 meters of this Moonwalk, more than six hours. When you keep on the computer while you are on holidays the moonwalk will surely have surrounded the whole world when you are back. It's amazing how much creativity is released in people. Does it stem from the reservoir which Michael incorporated and concentrated in himself and that is now available to us? Maybe. The server for the Eternal Moonwalk seems to be working to capacity. But if we renounce the server and dance the moonwalk ourselves, then it will surely turn into a never-ending moonwalk around the whole globe. Let some witnesses of the time period who knew Michael personally be talking who did not hustle into the media – as many pseudo-knowers - to comment meaningless things about Michael.

Soul Diva Siedah Garrett, who wrote the lyrics to "Man in the Mirror," and who often sang in the background choir, tells us on 3rd of July 2009 during a performance of this song together with the Agape International Choir, that she had been invited by many channels - CNN, Entertainment Tonight, MSNBC, Hollywood Tonight and other news media – to talk about Michael. "Everyone wants to hear whatever dirt I have to offer to feed in this media madness. I have nothing to offer. (applause) The only place where I felt comfortable to speak about Michael was yesterday in rehearsal with the Agape Choir. And I realized I really hadn't had chance to grieve and as I was explaining to them I was so pleased to have a place to speak about him and no one wanting me to spit on this man. I don't know nothing about his personal life, I know his music touched me and that's all I know." (YouTube)

Elizabeth Taylor did not attend the memorial at the Staples Center. Instead she said farewell to Michael on Twitter and tweeted on 26th of June 2009, "We had so much in common and we had such loving fun together. I was packing up my clothes to go to London for his opening when I heard the news. I still can't believe it. I don't want to believe it. It can't be so. He will live in my heart forever. But it's not enough. My life feels so empty. I don't think anyone knew how much we loved each other. The purest most giving love I've ever known.

Oh God! I'm going to miss him. I can't imagine life without him. But I guess with God's help I will learn. I keep looking at the photo he gave me of himself which says, 'To my true love Elizabeth, I love you forever.' And I will love HIM forever." And on 5th of July 2009 she adds, "I want you my friends to know that I will go to the hospital on Wednesday or Thursday to finish a test which I have started before. Even when my grief about Michael could not be deeper I will not be observed due to danger of suicide, as some cheaper rags want you to believe. I am one who survives, not only for my sake, but for my family and also for Michael. I will always love Michael from the bottom of my being and nothing can separate us." And on 6th of July 2009 she adds, "I was asked to speak in the Staples Center. I won't be a part of this public 'hoopla.' And I cannot guarantee that I would be coherent to say a word. I just don't believe that Michael wants me to share my grief with millions of others. How I feel is between us, not a public event....I love him too much." And twelve days later Elizabeth communicates once more through Twitter, on 18th of July 2009: "I am back from the hospital and intact. Naturally I'm still grieving about Michael. I will always do this. But as I said before,...I am someone who survives. There were many tragedies in my life, but I believe that they all taught me something. I have to look at it like this. I have to be stronger and to appreciate more what I have. I give love and I am surrounded by love, and I thank God for this."

Actor and bodybuilder Lou Ferrigno, who was also part of the video to "Liberian Girl," and earlier had played the role of the "Incredible Hulk," and last was Michael's personal trainer reports on 30th of June 2009: "When I heard of his death I thought it's a joke, especially at the age of fifty. I have met him one month ago, I had to train him. I worked with him on stretching on the floor, different moves. He was energetic, he was happy, animated. Fifteen years ago he told me he would only eat once a day. I think he said he is vegetarian. We met fifteen years ago, he was a big fan of mine. He loved the "Hulk" and everything....

When Michael met me the first time he had a mask on, came across the street and gave me a hug. It had nothing to do with the stage, it was simply Lou and Michael. We had a similar childhood, both much pain and bother. And we talked about it, his escape was the music, my escape was the bodybuilding and fitness. He had a passion for fitness, so we worked together, we were nearly like children. We never had a childhood....He didn't want to be like his father, neither me. He loved all people....He may seem eccentric from the outside, because he is a prisoner...He could not come to see me, I had to see him. There are all these people on the street, paparazzi, buses are passing, that's the house of Michael Jackson....We are talking about a complete prisoner." (You Tube)

Slash from Guns N' Roses lets us know after Michael's death how he and Michael came together: "I remember how I got a call from my manager, who told me, 'Michael Jackson is trying to reach you.' I was rather starstruck, really. In a certain way it was a feeling like: I have arrived. He called me in the hotel and I heard this voice and he said: I want you to play on my record....We had a relationship based on professionality, I was free to make my thing and he accepted it." (You Tube)

Michael not only named and shamed the ignorance of prejudice, but he himself was without judgment dealing with others. He lived the embodiment of love, which never interferes. In an exemplary way he succeeded to set an example of a sort of love that was not tied to conditions, a love which does not demand anything and not expect anything from others. This form of love is the highest form, which has to be searched for like a needle in a haystack among men. What we usually think of as love is only a limited form, which is similar to dependence and tied to conditions. True love can never turn into hate, when things run differently than our expectations or imaginations. The love of most parents for their children is tied to conditions and will be denied to them when the children are not behaving the way the parents want them to be.

Director Spike Lee shot together with Michael the video to "They Don't Care About Us" in the slums of Rio de Janeiro in Brazil. He remembered on 29th of June 2009: "Michael was great. He had a sense of humor. He worked hard. Michael said when you love what you are doing, it is not work. Then you can do it longer and harder and quicker, because it is no burden. You love what you are doing....Michael was a world citizen. I told him: 'Michael let's go to Brazil and do it.' And he said: 'Let's start on the way Spike.' And it is great when you work with people who say something like that. It is not a matter of budget. He wanted to do it. We started on the way."

It was a way full of magic, enchantment, wonder, and endless joy. "The heart of the awakening man is astonishment, admiration and deep wonder. Wonder is something unique. It seems as if the eyeless reality is looking, even if there is nothing to see in wondering, because the one who wonders is absent in the moments of wonder." (Mantese, 2009, p. 38) Michael is talking about this eyeless reality when he says, "Inside your heart sits a Seer." (Magical Child part 1, Dancing the Dream).

In the presence of the seer a stone will soften, glimmering glow will spark into a blazing fire, and death will come to life again. Michael represents a new world in an old crusty one, a new world which many only dream of, but don't have the courage to enter the gate. Michael represents a world which is lost to humanity, a sort of lost paradise. Michael was not able to see one living being suffering, but felt endless compassion with the weak ones. That reminds one of the story of the Buddha. The historic Buddha Shakyamuni (Siddharta Gautama) was born 563 (or 450) years before Christ. He came from an aristocratic family and grew up in a palace, where he was shielded from everything worldly. Yet one day he met the suffering, left his former life and his family behind and started as an ascetic the search for an escape of suffering. After having followed many religions and teachings, he looked for his own way and practiced silence. In his 35th year under a fig tree, which today is known as Bhodi tree, an all encompassing awakening happened. Since then the Buddha – the Awakened One – is the symbol for perfect wisdom and compassion. I think it is not exaggerated to assign exactly these Buddha qualities to Michael Jackson.

Humanity is as a whole not able to recognize such blessed beings. They are ahead of their time that everyone is only running afterward, because they feel that there is something attracting them. But as they cannot reach it the mind reacts with confusion and with harshness. He does not appreciate when he loses control, when the will of the ego reaches its limits. Recognition will only happen when the observer himself discovers and develops the qualities in himself which he admires and searches for in the other one. The less someone is tied to worldly ties, the more creativity and genius can express themselves in his work. Countless are the examples where Michael Jackson has perfected his handiwork and art. Unforgettable is the legendary moonwalk, which he performed to "Billie Jean" for the first time during the 25th stage anniversary of Motown, his first record label, on 25th March 1983. This performance was at the time the talk of the day in the nation. And who does not remember the enthusiastic performance at halftime of Super Bowl XXVII on 31st of January 1993, which had the highest Nielsen rating in the history of the United States. At the press conference Michael announced the foundation of "Heal the World," which would help the underprivileged children in the cities of America and was supported by former president Jimmy Carter.

"We have to get out the message of the need to heal the children and to heal the world,...to recognize that we need each other and must care for one another. Help and inspire us to develop this relief effort for children. To make a real difference, we must all care and commit to be a part of the solution....We must join together to make this world a better place for each of them."

On 10th of February 1993 Michael gave an interview of 90 minutes on the Oprah Winfrey Show with 100 million viewers, also a record. On 30th of January 2010 Michael received an Award posthum for his Life Work, which was received by his children in Staples Center in LA. On this occasion, all three wore red armbands – just as their father, who wanted to wear them as long there is still one child on earth suffering. Prince followed in his father's footsteps and promised: "Through all his songs the message was simple: love. We will continue to spread his message and help spread the word."

What jewels Michael has given to the world!

45. Philanthropist

Michael Jackson was a blessed artist, musician and dancer, but above all he was a great soul. This soul made people happy in silence besides his professional tirelessness. His outstanding quality was his philanthropy.

The term philanthropist comes from the Greek and means friend of men. A philanthropist believes in the goodness of people and is able to find it in everyone. His eyes look with love on everything and that is expressed in his service to people, nature and animals – each in his own way. Mother Teresa did it her way and Michael did it his way. Mostly Michael Jackson acted in silence and was not interested in making noise in the world. Thus in the public there is little known about his long-time respective activities. In the "Guinness Book of World Records 2000 Millenium Edition," Michael Jackson is not listed as the King of Pop, but as the "King of Charity," as the one with the most charities which were supported by a pop star. At least 39 organizations are known which Michael partly supported regularly. Besides addressing all social issues in his music, his films and in interviews, it was his concern to be active himself. Thus he led the attention of the public to issues such as the problems of AIDS, hunger, homelessness, street violence, racism, totalitarianism, destruction of the environment, child abuse, denial of animal rights, limitation of freedom of speech and much more long before the media discovered these themes.

Matt Semino asks in an article of July 2009: „Many may ask why this controversial figure, a man who has been the subject of intense criticism and public backlash, should be given such gravity in framing public discourse over the day's most important topics. Sometimes it takes a person, not just a political or spiritual leader, who stands out symbolically from the rest of society, to make that society reflects on the principles that it follows and the values it embraces. Jackson, throughout his life and in his death, has been ridiculed and revered, vilified and vaunted. In many respects, his story represents the highest possible highs and the lowest possible lows that life can present a human being. ... However, it is his broad cultural impact that truly transcends economic, social, political, racial, religious and generational barriers. Jackson rose from being simply a magical performer into becoming a humanitarian of historic import. He was a modern day messenger, a visionary storyteller who raised the level of consciousness for citizens across national boundaries. ... As history progresses and Jackson's symbol and work are analyzed in conjunction with the unfolding of human events, the important cultural relevance of his persona will be uncovered. Like a piece of Greek literature that embodies timeless themes of human strife and suffering, Michael Jackson's canon and celebrity will come to hold a similar place in the modern day cultural pantheon." (http://elitestv.com)

Michael Jackson would often donate the profits of concerts to local organizations or hospitals or to provide personal things for auctions, whereby the proceeds were given to UNESCO or other foundations. On 3rd of February 1992, some time before the start of the Dangerous Tour, Michael announced the initiation of the "Heal the World Foundation" (HTW), which aimed together with the "Ronald McDonald Camp" and the "Make A Wish Foundation" to fight AIDS and diabetes in young people. This day he declared: "The only reason I'm going on tour is to raise funds for the newly formed Heal the World Foundation, an international children's charity that I'm spearheading to assist children and ecology." At a press conference in London on 23rd of June 1992 Michael concretized the goals of the foundation:

"Our children are the most beautiful, most sweet, most treasured of our creations. And yet, every minute at least 28 children die. Today our children are at risk to be killed by diseases and by the violence of war, guns, abuse and neglect. Children have few rights and no one to speak for them. They have no voice in our world. God and nature have blessed me with a voice. Now I want to use it to help children speak for themselves. I have founded the 'Heal the World Foundation' to be the voice for the voiceless: the children. Please join with me and the children to help heal the world together....Finally and most importantly, I want to tell the children of the world, you are all our children, each one of you is my child and I love you all. Thank you very much."

At a press conference on the 24st of November 1992 Michael clarifies his views:

"Children show me in their playful smiles the divine in everyone. This simple goodness shines straight from their hearts. Being with them connects us to the deeper wisdom of life, especially young lives untouched by hatred, prejudice and greed. Now, when the world is so confused and its problems so complicated, we need our children more than ever. Their natural wisdom points the way to solutions that lie waiting to be recognized within our own hearts. Children are the world's foremost idealists and optimists....The world desperately needs their innocent perspective on the world's problems. We have to heal our wounded planet of the chaos, despair and senseless destruction we see today. The mission of HTW, my mission is healing. Pure and simple. To heal the world we must start by healing our children.... This Thanksgiving is particularly special to me with the launch of the single, "Heal the World." I wrote this song for everyone in our world, in an effort to help bring global harmony. All the proceeds of this song will go to the 'Heal the World Foundation.' Thank you ...."

In 1992, when Michael received "Best Male Solo Singer Award" at the U.K.'s Smash Hits Poll Winners Party, he thanks everyone and transmits the following message to his admirers:

"Now I'm asking you to do something again. The Heal the World Foundation is my most important mission. It is my heart and my soul. I have made substantial gifts to the foundation, and all the benefits from the song will also go to the foundation. If you can make a donation, please, do so."

On the 10th of December of the same year in the American consulate office, when he was honored by Pepsi for his engagement in the "Heal the World" foundation, he said:

"The innocence of children represents to me the source of infinite creativity, and I feel that this is where all my creativity comes from. This is not an intellectual kind of intelligence, but an intelligence that is full of wonder, magic, mystery and adventure. In this intelligence, there is love, there is trust, there is joy and there is beauty. It is the kind of intelligence that will heal the world. That is why I am here and that is why we are here. Thank you very much. I love you."

At the 20th American Music Awards on 25th of January 1993, Elizabeth Taylor presented Michael with the "Special International Artist Award" for record sells and humanitarian efforts. As Michael was the first recipient of a prize of this kind, Eddie Murphy announced that this prize would be named the "Michael Jackson International Artist Award" in the future. Michael gave thanks with the following words:

"Thank you all my friends. Traveling the world has been a great education for me. And if there is one insight that I've had, it is this: Wherever you go, in every country, on every continent, people yearn and hunger for one thing – to love and to be loved. Love transcends, love transcends international boundaries and upheaves the wounds of hatred, racial prejudice, bigotry and ignorance. It is the ultimate truth at the heart of all creation."

On 14th of February 2001 Michael Jackson presented, at Carnegie Hall in New York, his initiative, "Heal the Kids." He emphasized:

"...between parents and children, not just once a year over turkey and stuffin, but every day for peace and prosperity. Sadly that sound has become a lost melody, a forgotten refrain, an empty tune. And all we have in its place today is a dark and terrible noise. Instead of dinner conversations, there is the noise of video games. Instead of homework, there is the din of the evening news. And instead of regular conversations between parents and children about drugs or violence, there is the deafening sound of silence." (YouTube: Michael Jackson speaks at Carnegie Hall, New York 2001)

Michael cared in his doing about the ones without a lobby, and gave unimaginable sums in his generosity. The real amount which he spent is not known, but surely it must have been many hundreds of millions of dollars. It is known that he donated his complete share from the Victory Tour, Dangerous Tour and HIStory Tour to charities. Chris Apostle remembers: "This man gave people millions and millions of dollars to philanthropic stuff." And Cory Rooney adds: "In every city he would stop at a hospital and visit kids that were burned, ill or whatever. He took the time to do all of that." (http://thesportsinterview.com)

But most important for Michael was not the money which he gave so generously, but the joy he could bring others who were not so blessed by life as he was. He gave the disadvantaged the feeling that there is someone who cares as well as the faith in a higher force and a meaning through his presence. Michael fulfilled the last wish for deathly ill children, before they had to leave the world. And sometimes they recovered in a mysterious way. "Michael...had tried to help the Arvizo family...by doing everything possible to help heal Gavin of a mysterious form of cancer.... It was Michael Jackson who opened up his home and his heart to this family at a critical time in their lives. To this family...the superstar had become a savior." (Jones, p. 24)

Exemplarily and symbolically, Michael's care for his young friend Ryan White became known, to whom he dedicated a poem in "Dancing the Dream" and wrote the "Gone Too Soon," which gets under the skin. The global effects of Michael Jackson's compositions are always again shown impressively, as we could experience during the memorial for the 13-year-old great-granddaughter of Nelson Mandela. She was killed in an accident on the way back from the opening concert for the football world championship in 2010 in South Africa. The song "Gone Too Soon" went to the bottoms of the hearts of all people present. Michael was a personal friend of Nelson Mandela. In their encounters a connection on a deeper level was clearly apparent. In July 1996 Michael visited

South Africa and was a guest at Nelson Mandela's birthday party. In a speech he said,

"We are behaving like people without compassion and love for the most vulnerable section of society. The children of the universe are without a spokesperson, they are voiceless....We are all touched by the atrocities committed against children: sexual, physical abuse, child slave labor, educational neglect. We feel ashamed. Angry. Appalled. But there is no action, no action."

Besides the countless prizes as an artist, Michael as of the year 1999 had also received seventeen charity awards. Yet after the false allegations were discussed in the public, it turned more and more difficult for him to continue his caring activities. To many moths were spraying their poison. He suffered unspeakably under the gleefulness and agitation against him. The visits of hordes of children to Neverland turned more rare and random laughter of children no more filled the park and area so often.

The following charity organizations were supported by Michael Jackson: Initiation of the Heal the World Foundation - Neverland Ranch opened its gates every three weeks for underprivileged and terminally ill children, whose health costs were paid by Michael - AIDS Project L.A. - American Cancer Society - Angel Food - Atlanta Project Immunization Drive - Big Brothers of Greater Los Angeles - BMI Foundation, Inc. - Boys and Girls Club of Newark - Brotherhood Crusade - Brotman Burn Center - Good Times Camp Ronald McDonald - Child Help U.S.A. - Michael Jackson International Institute for Research on Child Abuse - Children's Defense Fund - Children's Diabetes Foundation - Children's Institute National - Great Ormond Street Children's Hospital London - Cities and Schools Scholarship Fund - Community Youth Sports & Arts Foundation - Congressional Black Caucus (CBC) - Dakar Foundation; Dream Street Kids - Dreams Come True Charity - Elizabeth Taylor AIDS Foundation - Family Caring for Families - Give For Life - Juvenile Diabetes Foundation - Love Match - Make-A-Wish Foundation - Minority AIDS Project - Motown Museum - NAACP; National Rainbow Coalition - National Solidarity Fund - Nelson Mandela Children's Fund - Opportunity Village - Rotary Club of Australia - Society of Singers - Starlight Foundation - The Carter Center's Atlanta Project - The Sickle Cell Research Foundation - T. J. Martell Foundation - Trust of Prince Charles – TransAfrica - United Negro College Fund (UNCF) - United Negro College Fund Ladders of Hope - Volunteers of America - Watts Summer Festival - Wishes Granted - YMCA 28th Street/Crenshaw - Youth Sports and Art Foundation L.A.

And here are some of Michael Jackson's personal engagements:
Jan. 1979: Michael donates books to the urban library, including Peter Pan, and promotes "Boogie to the Book Beat" a program to inspire youth to read - July

1981: Charity concert in Atlanta during the "Triumph Tour," which brings about 100,000 $ for the "Atlanta Children's Foundation." - 10 Jan. 1984: Visit to burn victims at Brotman-Memorial Hospital in Los Angeles - 9 April 1984: Michael Jackson visits 14-year-old David Smithee, who is suffering from cystic fibrosis, and invites him to Encino, where they spend a day together. To meet Michael was his last wish. He died seven weeks later - 14 April 1984: Michael equips a unit with 19 beds at the Mount Sinai New York Medical Center. It is part of the T. J. Martell Foundation for leukemia and cancer research - 14 May 1984: Michael is honored at a ceremony at the White House in Washington by president Ronald Reagan with a "Special Achievement Award" for his merits in a national campaign about the danger of consuming alcohol while driving - 5 July 1984: At a press conference in New York City, Michael professes his contempt for the high ticket prices for the Victory tour and declares that he will donate his part to three charities – The United Negro College Fund, Camp Good Times and the T. J. Martell Foundation - 14 July 1984: At a concert of the Victory Tour in Jacksonville, Florida, Michael meets eight children with incurable illness backstage, including 14-year-old Malanda Cooper, who had asked in a letter to the mayor to meet Michael. 700 underprivileged children are given the opportunity to see the show - July 1984: 1200 underprivileged children get free tickets for "The Jacksons" in Texas Stadium in Dallas - August 1984: After the failure of negotiations for a performance in Gary Indiana, "The Jacksons" care for the transport of 40 children of the Thelma Marshall Children's Home for orphans and kicked-out children of the Hoosier Boys Home and the Donzels Work-Study Program to Detroit, Michigan, to assist their third performance - 13 Dec. 1984: Michael visits the Brotman Burn Center. There he was hospitalized and treated after he was burned during a Pepsi shoot. He donates the honorarium of 1,500,000 $ to the center - 28 Jan. 1985: Michael and 44 other artists produce "We Are The World," written by Michael Jackson and Lionel Ritchie, for "USA for Africa." The proceeds of the sales are donated to hungry people in Africa -1986: Michael founds with 1,500,000 $ the MJ UNCF endowed Scholarship Fund - 8 March 1986: 14-year-old Donna Ashlook visits Michael in Encino after a heart transplant. Michael had invited her on 28 Feb. by phone, after he had learned that she was a big fan - 13 Sep. 1987: Michael supports the campaign of NAACP against racism and prejudice against black artists - Oct. 1987: After the BAD tour Michael donates personal objects to UNESCO. The proceeds are determined for the education of children in developmental countries - 1 Feb. 1988: "Man in the Mirror" is on the charts. The proceeds from its sales go to "Camp Ronald McDonald for Good Times" - 1 March 1988: Michael delivers a cheque about 600,000 $ for the United Negro College Fund (UNCF) - April 1988: Michael delivers tickets for 3 concerts in Atlanta, Georgia, to the Make-A-Wish Foundation - 22 May 1988: Michael visits children with cancer in the Bambino Gesu Children's Hospital in Rome. He promises an amount of 100,000 $ to the hospital - 16 July 1988: Michael meets

Princess Diana and Prince Charles in London. He delivers a cheque about 150,000 British pounds for the trust of the Prince and a cheque about 100,000 pounds for the Great Ormond Street children's hospital - 20 July 1988: Michael visits the children's hospital in Great Ormond Street and reads stories in a ward - 29 Aug. 1988: Michael gives a concert at his 30th birthday in Leeds for the English organization, "Give for Life" and delivers a cheque about 65,000 pounds - 23 Oct. 1988: Michael announces a donation for the Motown Museum in Detroit - Dec. 1988: Michael visits 12-year-old David Rothenberg, who suffered severe burns five years ago during a revenge act of his father against his former wife - Jan. 1989: The "Say Yes to a Youngster's Future" program honors Michael to appreciate his merits to inspire children for natural sciences with the "National Urban Coalition Artist/Humanitarian of the Year Award." - Jan. 1989: The proceeds of a concert in Los Angeles are given to "Child Help U.S.A." in appreciation of his support. Child Help founds the "Michael Jackson International Institute for Research on Child Abuse" - 10 Jan. 1989: For the BAD tour underprivileged children receive free tickets; Michael donates money to hospitals, orphanages and charity organizations - 7 Feb. 1989: Michael visits the Cleveland Elementary School in Stockton, California. There five children had been shot dead during gunfire by a 25-year-old man, and 39 children were hurt - 5 March 1989: Michael visits 200 disabled children in the "St. Vincent Institute for Handicapped Children" and invites them to Circus Vargas in Santa Barbara and his Neverland Ranch to visit his private zoo - March 1989: Michael receives, at the Universal Amphitheatre in Universal City in California, the Black Radio Special Award for humanitarian merits - 22 Sep. 1989: The Capital Children's Museum gives Michael the Best of Washington 1989 Humanitarian Award in appreciation of his merits to collect money for the museum and his relentless support of children - 13 Nov. 1989: 4-year-old Darian Pagan, who is suffering from leukemia, is invited by Michael to a staging of the Canadian Acrobats - 28 Dec. 1989: 17-year-old Ryan White, who is suffering from hemophilia and AIDS, spends his holidays on Neverland Ranch. He was infected with AIDS in 1984 during a blood transfusion and expelled from his school in Kokomo - 6 Jan. 1990: Michael invites 82 abused and neglected children of Child Help to Neverland - July 1990: 45 terminal ill children from the project Dream Street in Los Angeles visit Neverland - 18 Aug. 1990: 130 children of the "YMCA Summer Program" visit Neverland - 14Sep. 1990: The Council of the American Scouts honors Michael with the first "Good Scout Humanitarian Award" - 6 May 1991: Michael supports biologist Jane Goodall, who had been doing research on the life of chimpanzees in Gombe, Nigeria, for more than 30 years - 26 July 1991: Michael visits the "Youth Sports & Arts Foundation" in Los Angeles, which supports children of gang members and drug abusers. He gives a television and supports them financially – Dec. 1991: Michael's office of his company, MJJ Productions, finances a turkey dinner for more than 200 needy families – Feb. 1992: During 11Michael travels more than

30,000 miles in Africa to visit hospitals, orphanages, schools, churches and institutions for mentally retarded children - 3 Feb. 1992: At a press conference in New York Radio City Music Hall, Michael announces a further world tour to raise funds for his Heal The World Foundation - 6 May 1992: Michael pays the costs for the funeral of Ramon Sanchez, who was killed in riots in Los Angeles – 3 June 1992: The organization "One to One," which cares for the improvement of the living conditions of young people, honors Michael with an award for his efforts about disadvantaged youth - 26 June 1992: Michael hands over to the former Munich mayor Georg Kronawitter a cheque for about 40,000 DM for needy people - 29 June 1992: Michael visits the Sophia Children's Hospital in Rotterdam and hands over a cheque for about 100,000 $ - July 1992: Michael donates to "La Partida de Cuore" 821,477,296 Lire in Rome and 120,000 DM for children in Estonia and Lithuania - 25 July 1992: At a concert in Dublin Michael announces a donation of 400,000 pounds to various charities – 29 July 1992: Michael visits the Queen Elizabeth Children's Hospital in Hackney and brings with him Mickey Mouse and Minnie Mouse from Euro Disneyland - 31 July 1992: Michael hands over to Prince Charles a cheque about 200,000 British pounds for the trust of the Prince - 16 Aug. 1992: Michael meets backstage in Leeds 6-year-old Nicholas Killen, who lost his eyesight in a life-saving cancer surgery - Sep. 1992: Michael donates 1,000,000 Pesetas to organizations over which the queen of Spain presides - 30 Sep. 1992: In Romania, president Ion Iliescu inaugurates a playground for 500 orphans which was financed by Michael – 24 Nov. 1992: Michael is present at the Kennedy Airport in New York during the embarkation of 43 tonnes of medications, blankets and winter clothes under the supervision of the UN. In cooperation with the Heal the World Foundation and AmeriCares, goods worth 2,100,000 $ are brought to Sarajevo - 26 Jan. 1993: The project, "Heal L.A." of the Heal the World Foundation is announced at a press conference in Los Angeles. Michael receives 200,000 $ for it from the National Football League and 500,000 $ from the BEST Foundation - Feb. 1993: Together with the company Sega, an initiative is started whereby computer games and equipment for children's hospitals, children's homes and charity organizations in Great Britain worth 108,000 $ are distributed - 27 March 1993: Michael makes a speech in front of 1200 teachers and politicians in Los Angeles - 26 April 1993: Michael visits the Watts Health Foundation and two schools in South Central Los Angeles - 5 1993: The former American President Jimmy Carter and Michael promote their common "Atlanta Project Immunization Drive" - June 1993: 100 children from the "Challengers Boys and Girls Club" visit Neverland - June 1993: Michael promises a donation of 1,250,000 $ for children who have suffered from the riots in Los Angeles - 10 June 1993: Michael promotes the new "DARE Program," which sheds light on the dangers of drug abuse - 18 June 1993: Michael visits a hospital in Washington and plays chess with the children - July 1993: Michael receives from the American Friends of Hebrew University the

Scopus Award - Aug. 1993: Together with Pepsi Cola in Thailand Michael donates to the "Rural School Children and Youth Development Fund" of the crown princess Maha Chakri Sirindhorn 40,000 $ - Aug. 1993: In cooperation with "Pepsi Cola Int.," Michael donates new ambulances for a center for children in Moscow, and a hospital in Buenos Aires - Oct. 1993: Michael donates to the Children's Defense Fund, the Children's Diabetes Foundation, the Atlanta Project and the Boys and Girls Club in Newark 100,000 $ - 22 Oct. 1993: Michael visits a hospital in Santiago de Chile - 28 Oct. 1993: Michael makes it possible for 5000 underprivileged children to visit the Reino Aventura Park, where the whale from "Free Willy" lives - 5 Nov. 1993: Michael is guest at a children's party in the Hard Rock Café in Mexico City - Dec. 1993: Together with the Gorbachev Foundation, Michael organizes the transport of 60,000 doses of vaccination serum for children to Tblisi in Georgia - 16 Dec. 1993: The Heal The World Foundation supports "Operation Christmas Child," which delivers toys, sweets, gifts and food to children in former Yugoslavia - 1994: Michael donates 500,000 $ to the Elizabeth Taylor AIDS Foundation - 7 Jan. 1994: Michael gives a party at Martin Luther King, Jr.'s birthday for 1000 underprivileged children at Neverland - 22 Feb. 1994: The show, "The Jackson Family honors," is aired. The proceeds are given to "Families Caring for Families" - 12 Apr. 1994: During the 2nd Children's Choice Award ceremony in New York Michael receives the Caring for Kids Award - 6 Aug. 1994: Michael, together with his then wife Lisa Marie, visits two hospitals in Budapest, where they distribute toys - Mar. 1995: 4-year-old Bela Farkas gets a new liver. Michael and Lisa Marie had met him 1994 in Hungary and had searched everywhere to find a liver. They paid the entire health costs - 2 Nov. 1995: Michael receives the award, "Diamond of Africa" - 30 Mar. 1996: Michael receives "1995 Doris Day Award" for the short film "Earth Song," as this calls the attention to the plight of animals and the earth - 21 June 1996: Michael donates a four-fold platinum record of "HIStory" to support the Dunblane Appeal at the Royal Oak Hotel in Sevenoaks, England, and to support the families of 16 children who were shot dead at the Dunblane massacre – 18 July 1996: Michael deposes floral wreath in Soweto in South Africa for the young people who lost their lives during the apartheid fights - Sep. 1996: Michael Jackson was a special guest at the first Sport Festival "Hope" for orphans and disadvantaged children, where 3000 children and 600 volunteers participated - 6 Sep. 1996: Michael visits the children's ward of a hospital in Prague - Oct. 1996: Michael visits a hospital for mentally retarded children in Kaohsiung in Taiwan and donates 2000 free tickets for his sold-out concert - 1 Oct. 1996: Michael donates the profits of his Tunisia concert to the National Solidarity Fund for the fight against poverty - 3 Oct. 1996: Michael visits a hospital for mentally retarded children in Amsterdam and brings small presents. A room in this hospital, where the parents can stay together with the children, is named after Michael - 1 Nov. 1996: Michael donates a greater part of the profits of his HIStory concert in Bombay, India, for the poor - 7 Nov. 1996: At his first concert in Auckland, Australia, Michael fulfills the wish of Emely Smith with cancer to meet him - 25 Nov. 1996: Michael visits the Royal Children's Hospital in Melbourne, Australian, and brings gifts for the children. - 9 Dec. 1996: Michael visits a hospital in Manila, Philippines, during his HIStory tour and declares that part of the profits is destined for the renovation of the hospital - 25 Jan. 1997: Michael donates at his performance in Bombay 1,100,000 $ to a organization that supports the education of children in slums - 4 Apr. 1997: Magazine "OK" publishes photos of Michael and his son Prince. The honorarium of 1,000,000 pounds is donated to charities - 18 June 1997: Michael signs the book, "Children in Need," which is auctioned by UNESCO - Sep. 1998: Michael meets the 5-year-old Aza Woods, who is suffering from cancer, in Las Vegas and invites him to Neverland - 16 Nov. 1998: Michael visits as a member of an American delegation Harare in Zimbabwe, invited by the defense ministry - 1 May 1999: Michael receives at the Bollywood Awards an award for humanitarian efforts with the inscription, "Even coming from the young American tradition Michael is the embodiment of an old Indian soul. His action is an expression of the philosophy of the Vedas, which asks to work for human beings, not for their own interests" 4 Sep. 1999: Michael hands over to Nelson Mandela a cheque for about 1,000,000 South African Rand for the Nelson Mandela Children's Fund - 22 Jan. 2000: Michael and other celebrities finance the reconstruction of a park at the castle of Versailles in France, which was devastated by a storm. The costs are estimated at 20,000,000 $ - 28 Oct. 2000: Michael provides a self-painted disc for the auction at the Carousel of Hope Ball. The proceeds are destined for the research of diabetes in children - 6 Mar. 2001: Michael provides his black hat, his jacket and a birthday phone call for an auction of UNICEF. The proceeds are destined for the prevention of the transfer of HIV from mother to child - 26 Mar. 2001: Michael distributes books to young people at a theatre in Newark, New Jersey, via his new Heal the Kids initiative - 25 Apr. 2002: Michael performs at a donation event of the Democratic National Committee at the Apollo Theatre in Harlem, New York - 15 Sep. 2002: Michael provides 16 autographed objects such as CDs and videos for an auction to support the flood victims in Germany - 12 Oct. 2002: Michael invites more than 200 members of Team Vandenberg and their families – after return from a foreign assignment – to Neverland. This was to show his appreciation for the efforts of the military in his community – 19 - 29 Nov. 2002: Michael provides a teddy bear which is dressed like himself for an auction of Siegfried & Roy. The proceeds, 5000 $, go to Opportunity Village, an organization which supports mentally retarded children - 21 Nov. 2002: Michael provides his jacket for the Bambi Charity Event in Berlin, which brings 16,000 $ - June 2003: Michael meets the Wolf family at the Bambi Awards in Berlin. They had suffered great damage to their property from the flood catastrophe in Sachsen. Michael invites them to Neverland, where they spent three days - 13 Sep. 2003: Michael hosts a charity party at Neverland, to which 400 tickets at 725 $ each were available. Those attending included, among others, Aaron and Nick Carter, Mike Tyson, Penny Marshall, Pink, BoysIIMen, and Ashanti - 27 Oct. 2003: Michael's short film to his charity single, "What More Can I Give?" premieres in Las Vegas. The same day the official website "Music for Giving" goes online, where the song can be downloaded for 2 $. The proceeds go to 3 foundations: Oneness, Mr. Holland's Opus Foundation and The International Child Art Foundation. Michael receives the Radio Music Awards' first Humanitarian Award from Beyoncé - 9 Nov. 2003: Michael donates painted shoes to the Charity Event, "Shoes for Charity," an event originated by shoe factory owner Tatami - 1 Apr. 2004: Michael receives the Humanitarian Award of the African Ambassadors' Spouses Association (AASA) for his worldwide humanitarian efforts, especially in Africa - 14 Mar. 2007: Michael provides tickets for orphans and disabled children to participate at a fan event in Tokyo - 29 May 2007: Michael persuades an auction house in Las Vegas to donate a part of the proceeds from the sales of memorabilia of the Jackson family to charities.

   A sample of honors and Awards which Michael Jackson received: 28 Feb. 1984: Michael receives the Best Recording For Children Award at the 26th Grammy Awards - 14 May 1984: At the White House, then-president Ronald Reagan gives Michael an Award for Special Efforts, which honors his engagement at a PR campaign against drunk driving – 21- 23 June 1984: Michael receives the first Neil Bogart Memorial Fund Children's Choice Award at the Bobby Poe Convention - 25 Feb. 1986: Michael, together with Lionel Ritchie, receives the Song of the Year Award for "We Are The World" at the 28th Grammy Awards - 1Mar. 1988: Michael receives an honor grade and Award for Charitable Contributions - Jan. 1989: The "Say Yes to a Youngster's Future Program" confers to Michael the National Urban Coalition Artist/Humanitarian of the Year Award - Mar. 1989: At the Universal Amphitheatre in Universal City, California, Michael receives the Black Radio Special Award for humanitarian achievements - 22 Sep. 1989: Michael receives the Best of Washington 1989 Humanitarian Award from the Capital Children's Museum in appreciation for his efforts to collect money for the museum and his unwavering support of children - 11 Oct. 1989: The auditorium of the Gardner Street Elementary School in Los Angeles is named after Michael and he is honored with the Michael Jackson Auditorium plaque - 3 Feb. 1990: Michael receives a Role Model Award in Japan - 5 Apr. 1990: Michael receives the Entertainer of the Decade Award – 14 Sep. 1990: Michael receives the first Good Scout Humanitarian Award for his support of the Make-A-Wish Foundation, the Prince Charles Trust, the United Negro College Fund and Child Help USA - 23 Oct. 1990: Michael and Elton John receive the Award in Memory of Ryan White, which is handed over in 1991 - 1 May 1992: Michael receives the Points of Light Award from president George Bush for his support of children without rights – 3 June 1992: Michael receives from the organization One to

One an award for his tireless efforts in supporting young people - Aug. 1993: Michael receives the Our Children, Our Hope of Tomorrow Award.

46. HSU – Heart Soul Union

With Michael Jackson things came to reality which others did not even dare to dream. He was the fulfiller of the yearnings of people. When our deepest yearnings come true, we become more resistant to other addictions. We can become a complete part of this world, a healthy cell, which contributes to the flourishing of the whole earth organism. When we negate these yearnings in contact with ourselves, other people and our society, then the world gets lost.

The psychotherapist Wolfgang Bergmann has described the background of this escape in his book, "Computersucht" (computer addiction). The fascinating aspect of games such as "World of Warcraft" is the feeling of belonging. One is a member of guilds in which ethics and social values are held high. Whoever acts against these values is knocked out of the game. Many players have the feeling in the real world of being of no worth, to count as nothing, to be invisible, so they search for compensation in the experience of being something special and needed in the digital world.

The planet Joy is the place of joy for the reason that every fluffy transmits the message, "You are something special to me." When people have undergone ts traumatic experiences in childhood, they compensate for the shock and the experienced senselessness of the real world with grandiosity and narcissism in the virtual world. Bergmann claims that the basic problem consists in the fact that in our world there is no more mysticism, no more magic. There are no adventures, no excitement, no fantasy. These exciting things, which enrich lives, Michael has given in abundance. He has connected us with magic, wonder and the miracle of life, with excitement, adventure and fantasy.

"I am Peter Pan, in my heart I am Peter Pan....Peter Pan represents everything that children, magic and wonderment are about." (Living with Michael Jackson)

Michael made a rare exception for Martin Bashir and allowed him to accompany him for some months with the camera. He even showed him the "giving tree." There he often climbed up to be alone and to write his music. There, for example, "Black or White" and "Heal the World" originated. Michael even asked Martin Bashir to experience for himself how it was in the tree. It had been a big secret; he had never shown the giving tree to anyone.

"But Bashir didn't want to climb trees. He seemed to have other things he planned to climb: corporate ladders and roads to fame. For Bashir, this was a money tree....He wondered if Michael didn't prefer making love or performing." And Michael explained, that "climbing tress and water balloon fights were his favorite pastimes." (Jones, p. 31)

Michael lived in this world, but he was not of Bashir's world. To this world he had all access. He threw tonnes of pearls to the swine. If we would have the courage to open our hearts, then magic and enchantment would again find a place in our lives. Then we all could celebrate the Peter Pan in our hearts – instead of repeating in parrot fashion the things of people with dollar signs in their eyes.

In a world of Peter Pan there is no rage of destruction, no revenge, no hate, no murderers and no criminals. Here all would connect with each other to overcome the suffering of the world. All people would go to work with joy and even not perceive it as work, not as an unloved profession, but as a vocation, as a source of joy. The word work could step by step be forgotten and eradicated from the dictionary. If you do what comes from your heart, how could it be work? The employment agencies would be passé and replaced by enjoyment agencies. The employment agencies could only be found as a terrible historic relict in the history books.

The ZDF reported, in the week from 17th of August 2009, every morning in "Imprisoned – Life in Prison" about people whose freedom had been taken away. On 19th of August Ingeborg Haffert showed pictures which make one shiver facing the state of this society. A man from Morocco, who had lived seventeen years in Germany and studied engineering, and who had worked as a cook to finance his studies, was surprisingly arrested at the instigation of the Munich foreigners office and brought from one day to the other in deportation arrest.

Two days later his deportation to Morocco was planned. The morning of his arrest he did not understand what was happening to him. He never had seen a prison from the inside. He was not allowed to contact anyone or to inform someone in Morocco. He had no relationship to Morocco and no idea how he would proceed there. Then, he was at least allowed to talk to an employee of "European Home Care." This one reported that this is not a single case, but the usual practice of some foreigners offices to deport people without any warning from one day to the next. As in Morocco the term deportation arrest is not known, it would be very difficult to him to explain why he had been imprisoned in Germany. The crime of this man was that he had exceeded his study time.

This is an example of where humanity has landed, even having noble objectives, as they are described in the constitution and the "Grundgesetz der Bundesrepublik Deutschland" (Constitution of the Federal Republic of Germany): "Die Würde des Menschen ist unantastbar" (Dignity of man may not be touched) is only lip service and empty words. Borders and separation are more important to us than are human beings. Self-interest has priority in relation to the interests of community. When a cell obtains its well-being by harming another one, how can the result be a healthy organism?

I am always shocked by the hubris and arbitrariness beyond measure of people. Inside there can only be hate, envy and revenge; otherwise nobody would be capable of such heartless actions. For the one who works in such an agency and supports its un-rightful action, compassion and love seem to be foreign words.

Further reports of ZDF Morgenmagazin among others come from the JVA for women in Vechta The reports show that humanness has not yet decided to visit the world. The comments of the journalist are free of judgment and prejudice. Their purpose is to better understand how it happened that people got into their respective situations and to know how the stay there has changed them.

Prisons should not only be institutions for punishment, but also instruments for transformation. Due to sensationalist reporters we only get informed about the rare exceptions where this transformation did not happen. The public is not interested in the countless positive examples. The truth is trampled to death by ignorance. I was surprised in hearing that a female prison director spoke directly about the issue that not the inmates, but the majority of visitors is in urgent need of a visit of humanness. Visitors to the prison for women in Vechta, where mothers with children under three are housed, were considering life in prison too luxurious. Why? Because the building was not painted grey, but colorfully. Looking from outside it could also have been a hotel – if there were no bars.

What is so disturbing for us when we see people who have gone astray housed in a dignified way? I can only wonder, if envy, revenge, hate, hubris and boastfulness are the cause. These are the projections of one's own abysm, the shadow, the dark side, which we don't want to be aware of. Also in other areas we cover up true motives with sanctimonious etiquette; for example, greed as "profit maximization." Envy is camouflaged as "contest and competition," avarice as "ambition" (wordplay in German: Geiz = avarice, Ehrgeiz = ambition). Without the power of discrimination we are blinded by such expressions and give in to brainwashing by media, politicians and managers.

What a blessing it was when in autumn 2009 an alternative arose: the HSP – the Horst Schlämmer Party (Horst Schlämmer is an artificial famous figure of the comedian Hape Kerkeling), the only German party whose highest maxim is openness, honesty and where humanness is welcome. We could reflect to found a sibling party – HSP is in reality the abbreviation for "High Sensible Person" in form of a non-party. Party means separation; the word comes from the Latin partir.

How would it be to have a party whose goal is to undermine its own position or to destroy itself, a party where there is no judgment (wordplay in German: Urteil = judgment; Ur-teil; Ur is not separated; teil = part)? How would an HSU be, where Michael Jackson is nominated posthumously as honorary president? President honoris causae, president h.c. Michael Jackson? The Union of Heart and Soul? It could form a coalition with the HSP and garner more than fifty percent of the votes. There would not be election campaigns but election dances. And instead of speeches the cities would be flooded by singing.

Non-Party Program of the HSU – Union of Heart and Soul:
- The highest value is Truth.
- Power of discrimination is the instrument of insight.
- The heart is the instrument of perception.
- The most worthy Good is the Soul. Every human being is pure love.
- Judgment is abolished.
- Borders and separations are suspended.
- Everyone has the Right to live as he wishes.
- Everyone has the Right to learn as he wishes.
- Everyone has the Right to work as he wishes.
- There is one prohibition: Nobody has the Right to damage someone.
- There is one demand: Everyone has the Right to be left alone.

A society which prohibits light bulbs and where the succumber has no allowance to be crooked can then only be found in the history books. Whoever is against this program receives a fluffy. The deadly seriousness is left to the dead. (Wordplay in German: Bierernst = deadly serious; Biertrinker = Beer drinker) When someone starts laughing from the bottom of his heart without any reason, membership in the HSU follows automatically.

Whether Michael Jackson has changed the world by his work and consciousness or the world has changed despite Michael Jackson's work and consciousness cannot be answered. The fact is that everything is constantly changing: "Panta rhei" – "Everything flows," as Heraklit already said.

What was unthinkable some time ago is suddenly happening, as for example on 4th of August 2010 the foundation of the initiative, "The Giving Pledge" by Bill Gates and Warren Buffet. Since then forty billionaires are said to have joined to give at least half of their fortune to charities. Perhaps it is a good thing that the fortune is in private hands, and nations, communities and politics are insolvent. Private people can decide for themselves where the money goes and are not dependent on the approval and the applause of voters, who can only know what moths and tanners favor whose hands are tight. Michael Jackson was in any case convinced that the time has come where the world and the things are turning to good account, which is demonstrated in "On the Line," 1997. Perhaps we will still experience the blossom period of an HSU, the Golden Age on Earth.

"No sense pretending it's over, - Hard times just don't go away. - You gotta take that chip off your shoulder, - It's time you open up, have some faith. - Nothing good ever comes easy, - All good things come in due time, yes it does. - You gotta have something to believe in. - I'm telling you to open your mind. - Gotta put your heart on the line, - If you wanna make it right. - You've got to reach out and try. - Gotta put your heart on the line, - If you wanna get it right, - Gotta put it all on the line." (On the line)

Did you ever think about the fact that campaign promises are never seen through with and that promises that children make to their parents are always broken? The answer is simple. The dharma, that is the nature of a promise, consists in being broken. Therefore use the power of discrimination when something is promised to you, and be aware if you are expecting a promise from others. It has to be broken, because its only purpose is to be left alone. A promise is always the result of an expectation or a demand. In terms of Transactional Analysis, it is directed from the ego state of the parent to the adapted child. The critical parent expects the child to fulfill his demands. Promises are always part of a power game.

The reactions of many "serious" journalists and politicians to the "election campaign" of Horst Schlämmer were amusing. They thought the whole thing to be horseplay and comedy, so they were successful in suppressing what Hape Kerkeling was confronting them with in the mirror. When you look more closely you will notice that the impetuses for changes - and actually there are many – don't come from politicians, economists, scientists or businesspeople, but from musicians and filmmakers, from jokers, fools and people, who aren't taken seriously.

In Venezuela, for example, music already assumed a social function thirty years ago. "At that time the teacher Antonio Abeü founded regional symphony orchestras for children and youth from middle and lower classes. The enthusiasm for music kept them away from slipping into drugs and violence. Now there are more than 25 regional youth orchestras in Venezuela....When Venezuela's orchestras play it happens very vividly: During funny pieces every orchestra member is allowed to show his musicality and his temperament, to jump up alone or in groups or to twirl the instruments around and to dance thereby." The national orchestra in Caracas under its young director, Gustavo Dudamel, is in the meantime world famous and undertakes international concert tours, for example in 2002 to Berlin, where they were applauded enthusiastically at a concert in the Philharmonic. (Der Mensch" on www.apam-gesundheit.de)

Isn't this ingenious? It reminds me of Michael's reaction to Slash, when the latter came to rehearsal with a butt in his mouth and a bottle in his hand. The mind cannot accept something like that. For the heart it's quite normal.

What alternative is there for a promise? A clear purpose together with the wild power of determination makes possible the transformation from caterpillar to butterfly. When we are dealing with an agreement between two or more people it is the commitment or the contract. These transactions take place in the ego state of the adult and don't know psychological games. Purpose and contracts circumvent the parental ego and the adapted child, so that the adult can use the limitless energy of the free child to bring the purpose to manifestation. There are no longer opponents, but only interactors. Individuality and the individual don't play a role anymore, but bow to the cosmic order. "The driving force that has created the illusion of an individual life was extinguished....The void of existence, the ocean of peace and stillness was what I have ever been – nothing and everything, everything and nothing." (Mantese, 2006, p. 242) Undoubtedly Michael was permeated in his action and whole work by this power.

47. Soulguard

Today is the 29th of August 2009, Michael Jackson's 51st birthday. Even Google honors the King of Pop in Germany with a modified logo with Michael's trademark, his dancing feet on tiptoes with white socks – although not in the United States.

In his own country, the prophet is seen to have no value, as is commonly known. When will it finally sink in with the Americans? And when will they eat humble pie for all the injustice they committed to him? The biggest Michael Jackson tribute to his birthday is recorded in the "Guinness Book of World Records." In Mexico City at the "Monumento a la Revolución" on the "Plaza de la Republica," more than 13,000 people unite and dance together to "Thriller." Michael, to realize such actions, a multidimensional being like you is needed. Also in Germany some flashmobs were organized for his birthday. In Berlin at the Brandenburger Tor and at the main station, hundreds of people are dancing to "Beat It." In Munich there were flashmobs on 28th and 29th of August 2009 on the Odeonsplatz. Three hundred people in Seattle danced to "Beat It," as well as in Macau at the Ruis of St. Pauls. At the Romana Square in Bucharest in Romania on 29th of August, a tribute of 200 people took place to "Beat It." In Bucharest there was already a "Beat It tribute" on 8th of August 2010, a considerable achievement when you consider that the North is lacking the temperament of the South Americans. And when even Helge Schneider did his form of a tribute for Michael Jackson, on 31st of August 2009 in the Stadtpark in Hamburg: "Heal the World, world, world world,...erhaltet den Wald" (save the forest), then this is more than passing dimensions. That creativity is actually exploding is shown in the Michael Jackson Fashion Tutorial/Tribute on 29th of August 2009. Since that day also a tribute song from producer Al Walser from Liechtenstein and Jermaine Jackson is on sale, "Living your Dream," with the cooperation of Patrick Nuo and Jürgen Drews. (www.jacksontribute.us)

All these honors I find after returning from London. I travelled there as originally planned, because I had a ticket for the 24th of August 2009 in the O2 arena. Alone in this hectic city I had time to put myself in the position and life of Michael. What happened when Michael Jackson was seen in any arena in the world? It went around like a flash of lightning, and paparazzi, media and fans only knew one direction. Often Michael had to fear for his life and surely he would not have survived without damage in many situations without his bodyguards, who cared for his body and life. Sure he had bodyguards, but who cared for his soul? He did not have one soulguard. People subsisted by his energy, which James Redfield has called energy theft. Some people equal black holes and devour everything that comes proximate, even light. On earth it is just as in the universe – stars are devoured by black holes.

Michael has put his message, as well as himself, in endless disguises. When the disguise is very shimmering, it is difficult to concentrate on the content. Man loves to be blinded or to simply fall asleep. To get attention Michael loved to include a crescendo in his songs, small hints man tends to overlook due to his capacity of suppression. Often a tsunami, an earthquake or some other catastrophe is needed to awaken a "Sleeping Beauty." In such extreme situations, in many people the belief in the impossible becomes alive and they start to take initiative. The basis for success is self-faith, belief in one's vision, which overcomes doubt. On this belief Obama built his motto, "Yes we can." In 1991, Michael had already published a song which is dedicated to this faith:

"If you call out loud, will it get inside, - Through the heart of your surrender to your alibis? ... - The power's in believing, so give yourself a chance, - 'Cause you can climb the highest mountain, swim the deepest sea. - All you need is the will to want it, and a little self esteem. - So keep the faith, don't let nobody turn you 'round. - You gotta know when it's good to go to get your dreams up off the ground. So keep the faith baby, yeah, because it's just a matter of time, - Before your confidence will win out. - Believe in yourself, no matter what it's goin' to take. - You can be a winner but you got to keep the faith.... - Go for what you want, don't let 'em get in your way, - You can be better but you got to keep the faith.... - I know that keepin' the faith means never give up on love. - But the power that love has to make it right makes it, makes it right. - So keep the faith. - And when you think of trust it lead you home, - To a place that you only dream of when when you're all alone?... - I know that you can sail across the water, float across the sky, high. - Any road that you take will get you there if you only try.... - Just keep your eyes on the prize and your feet flat on the ground. - So keep the faith baby, yeah, because it's just a matter of time, - Before your confidence will win out.... - Lift up your head and show the world you got pride.... - I know that keepin' the faith means never givin' up on love - But the power that love has to make it right, makes it, makes it right, - So keep the faith." (Keep the Faith)

How much Michael himself believed in the effectiveness of confidence became obvious with the cancer-ill boy Gavin Arvizo. Aphrodite Jones describes Michael's words: "'You bring him to me and we will coat him with love,' Michael once told Janet. When the doctors were saying there was no chance for Gavin to live, Janet told the camera, 'Michael would say, "I will not have that." When the doctors said there was no hope, Michael said there was hope. 'By God's grace, God works through people,' Janet explained, 'and God elected to work in Michael to breathe life into Gavin and to my two other children and me.'" (Jones, p. 74)

Furthermore Aphrodite describes how Michael took the children under his wings and behaved like a father. When Michael met Gavin, his illness was so progressed that he could not move and could not speak anymore. Aphrodite describes how Janet Arvizo, the mother, experienced the contact of Michael with her children. "'He shows them the basic foundation of what life is, and that's a loving family,...Michael is filled with a lot of loving thoughts....And he's assisting me in fulfilling a father figure role they've never had....He spreads his wings and makes sure that the most important thing is that my children are safe and happy. It's a happiness they've never had in their life.' The exact words the Arvizos used to describe Michael were: honest, very trustworthy, humble, loving, caring, funny, unselfish, and attentive....Gavin said he never forgot Michael's words, asserting that, early on, he depended on those words of faith to get him through many rounds of chemotherapy....Janet...said that the doctors had told her to 'plan for a funeral.' She said the doctors told her that if the cancer didn't kill Gavin, the chemotherapy would. When Janet complained to Michael that her son 'was not going to make it,' Michael would tell her not to listen to that. Michael insisted that Gavin would live. Years later, Gavin would be told by doctors that there was no scientific explanation for him to be alive, that his cancer cure was a 'miracle.'" (Jones, p. 75f)

Can you imagine the breach of faith, and how great is the suffering of the soul, when this same family, to whom Michael gave his heart blood, later drags him to the qadi. Moths continue even today to claim that Michael's innocence is not rightly proven. In reality they don't have the courage to admit that they all erred and have projected for years their own blatant ignorance on an innocent soul. Pure souls serve excellently as projection surfaces, as often they don't even think of defending themselves or of a counterattack. Despite all resistance, Michael relentlessly screamed out his hope for a better world into the world.

"Shout" from 2001 was never released, and can be found on YouTube:

"Ignorance of people purchasing diamonds and necklaces.... - Kids are murdering other kids for the fun of it.... - Tragedy on top of tragedy, you know it's killing me. - So many people in agony, this shouldn't have to be. Too busy focusing on ourselves and not His Majesty. - There has to be some type of change for this day and age. - We gotta rearrange and flip the page..... - I wanna shout, throw my hands up and shout - What's this madness all about, - All this makes me wanna shout, - You know it makes me wanna shout, Throw my hands up and shout - What's this madness all about - All this makes me wanna shout, c'mon now. - Problems, complications and accusations, - Dividing the nations and races of empty faces, a war is taking place. - No substitution for restitution, - The only solution for peace is increasing the height of our spirituality. - Masses of minds are shrouded, clouded visions, deceptions and indecision - No faith or religion, how we're living? - The clock is ticking, the end is coming; There'll be no warning, But we live to see the dawn. - How can we preach, when all we make this world to be - Is a living hell torturing our minds. - We all must unite, to turn darkness to light, - And the love in our hearts will shine. - We're disconnected from love, we're disrespecting each other.... - The damage you have done is gonna last forever.... - Ashes to ashes and dust to dust, the pressure is building and I've had enough."

Michael's message was ever the same for decades. "Believe in yourself." "Be yourself." "You can be no one else but yourself," we hear in the long version of "The way you make me feel." "It's all about love. L.O.V.E."

In the media nothing has changed since Michael left the stage. I went through quantities of magazines, special editions and documentaries which were written after his death, and read various books. The speculation continues, the defamation continues and the trash is sold. In September 2009 a video is circulating in the media which shows Michael singing inside a car with the statement that this video appeared recently. In reality it could be found in the worldwide web since 2007, but a sentence like "appeared recently" is promotionally effective and costs nothing. One can make more money with it as with the news, "two-year-old film with Michael." Until then nobody was interested seeing Michael in a car and thus the film did not find its way in the news until that day. And ultimately such things have nothing to do with news.

But seemingly the moths are searching for stuff which brings bucks. And the news that is really to be found is not very interesting for them, because they would have to confess their own failing.

Let's hear some people speak who knew Michael, loved him for himself, as he was and is, instead of paying attention to insane minds. Michael was in the course of his career on the cover of the magazine "Ebony" fifteen times. In August 2009 a special edition was published which is only dedicated to Michael Jackson: "Special Tribute – Michael in his own words and notes from those who loved him."

Linda Johnson Rice, CEO of the Johnson Publishing Company, editor of Ebony, met Michael in the early 70's. "I knew there was something special about him even as a child....He was adorably cute at a distance and even cuter up close....(Michael had) an incredible level of trust with us – a rarity for a media company. But we worked hard to create that trust, to make it clear that we would always be fair. Michael especially took that to heart....

In 1984...he came over to our house to have lunch. There were no handlers, no security guards. No posse, no entourage, just Michael. He sat in our living room, very polite, very honored to be there, but also very relaxed. It was as if he were thinking to himself, 'I can just be with people.'...This book is to celebrate Michael's life, his accomplishments and to really bring to the forefront the archives and the history that our readers may never have seen. And so, it is an insight into the man, into his music and into the magic of Michael Jackson. We like to think of it as a family photo album."

Harriette Cole, editor and creative director of Ebony, describes her view: "Michael Jackson was and is an international icon. He made magic through his music and his creativity, through his generosity and his showmanship....In this special tribute, we do what Black folks do when our loved ones pass. We celebrate the great things. We applaud his body of work, which he consistently offered to us as an exquisitely presented gift. We choose not to go down the road of controversy. We do what we do best. We honor the life, the contributions, the talent, the brilliance, the joy, the effervescent love of one of the great beings of our time."

In this special edition we also read a long report of Reverend Al Sharpton: "In the age of president Obama, many almost forget the long, arduous process of normalizing an oppressed race to the masses and the years of self-sacrifice by individuals like my dear friend Michael Jackson....Every time they knocked him down, Michael got back up. He stood up and told us all to take a look at the man in the mirror and to heal the world. He told us to remember the time, and now we remember the plethora of great times he gave us: the sold-out international concerts, the largest album sales in history, the impeccable dance moves and, more important, his generous, humanitarian side. Donating hundreds of millions to charity, creating his own non-profit organizations and genuinely caring about the state of humanity, Michael will and must be revered for his distinguished and rare character....

In his sheer existence, he forced White America to confront some of its inherent biases and made it possible for many of today's artists, athletes and even the president himself to exist. Before Tiger Woods, there was Michael Jackson, and before Barack Obama there was Michael Jackson....A transcendent individual who crossed every single racial, social and generational line. MJ was much more than the King of Pop; he was and always will be a true groundbreaker and philanthropist. I pray history will finally serve him due justice."

Further from music producer Suzanne de Passe we learn: "Michael liked to hide in the closet, behind the shower curtain, under the bed, or he'd eavesdrop and jump out, and try to scare you....I (nicknamed) him Casper....It was such an innocent time and such a great time."

48. Genius

Michael Jackson worked together with Berry Gordy for many years: "At Suzanne de Passe's insistence, I was like, 'Well, I'll listen to them (the Jackson 5).' And when I saw them, they blew my mind, especially Michael....I could see so much in him, more than just his dancing and singing. I could see a knowingness about him. He would stare very closely at me to see what I was thinking. I thought he was reading my mind or something....Michael was a genius. Michael was a researcher. He'd study, study, study....I've never seen anyone exactly like Michael Jackson, and I don't think I'll ever see anyone like (him). He deserves to be the King of Pop and the greatest worldwide celebrity of our time." (Memorial Booklet, 2009)

Michael being a genius is not even denied by those who otherwise only deride and decry him. Geniuses, or more exactly, genies until today propose to humanity a conundrum. Since ancient times genies are androgynous, which means they embody the male and female aspects of nature in a perfect way in themselves. Thereby they overcome and transcend duality and thinking in opposites. In the meantime, in science there is also a change in thinking happening from the classical physical sciences to modern thinking in the science of life. The analytical linear and quantitative approach, which cares about dead matter, is taken over by a synthetic phenomenological and qualitative view, which discovers the nature of holiness and liveliness again.

The term genius firstly means "producer" and characterizes an extraordinary creative power of mind. A genie is not an imitator, but a fulfiller. A genie creates worlds and universes. The inner life of a genie is full of wonder, ecstasy and magic and in his creations he expresses his inner state. The vibrational frequency of this state of mind is so high that lower emotions as envy, hate and greed have no possibility to survive. They are quasi burnt in the high energy.

The American psychiatrist David R. Hawkins has done intensive research into the various levels of consciousness. The results of decade-long studies confirm the statements of wise people and mystics of all times, that the states of joy and of unconditional love carry such a power of action in themselves that the transformation of all those who come in touch with them happens on its own. One cannot deny oneself by staying far away of the source of love and joy.

All people who came near Michael confirm unanimously that they could not withstand his extraordinary presence. Even the biggest doubters noted that their prejudices melted away like snow at the sun when they came in close approximation with him. There is no explanation for this, because the relations of functioning transcend the level of mind, where explanations are located. Some try to stop the movement in themselves that is triggered by the contact with these high vibes, because they become afraid of death. And really they have good reason for this, because when one gets oneself involved with people of such high frequencies, the ego is endangered as it cannot stand them.

The whole fuss and rigmarole that media and press have made lifelong about Michael Jackson can be put in a nutshell as the endless forlorn fight for the existence of the ego. When the ego is endangered it would stop at nothing and has no problem in sacrificing the life of an innocent. More than two thousand years ago there happened exactly that. At that time – when there were not yet the modern media – the master was crucified with nails. Nowadays we have other forms of crucifixion – unbloody way, but nevertheless a crucifixion.

Aretha Franklin remembers: Michael "was huge on every continent. He transcended ethnic lines and color barriers. He crossed all of those lines with no sweat. What made Michael so special was the fact that people knew he was real. He was such a great performer, one of the greatest the world will ever see. He knew what he wanted and he knew how to put it together. Michael has left us a catalog of great music. His music and his spirit will never die; it will go on forever. Now he has just moved on up a little higher." (Ebony, 2009)

Quincy Jones belonged to those who knew and accompanied Michael since the beginning of his career; he says about the twelve-year-old Michael: "I was watching how aware and focused he was. Everybody said he could never be bigger than he was. I was seeing room for a lot of growth. I went to the Oscars one year and his big love song was 'Ben,' which was to a rat, you know. I said, 'We gotta try a woman now.' So we gave him 'She's Out of my Life,' about a marriage that didn't end well. It was amazing. He cried at the end of every take....He's my baby brother. I was always with him....I just value ever having had him in my life." (Ebony, 2009)

At the time of his death Michael was working together with composer David Michael Frank on a project to record a new album with his classical compositions accompanied by an orchestra. He announced the continuation of this project, but until summer 2011 there is no news available as to whether we will ever hear this music. (www.davidmichaelfrank.com) There was also a duet of Michael and Akon in the works. Akon describes the collaboration with Michael as an unbelievable experience. "I expected him to be a diva, not as talkative, you know what I mean, distant, send messages through other people....But he was just so direct, so humble, it was incredible." He revealed that they worked on a song, "Hold My Hand," whose lyrics include, "Life don't last forever, it's what you waited for." "It didn't really hit me until right now...life don't last forever...So once you're here, you've got to make the best of it and leave something behind that people can really cherish." (www.accesshollywood.com)

Michael was without airs and graces, even though he was said to be the biggest star of his time. He rather remained the embodiment of humility and humbleness. Corey Rooney, who often worked together with him reports: "Then you work with a guy like Michael Jackson who when he was late, he was supposed to be in the studio at twelve and he showed up about a quarter to one. He felt so terrible for being late he apologized the whole session. The next day he sent a big giant basket because we're talking about movies and that's how much I love movies. So he sent this giant basket. Oh my goodness, it probably had 100 DVD's. It had Popcorn, candy, all kinds of books and movie trivia, all kinds of stuff. Again, the card said, 'I'm very sorry for not respecting your time.'"

With such witnessing by people who worked with Michael in mind, everybody can review for himself the statement of Taraborelli that Michael was never on time. Following are some more appreciations to balance what the mind junkies are saying about Michael even two years after his death.

On 28th of July 2010, "N24" airs again the trashy documentation by Bashir. Was this due to sloth, ignorance or stupidity? I never received an answer to my mail regarding the matter. As long as journalism is mixed up with speculators we will be further sold trash instead of jewels.

Thank God there are some rare media like Ebony. "Michael Jackson, the consummate artist and creative genius I have known since he was a child, is dead. How difficult it is to construct that sentence. He was deceptively smart and strong. He also had a heart of love. 'We Are The World' is almost his autobiography. He made room for everybody....He took the soul and sounds of Blackness to the world stage....Michael was an avid reader of serious classics and a self-taught musician. He had a vision – a brilliant business sense. No artist has ever owned the musical catalogs that Michael did, which included the Beatles, Elvis and so much more. I was with him at Neverland through his darkest hours but, through it all, Michael was a survivor. Indeed, his story is one of unparalleled triumph; rarely have we seen the promise of youth fulfilled so brilliantly, so fully....I can only imagine the ovation he experienced in heaven. I can see James Brown, Sammy Davis, Jackie Wilson, Marvin Gaye, Otis Redding,

Sam Cooke, Elvis Presley, Frank Sinatra, Tchaikovsky, Mozart, da Vinci and so many giants from whom he drew inspiration, welcoming him home." (Reverend Jesse Jackson, Ebony 2009)

Cory Rooney and Chris Apostle state in the already cited interview with Chris Yandek the hope that people may remember the contribution of Michael to music, and recognize him as a musicologist. "Something about Michael that people don't realize is, I would call him a musicologist. This guy knew every song ever recorded, and every studio, the whole Sun studios thing, Memphis, you name it, Motown, New York, LA, everywhere. He knew everything, the musicians, the instruments, the mics. No one talks about this. No one discusses this and this is unbelievable. And by the way, unlike Elvis, this guy was doing it still for 43 years, Chris. My God man." Cory continues with the statement that he had waited his life and career long to someday get the chance to work with Michael, to be recognized, that Michael may recognize his talent. When finally the common work happened Michael taught him many things. (http://thesportsinterview.com)

In "Liberian Girl" and later in the film, "This Is It," we can witness what it means to artists to be "called" by Michael Jackson. People who are already successful as an artist, call working with Michael Jackson the absolute peak of their music career. Musicologist is the correct term. He is the music itself. Every cell in his body, every cell in his mind and every cell of his soul were filled with music. The same can be said of few other rare geniuses such as the Chinese star pianist Lang Lang and the German-American star violinist David Garrett.

"Michael has always been working on music. Always...always working on music. Like I said, he was never really happy with himself," says Cory. Later in the same interview, Cory states, "Michael to me, and I can only tell you to me, and I am sure I can get you dozens and dozens and dozens and hundreds of thousands of people who feel the same. Michael Jackson was like a Christ-like figure for us. To know that this man over the last fifteen years has been torn down, crucified, slandered, badmouthed, everyone would rather talk about something negative like he wanted to buy the elephant man's bones. So what? You know what? I would them buy too....but we are surrounded by hypocrites in this business. It's just a tragedy. I always wondered what it would be like if something God forbid happened to Michael. I don't think I ever really wanted to feel it. I just always kind of wondered like my goodness, what would happen? Well, here we are. And so far everything that's happened is pretty much exactly I thought what was gonna happen....He was one of the toughest men I ever met, and that's the truth. He was a rugged, tough guy. There was nothing timid about Michael Jackson." Then interviewer Chris Yandek: "You guys have told me a different story that the mainstream media is totally not focused on....What you're saying to me...is that the industry, that media, that is the industry, is not totally focusing on really how important this guy was to music as a whole." Cory states categorically, "They're not even scratching the surface."

Among the projects in which Michael Jackson was involved at the time of his transition included a collaboration with the then 30-year-old American R & B singer Ne-Yo: "He told me he views music like how I view music – in shapes and colors. That kinda blew my mind. The conversation ended with him saying, 'I just need melody, as melodic as possible – the songs need to say something.' From there I went into writing songs, putting songs together and submitting them to him....That was our relationship until he died. We were about to make it happen. God works in mysterious ways, and it's not our place to question what He does. There's a purpose and a reason for what He does. The songwriting experience was surreal....Jackson is half the reason why I sing. Period....I've definitely shed tears, but honestly, I'm kind of relieved. There is no one in the mass media who can reach him know. No backwards person can accuse him of anything now that he's beyond pain or suffering. I'm happy he's now in a place where he can't be harmed." (Ebony, 2009)

Michael's longtime spokeswoman Raymone K. Bain reports: "I think that most people feel that Michael's legacy will be the historic achievements and the accomplishments that he made in music; but Michael's greatest legacy is going to be Prince, Paris and Blanket. And I really believe that from the bottom of my heart." (Ebony, 2009)

And Songwriter Scott Paulson-Bryant says: "We will never stop loving Michael Joseph Jackson. Not only because he told us, that...we were the world but also because...he wanted us to help him heal the world. And he wanted us to do it as one. Rest in peace, Michael Jackson. You knew pain, you knew the love of millions. Without you, we'll have to start healing all over again. Together." (Ebony, 2009)

Michael himself says about his creative process:

„Ever since I was a little boy, I would study composition. And it was Tchaikovsky that influenced me the most. If you take an album like Nutcracker Suite, every song is a killer, every one. People used to do an album where you'd get on a good song and the rest were like B-sides. They'd call them 'album songs', and I would say to myself: 'Why can't everyone be like a hit song? Why can't every song be so great that people would want to buy it if you could release it as a single? So I always tried to strive for that. That was my purpose for the next album (Thriller). That was the whole idea. I wanted to just put any one out that we wanted. I worked hard for it."

Thriller sold, according to Michael's information, 104,000,000 copies. Michael comments this unbelievable success with, "God has answered my prayers."

Ebony asks for the roots of Michael's creativity: "So, the creative process, were you deliberate about that, or did it just kind of happen?"

Michael: „No I was pretty deliberate. Even though it all came together some kind of way, consciously, it was created in this universe, but once the right chemistry gets in the room, magic has to happen. It has to. It's like putting certain elements in one hemisphere and it produces this magic in the other. It's science." ...

„Quincy would say: ‚If the song needs something, it'll tell you. Let it talk to you.' I've learned to do that. The key to being a wonderful writer is not to write. You just get out of the way. Leave room for God to walk in the room. And when I write something that I know is right, I get on my knees and say thank you. ... When you know it's right, sometimes you feel like something is coming, a gestation, almost like a pregnancy or something. You get emotional, and you start to feel something gestating and, magic, there it is! It's an explosion of something that's so beautiful, you go, WOW! There it is. That's how it works through you. It's a beautiful thing. It's a universe of where you can go with those twelve notes." ...

"I direct and edit everything I do. Every shot you see is my shot. Let me tell you why I have to do it that way. I have five, no, six cameras. When you're performing – and I don't care what kind of performance you are giving – if you don't capture it properly, the people will never see it. It's the most selfish medium in the world. You are filming WHAT you want people to see, WHEN you want them to see it, HOW you want them to see it and what JUXTAPOSITION you want them to see."

Ebony changes the topic: „What do you thinks about the next presidential race, Hillary, Barack?"

Michael: "To tell you the truth, I don't follow that stuff. We were raised to not look to man to fix the problems of the world. They can't do it. That's how I see it. It's beyond us. Look, we don't have control over the grounds, they can shake. We don't' have control over the seas, they can have tsunamis. We don't have control over the skies, there are storms. We are all in God's hands. I think that man has to take that into consideration.

I just wish they would do more for the babies and children, help them more. That would be great, wouldn't it?" (Ebony, 2007, 2009)

On 30th of December 2009 CNN reports that "Thriller" was received as the first music video in history in the National Registry of the Library of Congress. There, US American films are kept permanently. (www.cnn.com)

49. The Place Where God is Visible

Let's once again give the word to Michael Jackson, because during his lifetime he was praised because of his music and dance, but his words were not given much attention.

"Some people say I live in a fantasy, because I see the world differently. Visions come to me in my sleep, I close my eyes to see what God is showing me - Close your eyes and imagine with me, see the wonder in every living thing - If we can live the way it is in my dreams, love will take us to a place where God can be seen - This is my dream. I have this dream, this I believe, the world a place for all humanity. If we could take love to its highest level, more than the world has ever seen. I have this dream, Let's put God's love on display, Angels of love come my way. It's really up to you and me, one world together in harmony. In my dream I see heaven, and the face of the One perfect being, I see people turning into angels, And God giving them their wings." (I Have This Dream, Eugene Kitt and Michael Jackson)

Together with Freddie Mercury, Michael recorded a song which was never finished. It is an expression of their compassion. A comment to the video on YouTube calls it, "Music of the Heavens." "There must be more to life than this, There must be more to life than this, How do we cope in a world without love, Mending all those broken hearts, And tending to those crying faces... There must be more than meets the eye. Why should it be just a case of black or white? There must be more to life than this."

Today on 14th of September 2009 I come across absurdity in the internet which only insane minds can invent. Greed for money must necessarily lead to lack of money, and so clever heads have thought about a solution to darn the holes: The air tax. In Austria it exists already longer than in Germany. When a businessman displaces public air, he has to pay air tax. The city Fürth in

Germany has decided to collect an air tax. This is made possible by a law that the government Merkel has passed, the PAT, - the private air-taking rate – which is indirectly hidden in the electricity tax. Greed does not stop in its inventiveness to line its pockets, even with air. (AZ Nürnberg 13 Sep. 2009)

The Bavarian Administrative Court in Munich yet judged on 22nd of June 2006 that the planned charge of the city for balconies which reach into the public space, is illegal. Nevertheless we can try it, and reword it a little bit. Somehow we certainly have to solve the world's urgent problems. I wonder when we will each be given a sensor which measures how much air we inhale, so that we may pay a respective fee.

Michael Jackson was all his life a victim of rapacity – from individuals as well as the media. What is the motive of paparazzi to follow celebrities at every turn, to shoot them with huge objectives and circle with helicopters above their compound, if not greed. Aphrodite Jones proves in her research without a doubt that the allegations in the Chandler case in 1993 as well as the charges in the Arvizo case in 2003 were exclusively motivated by greed for money and revenge, greed and wounded vanity. "Witnesses showed not only that Jordies parents get separate payments, but June Chandler's former new husband, David Schwartz, had decided to reimburse himself a complaint against Michael Jackson - to get replaced so that its own financial implications. During the negotiations it was also obvious that to five former employees who had charged Michael, money flowed in the amount of $32,000 from television with shows like "Inside Edition" and others in which there were all about gossip. Also on the sale of stories about Michael and Lisa Marie Presley was negotiated. During the negotiation turned out also that, in the case of Chandler, a psychologist Dr. Stanley Katz had been called, and that the same psychologist was also switched from the attorney of Arvizo. Observers of the trial considered this a very strange coincidence." (Jones, p. ???)

What is the reason for people to buy gossip and scandal prints? Pure craving for sensation. Craving for sensation is greed too, greed for thrill, excitation and excitement. The motive is not the search for information, but it's about self-satisfaction. The confirmation of one's opinion and prejudices is a satisfaction for the insatiable mind. The main occupation of most people is everyday self-satisfaction, in the form of mindfucking as well as of bodyfucking. Self-satisfaction is not limited to the physical pleasure principle, but there are also forms of mental self-satisfaction, the simplest being explanations and the most complex being slanders. The mind is always searching for explanations for incident and observations and only content when it has found them. Whether the explanation is meaningful and accurate, whether it is truth or pure fiction, is absolutely negligible. The unconscious motive behind the search for explanations is not the establishment of the truth, but the satisfaction of the mind.

The mind only comes to rest and stops keeping on and on when it is served a theory. Then it settles back. Madonna held a moving speech on 13th of September 2009 at the MTV Special Tribute of the Video Music Awards (VMA): "There is no question that Michael Jackson was one of the greatest talents the world has ever known....His music had an extra layer of inexplicable magic,...actually made you believe that you could fly, dare to dream, be anything that you wanted to be. Because that is what heroes do, and Michael Jackson was a hero....

He seemed otherworldly, but he was also a human being....In that moment I could see both his vulnerability and his charm....And then for one reason or another we fell out of touch. Then the witch hunt began, and it seemed like one negative story after the other was coming out about Michael. I felt his pain. I know what it's like to walk down the street and feel like the whole world has turned against you. I know what it's like to feel helpless and unable to defend yourself, because the roar of the lynch mob is is so loud that you are convinced your voice can never be heard.

But I had a childhood, and I was allowed to make mistakes and find my own way in the world without the glare of the spotlight. When I first heard that Michael had died I was in London....All I could think about in that moment was, I had abandoned him. That we had abandoned him. That we had allowed this magnificent creature that once set the world on fire to somehow slip through the cracks. While he was trying to build a family and rebuild his career, we were all busy passing judgment. Most of us had turned our backs on him.

In a desperate attempt to hold onto his memory, I went on the internet to watch old clips of him dancing and singing on TV and onstage, and I thought, 'My God, he was so unique, so original, so rare. And there will never be anyone like him again. He was a king.' But he was also a human being and alas, we are all human beings and sometimes we have to lose things before we can truly appreciate them. I want to end this on a positive note and say that my sons, age nine and four, are obsessed with Michael Jackson. There's a whole lot of crotch-grabbing and moonwalking going on in my house, and it seems like a whole new generation of kids has discovered his genius and are bringing him to life again. I hope that wherever Michael is right now, he is smiling about this. Yes, yes, Michael Jackson was a human being, but dammit, he was a king. Long live the king." (MTV 13th Sept. 2009)

The number of people who are bestowing honor on Michael in every imaginable way is slowly but steadily growing. Besides others David Garrett on 7th of November 2009 on the TV show, "Wetten Dass," honored Michael with "Smooth Criminal," which he played on his Stradivarius. Thank you David! On 9th of July 2010 David again enchanted us with an homage to Michael, when he together with the then 24-year-old Australian Orianthi, on "Sommernachtsmusik" on "ZDF," scintillated with "Smooth Criminal" – a treat for the eyes and the ears. Such genre-transcending cooperation was only made possible by Michael Jackson.

On 30th of January 2010, during the Grammy Awards, Celine Dion, Usher wearing a black armband on the left, Jennifer Hudson, Carrie Underwood and Smokey Robinson performed, together with a recording of Michael, in front of a 3D-projection of "Earth Song" from the film, "This Is It." "Unbelievable" was Lionel Ritchie's sole comment, and then he welcomed to standing ovations Michael's children, Prince and Paris, who – both wearing red armbands on the left – received the "Michael Jackson Lifetime Achievement Award" for their father.

Every time such tributes for Michael take place and when people gather who feel connected to him, the immense influence which he had on the world is directly apparent, which now continues even people not noticing it. Love keeps up its invisible work.

On 17th of August 2010 a partnership is forged between the project "MJTP" (Michael Jackson Tribute Portrait) and "A Million Trees for Michael," which cooperates with the non-profit organization, "American Forests," who plant a tree for every donated dollar and dear to Michael. In the film, "This Is It," we hear that he concedes to us only four years to save the planet. Love keeps up its invisible work.

In April 2010 Renia tells me about her experiences: "I don't know how it happened, I always loved Michael's music, but after seeing 'This Is It,' my life has changed forever. I don't know who did it, why I, why so late. I don't have answers, but I know for sure that I don't need them either. I am happy, how much luck every day is bringing."

When someone is ready to allow that IT works, explanations are superfluous. Michael's friend Cory Rooney confirms that most people turned their back on Michael in the most difficult times of his life: "When Michael was on trial, nobody, nobody stopped to go and support him at the trial. The guy is acquitted on ten counts of child molestation. No one said, 'Sorry Michael.' No one said, 'Michael we knew you were innocent.' No one did a BET tribute to him then. Nobody played his music and did a marathon then. Nobody rallied up and did a concert....How come all the artists didn't band together back then and say: 'Hey! You know what? Let's do a tour like Michael did when he did the 'We Are The World' tour and let's raise some money. Let's get this thing going.' No one did that....Half of Hollywood showed up for this man (Tookie Williams, a murderer, who made an inner change in prison)....He was nominated for the Nobel Peace Prize.

Well, how about the millions of children that Michael Jackson has helped over the span of his career? Yet two children come with some false allegations and those two children become the two children that destroy him. It's crazy, so it makes me look at the entertainment business and just say I'm surrounded by a bunch of hypocrites....Everyone's gonna do their tributes, but the tributes now if you look at it, it's all because now everyone's gonna get some spotlight, they're gonna get some shine. Now all of a sudden everyone wants to say something good about him." (http://thesportsinterview.com)

50. Michael in Private

Anyone is sincerely interested to get to know Michael Jackson better, to experience how he was privately, can find plenty of material on YouTube, for example the video where Michael is grooving to the song "Ignition" by R. Kelly in the back seat of a car, together with his friend Brett Ratner driving.

Besides on YouTube the series, "Private Home Videos," is available, where we can find ninety minutes of enlightening, surprising and touching things. Originally these films were aired on FOX News in 2003, but due to the massive counter-propaganda of the moths, they seem to have made no permanent impression on Americans. Part one shows Michael's childhood home in Gary, Indiana on Jackson Street, all nine Jackson children, the brothers in the snow, Michael at age six rehearsing in the living room, the Jacksons at a party.

Michael commented, "We traveled, traveled every night,...I don't like to tour, I do like relating to the fans...the energy is great, it's fantastic....it is a difficult thing to tour, you go from one continent to another, you're sleepy, the time zones are different, you can't sleep after the show..." Someone off camera says, "Can we just do it again without the negative...?" "I don't like it though......I'll make it positive then, but you do know the truth." Off camera we hear, "Action Michael," and he says, "I love to tour," which causes everybody to erupt in laughter. He asks, "Why are you all starting laughing...No but seriously....I love my fans,...they know all the songs, all the dance moves, everything, they even come with the tape on their fingers, the hats and the glove...it's just a wonderful experience, I love it. The fans are the reason why I do the tours, and it's very important to give the best show that we can possibly give them....It's a spiritual thing also, because when, certain songs we play, like 'Heal the World,' 'We Are The World,' or 'Man in the Mirror' - the whole stadium is lit up with these Bic lighters they use, and they know when to do it...it's very emotional, it's fun, and I love to entertain, that's one of my favorite things. I think the fans see that. Actually I know they see it, because when I walk out on stage they give me so much love....It's my birthday...and then they brought me this huge, beautiful birthday cake. I realized I've got family all over the world." (YouTube, Home Movies 1)

Never has any fan doubted that Michael loves his fans. There is an invisible mysterious relationship between Michael Jackson and his fans. In the book, "It's all About L.O.V.E," which was published 2010 in English language and includes reports of fifty fans from Germany, Spain, Sweden, United States Oman, Great Britain, Denmark, Norway, Australia, France, India, Romania, Italy, Poland, Hungary and Argentina, we can find numerous evidence for the magic that connected both sides.

In a certain sense Michael needed his fans and they needed him. For many he is the anchor in the dark nights of their soul and gave them hope and new courage to face life. "Yet his powerful music and lyrics gave me the strength I needed to go on and find my own way. He was my anchor in the sea of uncertainty, my guide through the jungle of my confusion and my guidepost in the search for values in my life." (Marina, It's all About L.O.V.E., p. 54)

On the other hand, fans supported Michael in overcoming all the misdeeds that where done to him in his life. "As the criminal trial progressed, Michael began to suffer a subtle physical meltdown. His fans gave him a sense of hope as he battled through a legal storm. But the remaining media continued to pick Jackson apart, focusing on the possibility that the testimony from past accusers might be allowed into the trial. More than ever, Michael needed to feel the energy of people who cared about him. It seemed that his fans were just as important to him as his family, and both groups were outraged about Michael's public humiliation. His fans, even more than his family, were outraged that Michael was being so harshly judged. In the midst of the chaos, Michael appeared to become closer to his fans than anyone might have imagined. He certainly was depending on Tom Mesereau and his defense team, but in the end, Michael's strength came from the people who loved him and admired his life's work. Die-hard fans, people who were camped out at the fences surrounding the courthouse, people who were camped out at the gates of Neverland, had become enormously important to Michael's mental state.

They were strangers, really, but to Michael, they were the people who sustained him throughout his life. The stage was all he'd ever really known. Fans stayed the course with Michael through his worst public ordeal....No other entertainer could have drawn people from so many walks of life; every creed, race, and nationality was represented....The fans who were there created a synergy that was undeniable.

But the media thought that Jackson fans were completely off the wall....'Hey, hey, we're here to stay. We shall not be moved...by all this negative media...Hey, Hey, hypocrisy was never a friend of mine. You commercialized, to victimize, deceiving minds,' people chanted. 'America is supposed to be...the land of milk and honey, overflowing in equality. Michael Jackson should be treated with dignity. He's a part of humanity...Flesh and blood like you and me...You need to stop being greedy, using Michael as a commodity, trying to sell your philosophy.'" (Jones, p. 128/129)

51. Michael's first Christmas

Let's look at more important things than the endless controversy and offences woven about Michael Jackson, like for example the first Christmas that Michael experienced. As Michael was raised as a Jehovah's witness, the Jackson brothers used to look out the window at Christmas with sadness, wishing to be just once a part of this celebration.

Elizabeth Taylor finally fulfilled this wish for Michael in 1993, when he was already 35 years old. In the home movies from that day, both can be seen in nightclothes, when Elizabeth is knocking at Michael's door to call him for the handing out of presents. Michael comes cautiously closer to the shining, decorated Christmas tree and touches it softly, as if it were made of glass.

"I've met a lot of people in my life and very few are real real real friends; you can probably count them at one hand. And Elizabeth is one of the most loyal, loving, caring people that I know. She decided to transform Neverland into its first Christmas."

Elizabeth continues to tell the story: "It is 1993 and this will be Michael Jackson's very first Christmas. It has taken me I think five years of talking him into celebrating Christmas at Neverland, because I understood that if you're a Jehovah's witness, they don't celebrate Christmas. When he quit being a Jehovah's Witnesses, I said to Michael, 'I think Christmas is a wonderful way of celebrating love. It's a celebration of love.' And I can't see Christmas without Michael or Michael without Christmas."

Michael continues: "I had no idea she was planning this....At the same time it was exciting, I felt guilty too at the same time. I remember going in the bathroom and crying later, because I felt I had done something wrong."

"In the video we see four "Super Soakers," the giant water gun, being unwrapped, each time with much laughter. Michael declares, "If you're wondering why I love Super Soakers so much...if you come to Neverland it's a rule that you are bound to get wet, either be thrown in the pool, or you have a water balloon fight or a Super Soaker fight."

We then see rollicking play with the Super Soakers, with Michael's sister Janet and his friend Macaulay Culkin.

Michael's commentary: "We're preparing the water balloon fight. We have teams. We use the whole ranch. My favorite thing in the world to play, if you call it a sport, is a water balloon fight....I've never lost a water balloon fight. I'm the Michael Jordan of water balloon fighting. I went through this entire water balloon fight completely dry."

We see Michael dancing upon the two meter diving board over the swimming pool, until Macaulay Culkin pushes him, fully clothed, into the water. Did you ever see Michael fully clothed, under water, and then again arising spluttering? (Home Videos 2) Later Michael gives a statement as to his life philosophy. "I don't want to copy people. I like being an innovator, a pioneer." (Home movies 3)

These private records prove how distorted and mendacious the picture was that was painted of Michael in the public. Michael was also always a family man and held the tradition high.

In the next part we witness how the Jacksons celebrated a day for their father and a day for their mother. "Joe Jackson Day represents the day for our father. We don't celebrate birthdays really, so we created a day for our father and a day for our mother. All the family comes and we present them with speeches, how we feel about them, and we give them them presents....My father loves animals. I think that's where I got my love for animals from. But this was his day....But the real fun is when you see 500 kids, you know, terminally ill children having fun...That day Janet and I gave my father a boat. He loves to fish, he loves fishing, he loves the outdoors." (Home Videos Part 5)

The film continues with parts of the making of the film to Michael Jackson's song, "You Rock my World," where Chris Tucker plays a role. Michael reports that the collaboration with Chris was quite difficult because they could not stop laughing. (Home Videos Part 6)

That the friends of Michael and he himself could not stop laughing shows another part of the Home Movies. The scene shows a supermarket where Michael is going to shop. He can hardly fend off the capers of his friends. It shows his extraordinary sense of humor and his delight in comic and fun.

"A good friend of mine who owns this mall, he had them close the whole shopping mall and he had people in there that I knew pretending as if they were shopping...I went shopping, it was great....it was a lot of fun...it gave me a chance to see in my way kinda what the real world is like, even though it wasn't the real thing.... Everybody was messing with me, trying to steal my cart."

One of the participants calls out, "If you can't keep track of your cart you shouldn't shop." Michael comments, "I got to do something that I usually don't get to do." (Home Movies 3)

What do you think about a superstar who does not need anything as source of joy and contentment but a supermarket? What do you need to enjoy and to be content? At the end we see parts of "The Making of Bad." "Bad - we did this in a subway in New York and Martin Scorcese was the director. That's the rehearsal....It's mostly just spontaneous movement, which it should be, because to have everything choreographed would be hokey for this type of song."

The eighteen-minute video version of "Bad" illustrates this clearly. The conflicts of rivaling gangs and the provocations and the attack of uninvolved people remind us of the violence acts of young people in underground stations and public traffic, which have been increasing for some time.

"Bad" conveys the clear message that the bad image, the profiling, and venting one's rage on others is the wrong way. "You're doing wrong, you're doing wrong, you're doing wrong," Michael sings nearly conjuringly – until the aggressors cut and run, because there is no more an opposing wind blowing, similar to what happens in "Beat It."

One who does not experience resistance ceases his aggressive behavior, which was only kept up by counteraction. Michael appeals to the hurt inner child, which is deeply longing for recognition, wants to be really seen, wants to be as it is. This one is not at all interested in fighting and aggression, but only trying to get attention which has usually been denied to it in life. At the bottom of its heart it is searching for joy and peace. Michael explicitly emphasized that he created Neverland for this purpose.

"Neverland appeals to the child inside of every man, woman and child. It's a place where I feel that you can return to your childhood. You find grownups doing things they haven't done since they were like ten years old and it's just a fun, wonderful place to be....There is just unlimited space,...mountains and horseback riding and all kinds of fun things, so it's a just a fun place, I love it, and I will always love it. Neverland is me. It represents the totality of who I am, it really does. I love Neverland." (Private Home Movies)

Those who understand what Neverland really meant to Michael Jackson realize that the invasion of Neverland by the sheriffs in 2003 was a dagger thrust into Michael's heart and soul. With the support of the state and the law at that time, a legal murder in installments was initiated in front of the whole world. Even though the physical body, despite a pierced heart, was kept up for a while by his life energy, and Michael Jackson himself also wanted to live, nature took its natural course. The leak where his life energy was bleeding away was no longer closeable, the process of dying that started in nano-velocity.

To Aphrodite Jones it is crystal clear, "as to why Jackson needed to create a life that was free of adult constraints. Given the constant scrutiny, the ever-present expectations from adults, it seemed understandable that Michael had taken such great pains to build a self-contained world at his home. Neverland was his getaway from the TV cameras, the flashbulbs, the gossip columns, the gawkers, the whole universe of adults who placed him in a fishbowl from the time he first became star." (Jones p. 50)

Michael loved Neverland, because it was his house and home – and part of this home were all those who were visitors in Neverland. This home was completely destroyed by rakes and invaders – under the mask of legality, in the cosmic sense a crime to humanity. The peace which surrounded Neverland became history in just one day.

Another part of the Home Movies shows Michael rehearsing moves that were inspired by Charlie Chaplin. Michael's comment thereto and to "Smooth Criminal":

"Every time I do an album I write almost literally 100 or over 100 songs...and Smooth Criminal almost did not make it on the album....I decided that I would make a short film, I'd do a Western....At the last minute, I said no, I don't want do it as a western, it should be like a hot summer night in Chicago in 1945, an underground kind of thing going on,...that was the best way to go. It's one of my favorite pieces." (Home Videos part 6)

We also see a meeting of Michael with the Princes of Wales. Michael about his relationship to Princes Diana,

"Lady Diana in real truth was one of the sweetest people I've ever known, because we could relate to each other. We shared something in common, with the press. I don't think they hounded anyone more than her and myself. And we had a relationship, a very good relationship, where we would call each other late at night for me, and we would just talk about, just cry on each other's shoulders, how hard and difficult and how mean the tabloids can be, and how they lie and twist stories around. She came to a concert at Wembley stadium in London,…when the royal family come, you have to line up….She called me away from the line…She said, 'Are you gonna to do Dirty Diana tonight?' I said, 'No, no I took it off the show out of respect for you.' She said, 'That's my favorite song.' I said, 'Are you serious?'…She was just a wonderful, warm, compassionate person, very caring, very caring. It was real. It wasn't publicity….She really cared. I'm the same way, I feel the same way that she does about children and the future of our children and the future of the world."

His caring about the welfare of children Michael already expressed at the age of 27 at the 28th Grammy Awards, when he was given the Song of the Year Award together with Lionel Ritchie. His acceptance speech ends with the request, "And I'd also like to say, when you leave here, remember the children. Thank you."

On YouTube we can find sufficient examples of Michael's visits to institutions and hospitals during his concert tours, how he helped needy children. Michael saved the life of the deathly ill little Bela Farkas from Budapest.

"On my off days I do as many hospitals as I do concerts….But because it's good news the press don't cover it. They want bad news. But I do it from my heart….We bring bags of toys and posters and albums, and you should see how it transforms kids, they jump up and down and they're so happy. This is Lisa Marie and myself at a hospital in Budapest, and I saw this little kid, his name was Farkas. He was very sick, he was green in the face, but he had this glow and this sparkle in his eye. I asked his nurse, 'What's wrong with this kid?' She said that he needs a liver. So I said, 'Does that mean he's gonna die?' She said yes he's gonna to die unless he gets a liver. I said, 'I'm not gonna let him die, this sweet angel. No matter what it takes I'm gonna find a liver for him.'…We went all over the place, and it took a long time. I said, I'm not giving up, I'm not going to have this child die. I was so happy when I got a phone call, they told me we found a liver, and he has his life, and I'm so proud that I could help him. God bless him. I love you Farkas." (Private Home Movies Part 7)

Michael Jackson has earned hundreds of millions of dollars and at the same time given away hundreds of millions of dollars. All his life he has been the embodiment of generosity. Even as a child he bought sweets for his classmates from his hard-earned money. Kenny Ortega, director and choreographer, who was friends with Michael for 25 years, confirms it: "This guy had the biggest heart...and really, really did care about improving the human condition, especially for children. That was part of his mission. While he was on tour...he always wanted to know what he could do in each place so that when he left, he left the place better." (http://mjtruthnow.com)

Kenny produced the film, "This Is It," and says in a conversation with Oprah Winfrey, "for the last couple of years we had been talking about finding the right project. That it had to have meaning, real purpose behind it for him to want to do something. And when he called me, he said, 'This is it.' That's where the title came from. He wanted this so much for so many reasons. For his children, who are now old enough, and really, you know, curious (about his performances)."

The last time Kenny saw Michael was 14 hours before his death. He says working on the film has helped him begin to heal. "Being there with the material just gave greater value to the history I shared with Michael, a greater importance to how lucky I was, honored to have him in my life." (www.oprah.com)

Even now that Michael cannot follow his earthly mission further, there are successors who have recognized the power of transformation of music and of children. We don't even know most of them, and they do their work in silence.

The Chinese star pianist Lang Lang, who also like Michael had to sacrifice his childhood to fulfill his dream, closes his autobiography from 2008, which he wrote at age 26, with the confession, "I always have had big dreams and it may perhaps seem idealistic or naive, when I believe that I am able to make a better world by making the life of children better through music. I always have to think of the statement of Laotse: that a journey of a thousand miles begins with one step." (Lang Lang, 2010, p. 274)

Other artists have also utilized their work and creative force for the welfare of children, for example Peter Maffay with his musical Tabaluga and the-same named foundation.

Michael was not a star at Neverland, but a simple human being, a happy man, who liked to scamper and frolic around with children. There he was simply himself and was allowed to be himself, jumping on a trampoline and searching for Easter eggs. As a cocky visitor breaks an egg on his head, he simply puts on his hat again and it goes on. How would you react if someone were to break a raw egg on your head? Even Gregory Peck and his wife were as visitors in Neverland, riding the carousel and the ferris wheel.

In one part we see scenes from the making of "Jam," with the basketball superstar Michael Jordan. In another part, the whole Jackson family is assembled – brothers, sisters, aunts, uncles. Especially funny is the trick they play on John Landis, the director of "Thriller." While Michael is thanking him sanctimoniously and expressing his appreciation for his work, Macaulay Culkin is sneaking from behind with a pie in his hands calling "John, John." And as he turns around, the pie is landing on his face - and the scene continues on with a huge pie fight. Just before John had sat down, Michael narrated, "He knows something's up," and really, John had taken off his glasses before turning around.

Anyone who is not yet satisfied with Michael privately should have a look at the part where Elizabeth Taylor gives an elephant to Michael, and the same day Michael gives her a huge tapestry portrait of herself. Michael, all American, is all the while chewing gum. (Home Movies Part 8) Then follow some insights behind the scenes of "Remember the Time," where Michael discloses what a funny guy Eddie Murphy is and how much fun it is to work with him.

52. Michael as Dad

And finally Michael gives us some insights into his most holy place in scenes together with his children.

"You've seen a lot of footage tonight of my life, my joys, my happiness, you know, but what you're gonna see now is what I'm most proud of, what I think life is really all about." We hear Michael's song: "You are the sun, you make me shine, or more like the stars,...you are the moon, that glows in my heart, you're my daytime, my nighttime, my world. You are my life."

"I love and adore my children. They mean everything to me. When they're in public, though, I conceal their faces, because I want my children protected. At home they have a normal life. They play with other kids and they have a good time, they're laughing a lot, they run around. They even go to school. It's a normal life for them. But in public I must protect them....I love my children very much. I'm proud to be their dad."

Michael Jackson published his love declaration for his children and all the children of the world in 2001 on his album "Invincible."

"Once all alone I was lost in a world of strangers,

No one to trust, on my own, I was lonely,

You suddenly appeared.

It was cloudy before, Now it's all clear.

You took away the fear, and you brought me back to the light.

You are the sun, you make me shine,

Or more like the stars, that twinkle at night,

You are the moon, that glows in my heart.

You're my daytime my nighttime, my world,

You are my life.

Now I wake up every day with this smile upon my face,

No more tears, no more pain, 'cause you love me.

You help me understand,

That love is the answer to all that I am.

And I'm, I'm a better man, since you taught me by sharing your life.

You gave me strength, when I wasn't strong,

You gave me hope when all hope was lost,

You opened my eyes when I couldn't see,

Love was always here waiting for me." (You Are My Life)

The video, "Michael Jackson The Daddy" is a very touching and shows Michael as father with his kids. Do you really wonder that Michael wanted to protect his children from the hell to which the media and the public have subjected him? Do you wonder that he wanted to protect them from the lies, gleefulness, the derision and the torrents of abuse that were poured on him? Wouldn't it rather be strange and abnormal if he were to allow the paparazzi to persecute his children, as they did for example with the children of Diana, William and Harry?

The following videos give us further direct insights and impressions of life in Neverland: "Michael Jackson with his children – LOVELY," "Michael Jackson loves his children," "Michael Jackson loves his children part 2," "Michael's Children" and "Blanket Jackson New Pics." In "Paris, Prince, Blanket and Michael Jackson – Last Christmas" we can marvel at a complete photo album with the kids.

These are only some of the countless films that YouTube has the courtesy to provide for us, so everyone can get an idea of the facts for themselves instead of relying on the crooked and one-sided reports of the media. In "Michael Jackson Family Home Movie plus Christmas Rare Video" from 2000, Michael teaches his then three-year-old son Prince, with the nickname "Applehead," to play chess. Then follows a scene where the whole family is unwrapping presents at Christmas. To understand Michael and to empathize how he is overall, words are not sufficient. Also this book can only transmit to the reader the essentials when you also go back to the internet and the videos on YouTube.

Here are some more examples: "Rare home video – Michael Jackson playing hide and seek," "1987 Michael and Bubbles Moonwalk," with his ape who is imitating Michael, Michael with his typical Namaste gesture and his moonwalk. In "The unauthorized Interview of MJ, Part 1," we see the fifteen-year-old Michael in 1983 with his llama at his home in Encino in California. It's amazing what this guy at that time already reports about the source of his creativity:

"When I say magic, I mean wonderment, excitement, the unexpected, escapism, creating something that's so incredible, an illusion...I like creating magic, excellence....I don't write my own songs,...I'm just a source, I'm just a tunnel too through which they come...they've all been written before...."Beat It," all those songs have been up there somewhere,....some other higher force that's making it happen."

In part two of the video Michael is sitting at dawn, we hear the sound of the water fountain and all the other inherent noises in his garden, and fancying of his fondness for this time of the day.

"The moon is out, the most beautiful part of the day,...Everything comes to life,...everything's becoming magic,...I would say this is my favorite part of the day, dawn and dusk. There's a certain magic about it....Some psychologists say that at dusk, for a lot of creative people, you reach your alpha state, subconscious, you become more creative, ...but for me it could be any time,... there's no special time,...It's like a painting, it's very artistic, it's magic....Just the sound of the water is magic. So beautiful,...I'm a fantasy fanatic, and anything that take you off into another world, escapism, that's what I like. I'm not so crazy about the reality of everything, I like a lot of fantasy and that's what I try to create..."

I already have cited various times from the book of criminal reporter and author Aphrodite Jones, "Michael Jackson Conspiracy," which describes the truth about the trial against Michael firsthand. She covered the trial from the first day and reported about it on American TV. Michael's attorney, Thomas Mesereau, confirms in a video on YouTube the accuracy of her analysis and the excellence of her book.

When Aphrodite was searching for a publishing company in the United States in 2007 she got the response that pro-Jackson books were not welcome. Therefore she decided to publish it herself. The book is a must-read for everyone who is really interested in the truth, instead of continuing to carry the wrong picture that was drawn by the media throughout Michael Jackson's entire life. At the beginning of the trial in January 2005, Aphrodite Jones was sure that Michael was guilty and proclaimed this opinion also in her reporting.

"Certain reporters had slanted TV and radio coverage to suit the prosecution, and I was one of the people who followed that dangerous trend. Somehow, I had missed the truth. When I read the accounts of the NOT GUILTY verdicts in all the newspapers, I felt ashamed to have been part of the media machine that seemed hell-bent on destroying Jackson (p. ix)....If there was a media conspiracy, I was guilty (p. xi)....I was devastated. But then I thought about Michael. I wondered how *he* felt, and realized that he was the one who'd been through hell. He was the one who was subjected to a mainstream media machine that wanted him destroyed. *He* was the one people trashed behind his back (p. xii). I felt that, no matter what the media, the skeptics, and even my friends and family had to say, I needed to stand up for Michael Jackson.

As I began to write, I noticed that people everywhere were making fun of me. *A pro-Jackson-book*? Impossible....It became my most arduous work, ever, and at times it felt like I had the whole world on my shoulders. I wondered if Michael lived his life this way....I hope this book reaches beyond Jackson supporters, and gets to the millions of folks who've been trusting the tabloid media, way too much. If the truth prevails, then one way or other, people will open their hearts (Jones, p. xiii)."

"As Michael approached the court (on the day of verdict)...made it seem like the whole earth stood still. Whatever his health condition was at the time, whatever toll the trial had taken on him – Michael didn't show it. He waltzed up to his lead attorney, Thomas Mesereau, and, just before he walked behind the closed doors of the court, Michael stood up tall as he waved to his fans, happy to see them out in full force.

For the people behind the gates and cyclone fences who were screaming and cheering, there seemed to be a communion. Something about Michael made hearts pound. Everyone in his presence could feel the music. They could feel the dance....

At 2:10 PM, Judge Rodney Melville finally began to open up the verdict envelopes. As each envelope slid open, the judge's face remained still. Not a word was spoken in the court, but a few female jurors had tears in their eyes. Time stood still. It seemed like forever. And then, suddenly, the Superior Court Clerk Lorna Ray actually read the words:

'Count one – conspiracy – not guilty.'
'Count two – lewd act upon a child – not guilty.'
'Count three – not guilty.'

'Not guilty' were the words being read over and over, fourteen times in all....Judge Rodney Melville, who had handled the case with such dignity and clarity, who had kept everyone safe and sound, who had not tolerated any disruptions whatsoever, now read a statement to the court:

'**We the jury, feeling the weight of the world's eyes upon us, all thoroughly and meticulously studied the testimony, evidence, and rules of procedure presented in this court since January 31, 2005. Following the jury instructions, we confidently came to our verdicts. It is our hope that this case is a testament to the belief in our justice system's integrity and truth.**'

With those words, Michael, from behind the defense table, resumed his vast composure. In some strange way, Michael seemed to have the appearance of an ancient king. There was something imperial about him. So absolutely commanding with his presence, Michael listened with quiet intent as the statement from the judge was being read. With his head held high, the superstar remained motionless. Only those who could see him close up, could detect a slight tear running down Michael's face." (Jones, p. 2ff)

53. I Am the Light of the World

On October 26, 2009, the first posthumous album of Michael Jackson was released. It contains among others a song which Michael together with Paul Anka had written in 1983, and which was originally published in 1991 on an album of the singer Safire from Puerto Rico, as "I Never Heard." With the name "This Is It," Michael had announced his planned concerts in London and this is also the name of the film, which premiered on October, 28, 2009 in the cinemas. Always again "This Is It." What does it mean? What is it?

"This Is It, here I stand,

I'm the light of the world, I feel grand.

Got this love, I can feel,

And I know yes for sure it is real.

And it feels as though I've seen your face a thousand times,

And you said you really know me too yourself

And I know that you have got addicted with your eyes

But you say you're gonna leave it for yourself

Oh, I never heard a single word about you,

Falling in love wasn't my plan,

I never thought that I would be your lover,

C'mon baby just understand.

This Is It, I can say
I'm the light of the world, run away.
We can feel, this is real,
Every time I'm in love that I feel
And I feel though I've known you since a thousand years,
And you tell me that you've seen my face before.
And you said to me you don't want me hanging 'round,
Many times, wanna do it here before, ...
I never heard a single word about you,
Falling in love wasn't my plan,
I never thought that I would be your lover,
C'mon baby just understand.
This is it, I can feel,
I'm the light of the world, this is real.
Feel my song, we can say,
And I tell you I feel that way.
And I feel as though I've known you for a thousand years,
And you said that you want some of this yourself,
And you said you want to go with me, all the while,
And I know that it's really cool myself ...
I never heard a single word about you,
Falling in love wasn't my plan,
I never thought that I would be your lover,
C'mon baby, just understand.
(Michael Jackson, Paul Anka, 1983, released 2009)

The truth is not easy to discover, else it would have been common knowledge among mankind for a long time. Indeed it is fact that mankind is laughing at the truth and equally at people who serve as vehicles to bring it to earth. When Michael Jackson sings, "I'm the light of the world," he is not talking about "I" in this physical form with the name Michael Jackson, but he talks or sings of that which is the essence of man by itself, the essence of each human being, of that which makes a human being really human. Light, clear pure light, without limits, without separations – only light. Not physical light, not light in a form, but light without form and without name. Light which penetrates everything and radiates everywhere. This am I. This I is not "I," but "i" am here to realize "I." "Each one of us has an exact role in the cosmic drama, which manifests on the material plane, where we are present. The personality equals a role under thousands of roles. When I pretend to be 'myself' then we only drop one mask after the other to reach to our real identity. The synthesis of the earthly way is to bring about that our real being takes possession of our body in a way that we are not personality, but that I AM in big letters....The individual who is distracted by the material world only believes in a small part of itself and gives it a fantasy value, which has no meaning at all, while the only thing which could save it to follow the cliffs of life like a snow ball." (Puigchinet, p. 55)

Many of the lyrics of Michael Jackson talk about this I AM in big letters. Yet 25 years ago, when "This Is It" was written, he had realized the true essence of the human being. "The I is below, above, in the West, the East, the South, the North: The I is the whole world," the Chândogya-Upanishad says. (Upanishaden, p. 120)

Another name for "I" is "Self" or "Soul," in Sanskrit Atman. As Great Self or Great Soul, as Mahatma, Michael Jackson has won the hearts of millions and at the same time provoked the lower animalistic instincts in man. By his actions, without even meaning to, greed, envy, hate, ignorance, prejudices and abuse were brought to light. Unimpressed by these cosmic events, Michael Jackson has gifted us with his music. Love declarations to "IT," to "THAT" and not only to a single human individual – as one could guess on first sight. Songs like, "You are my Life," "Invincible," "Cry," and "Speechless" are addressing different consciousness levels at the same time. Everyone understands them according to how many layers of the onion he has already peeled. As the masses necessarily count among the stragglers and not to the vanguard, the mass media naturally did not understand his words and in their ignorance had referred his lyrics and words to his person and personality.

I wonder when humanity will be ready and prepared to eat humble pie in relation to Michael Jackson and in all humility and humbleness will confess, "We have missed the truth." Such an admission requires such a mental and spiritual greatness which only a few opinion-makers bring with them, for example, Aphrodite Jones, DeBorah B. Pryor, Charles Thomson, Matt Semino, and Larry Nimmer.

"This Is It" – the wise scriptures indicate this "IT" as "THAT," in big letters, so that the superficial mind can stop and does not capture "IT" in its mediocrity. There is nothing greater than IT or THAT and there is nothing smaller than IT or THAT. Laotse called IT in the second century before Christ the Tao. "The TAO produces the One. The One produces the Two. The Two produces the Three. The Three produces all things." (Laotse, verse 42)

And what is the answer of Inesita from Chile at her seventh birthday in 1957 to the question of what she will become later, artist or ship's captain: "When I am one, I will become two, and when I am two, I will become three, and when I am three, I will create another one." (Puigchinet, p. 16)

Perhaps we should listen more often to innocent children, who have not yet been squeezed with the force of Procrustes into the solidified ties of adults and still have access to the original source, where there is no separation, no second, only one. Who are directly connected to the level where creation begins and who do not yet suffer from amnesia. Who know that the Two and the Three and the following many are THAT. Who did not yet forget that their father and mother are One – I, ICH, YO, ES, DAS, TAO, ATMAN, GOTT, ALLAH, BRAHMAN, JEHOVAH, BUDDHA, AHURA MAZDA, CHRISTUS or one of the countless other names.

On October, 11, 2009 I hear from Inesita: "I have until now only known one or two poems from Michael's book ‚Dancing the Dream.' And now I read it in the internet. I was so astonished that I could not continue to read. My book "La Clave del Sol" – "The Key to the Sun," with poems, which I have written since my childhood and which was published in 1990, contains the SAME WORDS, the same wish to express spirit...the same words in the same sequence. How is this possible? I believe we were one soul in different bodies." In reality we are all one soul in different bodies. The only difference between Inesita and the people who feel separated from God is that their soul is slagged by superpositions in a way that the fire of the soul is extinguished. As soon as these superpositions are removed, the fire will again be ablaze. "I am the light of the world." Isn't it wonderful and soothing that we have no need to search for anything or to find anything to strike this light, but only to remove that what is only a waste? Isn't it wonderful and soothing that we don't have to calculate endless time of effort and not wait for years of processes of growth and development for the light to radiate? It is sufficient to dis-cover what was covered, to un-fold what was folded, to make a reality what is already real. What was is and will be. This is not a big stretch – and yet it seems to be unreachable for many people. Why does it seem to us that the nearest of the near is so distant? Because we are identified with our mind, with our thoughts. We believe the things we are thinking about. We are not sufficiently awake to realize that a thought is nothing but hot air or cold air – no more, no less. And this hot or cold air is the basis of our world, is the basis and the foundation, where we live. Let the air be air and don't care about it - and you will realize that you are One, and that there never was a second. This supposed second is the ego, an illusion.

"He was Michael Jackson. He could do whatever he wanted but he had no ego," says Orianthi Panagiris, who had rehearsed with him for his tour only 48 hours before Michael's death. The 24-year-old Australian exceptional guitarist experienced for a month how Michael was: "He had a presence, but he had no front and would joke around and have fun." (www.examiner.com) "He was staring at me from the couch. I played 'Beat It' for him. He had an amazing aura." (www.bilde.de, October, 14, 2009)

Many fans, especially the hardcore fans, who followed him everywhere, also report about Michael's huge aura, which could already be sensed when he came nearer, even if one could not yet see him. "The black shimmering car slowly rolled through the gate (of Neverland)...Once it came closer towards us we actually felt that Michael was in there. His aura was immense. We had experienced it several times before on our trips. You could feel him before you saw him." (Marina: It's all about L.O.V.E., 2010, p. 57)

"But his immense aura made us feel like being in a vacuum, everything around became insignificant and even the screams and thunderous whistles seemed so much softer then. Unlike most people who walk on the face of earth he had something mysterious about him that puts one under a spell and amazes one, for he himself was magic without being depending on any conjuring tricks at all." (Marina and Katharina, p. 401)

As wise masters and awakened teachers who have overcome the ego are pure presence without personality, clairvoyants were able to observe such oversized auras. While an ego takes everything personally, a presence does not react to outwardness, personal animosities and identifications. An ego has likes and dislikes, a presence not. It follows the flow of life and takes everything as it is, without the wish that it should be different as it is. That's the reason that a presence is apperceptive for inspirations and visions from the greater energy field.

The biologist Rupert Sheldrake researched these fields in the 1980's which he called morphogenetic fields and pleaded for a new understanding of the liveliness and holiness of nature. (Sheldrake, 1990) Egos are not interested in presence, but use it as projection screen for their own conditionings. Unconsciously a present being serves as a screen, so that they see every film in them which their own projector is sending out. That is also the simple but plain explanation for all the rubbish and trash that is produced by the media. Among the media people the bloated egos are are romping about in droves, and. 99.9 percent of all reports about Michael Jackson are projections, which means they are stories of the writer or filmer which are projected onto Michael.

As the presences on this planet are still rare, there are actually only a few testimonies of pure perception without the filter of unconsciousness. Despite their projections, egos are so bold on the other side as to swear an oath on the truth of their arbitrary interpretations. Egos are basically not interested in the truth, but only in the survival of the ego. With the realization of the truth the, ego dies an unspectacular death. As long as there are egos, ignorance will continue to reign. Ignorance is not a crime, but ignorance is the root of all evil. The light of the presence changes not only consciousness but also the vibrational frequency of the physical body. People who were near to Michael Jackson in the last weeks and months before his death and capable to perceive things, to really perceive them, reported that his physical body had problems in the end in holding the light of presence. The perception of this light equals the sensation of burning inside. In this state certain physical food may be too gross to be digested and absorbed without having problems. It's undeniable that Michael Jackson had eating problems and extreme sleeping problems in June 2009. When the physical body does not get enough food and sleep, the life energy slowly fades out. During the rehearsals for the This Is It tour, new ideas constantly came to Michael for the stage show which outweighed everything seen before. He mentioned to Kenny Ortega, "God channels this through me at night. I can't sleep because I'm so super-charged," to which Kenny answered, "But Michael, we have to finish. Can't God take a vacation?" And without missing a beat Michael's answer was, "You don't understand. If I'm not there to receive these ideas, God might give them to Prince." "You don't understand" – this feeling Michael Jackson would have often. "No one understands me." (Childhood, 1995) Even when he did not always say directly, one can witness in many interviews and conversations that he tried desperately to convey to the world his thoughts and perceptions, in interviews with Diane Sawyer, Ed Bradley, Martin Bashir, Oprah Winfrey and others. And mostly the interviewers answered with doubts and never-ending questions, which on closer look had the purpose of confirming their own pre-conceived stories. Nevertheless Michael did not give up hope that the truth and the power of love would finally win. When Kenny mentioned his worry that Michael was pushing himself to much for the last tour, taking not enough food and not resting sufficiently, Michael shall have said: "Don't worry, just put the people all crushed up against the stage, they're my fuel, they're my food. Their love will get me to the end." (http://blogs.usatoday.com)

Rosi, who did not know this statement of Michael, wrote to me on January, 31, 2010, "Some songs of Michael are like a divine service, for example 'Will You Be There' and 'Speechless.' Suddenly I thought, oh God, he is talking to God. This recognition nearly knocked me out and I started to shed tears; I cannot put it into words."

We also know reports of similar experiences with overloading by the divine power, for example in „Kundalini" from Gopi Krishna and in the autobiography of Meister M, "Im Herzen der Welt" (In the Heart of the World) It is not hard to see that humanity as a whole is not yet prepared for the ascent to this level of consciousness. But Michael Jackson was a mature soul and far ahead of his time. Orianthi, who was lucky enough to be near to him for weeks, is convinced: "It was a completely surreal crazy experience. I still cannot grasp it today, what happened. How terrific this man is, we will certainly only understand in hundred years." (www.bild.de)

I hope that it will not take another a hundred years, because firstly we are living in a time near to the quantum leap, and secondly I want to experience while still in my earthly body that the world offers Michael Jackson the place he deserves. When, at the time 25 years old, Judith Hill, who was to perform the song, "I Just Can't Stop Loving You," with Michael on the planned tour and had rehearsed with Michael for weeks, talks about Michael, it sounds like a declaration of love: "When he first came in where we all were, he was so sweet and endearing. He had a big, big spirit. His spirit was so sweet. He was very kind towards people. He was so nice to all of us and so warm. Michael had such a gift. I mean, to be so warm and to embrace us like he did with everything he went through is amazing. After all that he had endured in his life?...He went through a lot and still gave love back." To the question of what lesson Judith was taught by the experiences with Michael, she answered immediately and decisively: "Musically he never apologized for what he was. He was completely himself. Not following anyone. He was locked in his own world. He was true to himself no matter what was said. That is a good lesson for me, I think. To stay true to my vision, to my music and to myself." (www.urbanbeautycollective.com)

Jan Delay, who was on radio the night Michael's death became known, has his own assessment, and says that Michael Jackson was four times as big as Elvis was. (December, 3, 2009, WDR 3, 10:40 PM) Similar things we hear from Cory Rooney: "Michael is not comparable to these people (Elvis Presley, Bruce Lee, Marilyn Monroe). I would say Elvis Presley is the closest you'll get to that....I'm not gonna discredit Elvis Presley, but they're two different people. And Michael as far as I'm concerned surpassed Elvis and everything that Elvis was about, a long time ago."

54. This is My Dream

"This is my dream," which is the dream of Michael Jackson, Martin Luther King, Princess Diana and so many known and unknown souls in every nook and cranny and corner of the world. Whether humanity has already ordered the moving boxes for its entry into the media, I cannot judge, but it has ever knocked on the doors of the field. In the field of music, Usher writes of Michael Jackson to this merit: "He has brought humanity into the music industry." (N-TV, 5th Avenue, 06/27/2010)

Dawning recognition that transforms the world and the people and begins to heal old wounds, when joy and appreciation prevail over competition and judgment. Everything that happens is part of a larger plan, and serves a purpose. It is not for the people who go into the pot to sort the bad and the good guys into the crop, or vice versa, break things into likes and dislikes, start things up or shut them down. It is the task of everyone, to live his dharma, that means be be human and to appreciate everything in its place and to be respect it as a necessary part of the whole. Anything and everything, the whole variety, contributes its share to the world itself and to the process of transformation of the world and humanity and the needs the space it deserves - whether it is a saint or a criminal. Judgment and prejudice are the result of lack of self-knowledge and blatant arrogance. One who himself goes through life in his love, with joy, does not even think of wasting his time trying to judge others and to seek a drawer for them. A judgment is always the result of one' own dissatisfaction or destructive emotions such as envy and hatred. Destructive, especially for oneself.

Norma Gentile, sound shaman, one who had been gifted from an early age with a fine intuition, gives us some interesting insights into the deeper connections of current events in the world. Astronomically in summer 2009 we could observe some "homeopathic" eclipses, which are connected with the "planetary shift away from judgment. The first eclipse ... occurred the day of Michael Jackson's funeral. On July 7th 2009...we experienced a minor lunar eclipse. Think of it as a homeopathic eclipse meant to expose our own inner issues and help us clarify emotional boundaries" and learn more about opening our hearts. (www.spiritofmaat.com) It creates an awareness that we, as a personality have both sides of any polarity in us and therefore consider each for what it expresses, and not judge it. The judgment on the one hand and the fear of the judgment on the other hand, are the reasons that we shut ourselves off and do not express what moves us inside. We try to make a good impression, which has nothing to do with ourselves and our inner experience, but hypocrisy and masquerade. The most destructive thought that has been inculcated in ourselves is, "What will the others think?" This is a killer argument for honesty, authenticity and humanity. This conditioning creates liars, hypocrites and zombies.

Norma Gentile transmits us the following message: "It is not a coincidence, says Archangel Michael, that Michael Jackson passed and how he did. Both the clarity of his artistic vision and the murky waters of his personal life, especially around his ability to care for himself, are reflections of what each of us deals with in our own way. None of us is perfect. And the higher voltage energies brought into one's aura by public scrutiny and attention makes it even more difficult to balance inner self-care and outer world doing." (www.spiritofmaat.com and www.healingchants.com)

People are not aware that they build up an energetic connection to others by judging them. A judgment constricts us emotionally and closes our hearts. This results at the same time in the fact that we are no longer able to love ourselves. "We lean mostly on the crooks of things that we judge to be bad. Because when we define something as bad or evil, we automatically define the contrary, what is desirable and good. And we all want to believe in our innermost is that we are good. In our polarized belief system we were taught to love what is good and to reject what is bad. ... This contributes greatly to our comfort. But none of both furthers love."

And exactly this was Michael Jackson's main concern. "It's all for love, L.O.V.E.," he conjures for the last time in the film, "This Is It." This message Michael lived and expanded for decades – even when the mainstream of humanity was and is not able to realize the essence of what Michael Jackson is – the embodiment of unconditional love. Love does not mean to accept one thing and reject another, but to realize the polarization of our perception, thinking and acting, and acknowledge and appreciate both sides. In this consciousness of oneness everything has its place and both sides are seen and included, the so-called "good" and "bad" ones. Who appreciates what is and how it is envelops compassion for all living beings.

Every judgment excludes compassion. Can you feel it? The seven minute video to the song, "Can You Feel It" of the Jacksons from 1980 is already a vision of paradise on earth, an anticipation of the Golden Age, which was long ago announced in the vedas, the fluid fire that emanates from Michael's hands, his radiating smile, his shining aura and the golden halo around his head. Michael is not only the embodiment of unconditional love, but also of non-violence, humility, devotion, integrity, authenticity, generosity, compassion, empathy, forgiveness, selflessness.

The vision of Michael Jackson is not only internalized by many fans – as many media want it to be - but also the heads of churches. So we hear on June, 10, 2010 at the opening concert of the football world championship in South Africa from the mouth of Archbishop Desmond Tutu the actual words, "Can you feel it?" and "We are the world," and "It helped the caterpillar to turn into a butterfly...."

Is there justice in the world? Perhaps not in the earthly world, but now and then we experience how life follows its own laws and produces justice, even late. On November, 18, 2009 the news was spread that Evan Chandler, the father of Jordan Chandler, who started in 1993 the most inhuman story in history that one can imagine, and which was the beginning of an incomparable martyrdom of Michael Jackson, had committed suicide on November, 5, 2009 by a shot to the head. He was found in his apartment in a luxury building complex in New Jersey on his bed with a pistol in his hand. He died, according to neighbors, lonely and sick as a broken man. All family members had long before distanced themselves from him, so that there was nobody to care for him in his old age, it was said. In 2006, his son Jordan, who today is living with a new name, is said to have solicited an interim injunction against him. A tragic end or cosmic justice? Can you feel it?

Michael Jackson blew all earthly dimensions all his life, yes, he was greater than life, inconceivable, incomprehensible and inimitable. We can conceive and comprehend only things which we can hold in our hands, imagine only things which we can hold in our minds. When hands and minds are too small then we need bigger vessels.

Patrizia Alexandra Pfister , who channels messages of Kryon and Lady Gaia, the planet earth, reports: "Let me...shortly go into the life and death of Michael Jackson. All negative things you have ever read from him or about him have little to do with who and how he really was. He was a master, master of the Hathors, those species who succeeded to ascend...by engrossing the mind in the study of sound and collected so much knowledge as no human race before. They were humans, even when we would not conclude it due to their look....Michael Jackson thus belonged to those beings who understand more of sound and its effects than anyone else. He combined the effect of sound with the effect of body movements and thus addressed millions of people. By his work he could reach people, who did "not care two figs about" spirituality. But you would be surprised if you knew how many people were indeed brought through on the conscious path by his work. Why did he go right now? Well, like by many masters their death affects people more than their life – and so the time was chosen purposely, because the energy for the ascent was thus canalized. He thus has let go consciously, as his life by the assessment of people had no more positive aspects. Therefore honour his life and death as a huge gift and don't believe everything that you hear about him, but feel it when you are hearing or seeing music or videos from him. Feel! Feel! Feel! Can you feel it?" (www.licht-arbeiter.eu)

Tom Kenyon and Virginia Essence have done research about this unknown civilization of the Hathors and received the following message from them: "We come in love, with the sounding of a new dream reality for your earth. If you are ready to build the new world, we invite you to join us on a journey of the mind and heart. We are your elder brothers and sisters. We have been with you for a very long period of your evolution on this planet. We were with you in eons past - even in the forgotten days before any trace of us is known in your present written history. Our own nature is energetic and interdimensional.... In the past we have spicifically worked with and through the Hathor fertility goddess of ancient Egypt. We also made contact with Tibetan lamas in the formative period of Tibetan Buddhism....Therefrom come some of their unique techniques and practices on the use of the sound of our lineage and our teachings....We vibrate at a faster rate than you. Nonetheless, we are all part of the mystery, part of the love that holds and binds all the universe....We are not saviors; we're not messianic. We want to clearly step out of that projection so that the reader understands that we are simply elder brothers and sisters offering our understanding and what we have learned. You may take or leave it but we offer it freely....The hope that someone or something will save you, that you will not have to make any changes in yourself, that you will not have to be responsible, is unrealistic....Ascension is a process of self-awareness and self-mastery on all levels." (www.licht-arbeiter.eu)

Reiki Master Lynn Brewer sees Michael as such: "Michael Jackson, as many of his loyal fans have suspected, was not only human. In the depths of his soul,

Michael Jackson also belonged to an intergalactic, interdimensional species of Christ-conscious beings who were known to the ancient Egyptians as the Hathors....Maureen St. Germain, a facilitator for the ancient mystery school teaching...describes the Hathors as the 'most intelligent, most advanced race in the solar system.' According to her they 'only represent peace and love,' 'function only through sound,' and 'hold the flame of absolute love on the planet Venus.' The Hathors are 'a race of fourth-dimensional beings, who come from Venus. You don't see them in the third-dimensional world, but if you tune to Venus on the fourth dimension, especially on the higher overtones, you'll find a vast culture there....The Hathors are beings of tremendous love. Their love is on a level of Christ consciousness. They use vocal sounds as their means of communications and performing feats within their environment....They have almost no darkness to them at all; they're just light-pure, loving beings. Hathors are very much like dolphins. Dolphins use sonar to do almost everything, and Hathors use their voices to do almost everything....As I noted at the outset, Michael Jackson was, in the depths of his soul, also a Hathor. At some point in the journey of his soul, perhaps many thousands of years ago, Michael Jackson answered the call of the Galactic Command for more highly evolved, higher-dimensional beings to come to planet Earth to help raise the planet's vibration and thereby prevent its self-destruction. As many higher beings...Michael Jackson's soul sacrificed his higher level of consciousness to incarnate as a third-dimensional human being for the purpose of helping humanity....Michael Jackson worked primarily through sound, using a high, pure vibration to fill our airwaves with messages of hope, love, light, harmony, peace, unity, beauty and goodwill. In so doing, he touched the consciousness of millions (if not billions), brought healing to our hearts, and fulfilled his soul's mission of helping to 'make the world a better place for you and me.' Moreover, by incarnating as a black man in this lifetime, through his own DNA Michael elevated the vibration of the continent of Africa, and of all people of African descent. As is evident to us all, in the fulfillment of his soul's mission, Michael Jackson suffered greatly. This sensitive soul was crucified by the corporate media – a media which nowadays serve as one of the foremost, modern-day crucifiers of human beings who stand for a higher frequency of love, light, beauty and truth on Earth. Michael Jackson was often misunderstood, and more than this, he was repeatedly flogged, mocked, scorned, derided, and ridiculed before the public. So was Jesus Christ in his day: They hung him high, they stretched him wide, he hung his head, for me he died. That's love." (http://lovelightbeautytruth and www.lightworkers.org).

Dr. Monica Burns-Capers, author, life coach, as well as management & behavior consultant with her own organization, sums Michael Jackson's activities and qualities as spiritual teacher: "Michael Jackson's stage presence was undoubtedly incomparable. He performed with an energy and a divine ambiance that was clearly not of this world. No one else in our lifetime will ever come close to the magnanimous and influential powerhouse that was…Michael Jackson. But in now ponder, were we just too enamored with the performer and his image, to realize the profoundness of the spiritual and life lessons he was teaching us all along – contained in the lyrics of his songs? Michael Jackson's passion, purpose and message was for peace, harmony, and equality in the world. He longed for simple experiences that we, today, continue to take for granted. He wanted normality, he wanted to experience a childhood. Was his behavior as a 'childlike man' a bit strange for some? Yes…maybe. If you have never experienced NOT having a childhood, you have no grounds for judgment. According to the Bible Scriptures, Luke 18:16-17 states: 'I tell you the truth, anyone who doesn't receive the Kingdom of God like a child will never enter it.'" (http//searchwarp.com)

Michael once mentioned in an interview that "Childhood" says all that is important and meaningful for him. "I'm searching for the world that I come from. 'Cause I've been looking around, in the lost and found of my heart. No one understands me." (Childhood)

What hubris of the media people who wish to analyze and describe Michael Jackson, and don't have the slightest clue how to enter the space of the heart, which moves a being like him, which is the source of his creations. They are pearling along the shallow banks and fancy themselves to have found pearls. Yet everybody knows that one has to dive deep to find pearls, and not even every diver has enough breath to reach to the bottom. To pretend that the colored pebbles at the banks are pearls is nothing other than a smooth betrayal and trap, which the mass of humanity always falls in – and is even willing to pay money for, paper notes for a illusory world (wordplay in German: "Papierschein" = paper note; "Scheinwelt" = illusory world).

Nobody is really interested to see the wounds and deep hurt that arise from such ignorance. While physical injury is a criminal act, even when every body will heal after a while, the injury of the soul is ignored. Thus a wounded soul will suffer life long from inflicted hurt and does not heal as quickly as bodily wounds.

"Speculate to break the one you hate. Circulate the lie you confiscate. Assassinate and mutilate. As the hounding media in hysteria, Who's the next for you to resurrect….It's slander. With the words you use, you're a parasite in black and white. Do anything for news. And you don't go and buy it. To read it sanctifies it." (Tabloid Junkie)

With injuries of the soul money cannot be earned in a reversed world, and not one court of this world puts a stop to the whole thing.

Dr. Monica Burns-Caspers adds, "Michael Jackson has served his purpose, has carried out his mission, and has delivered his message. He has entered the gates of heaven where he's entertaining God and his fellow Angels. And he can finally rest in the comfort and peace of his true father's arms, as he now knows and feels acceptance. He can now be that 'child' without judgment. And most of all...he has heard those approving words from his true father in heaven – '*My child ... Yours Is Indeed A Job Well Done!*'"

Sir Bob Geldof said many years ago: "When Michael Jackson sings, it is with a voice of angels, and when his feet move, you can see God dancing."

The late astrologer Linda Goodman has analyzed Michael Jackson's horoscope and confirms what everyone who sees reasonably already knew, that he carried "a heavy karmic burden." The vibration of his birth number 29, which Michael Jackson had, "proves man in relation to his spiritual power by 'trials and tribulations,'" as in the story of Job (23:10 and 34:36) in the Old Testament.

Life is full of uncertainties, full of betrayal and disappointments by unreliable friends, unexpected dangers and considerable sorrow and fear, caused by members of the other sex. There is a number of severe warnings in every area of his personal and professional life. Wasn't the the life of our beloved Michael Jackson with all its highs and lows, and with all its sadness, fragility and glory?...

Even when he was bent and broken on earth he now has ascended to the Christ consciousness, where he originally came from. That is the revelation, the good news. I am extraordinarily blessed to bring this message to his fans. Michael has freed himself from the wheel of life – death and rebirth – and joined the great brotherhood of Christ consciousness, which has silently served mankind and the earth for countless ages: the Ascended Masters of the Brotherhood of Light....To be with the Lord, where he will continue to serve mankind in his own wonderful, gorgeous and silent way. He was received from this blessed heavenly crowd with all the love, glory, respect and honour – and with a thundering applause for the life that he lived on earth." (www.spiritofmaat.com)

Michael's work will continue to spread, there can be no doubt about this. "Now I understand what the great mystery is like. The lyrics all really carry out their duty; every single word makes sense. Some messages are exactly what I need at a certain time. So what? It is not the song, not the music, not the arrangement, the chorus, the musicians. NO, IT IS MICHAEL'S VOICE. The deepness of his voice, his sound, his tempo, the flow in his throat. The voice of Michael tells me more than his words. His voice touches a part of my soul and breaks my own system of parameters, so that the pieces are lying shattered at the ground. His voice makes sure that I will feel whole again, that I am again am who I am....And my wings again will be freed....Michael's voice gives me the true meaning of life, the true REASON why I am here on the earth. Nothing misses, no religion, no philosophy or esoteric school, only Michael's voice....The rest of the time I am not from this planet and perhaps forever like a big amen, that resounds in a great space named heaven." (Inesita, 19 April, 2010)

Earthlings in the meantime try to make up for the deference which was not given him during lifetime sufficiently or too rarely. On March, 4, 2010 Michael Jackson was admitted in the Hall of Fame at the Echo Awards. As a tribute was performed, an energy-laden dance to the music of "Smooth Criminal" choreographed by Detlef D. Soest. Let's rejoice about the blossoming of all the seeds that Michael Jackson has sewn on fertile ground.

55. One Year Later

From June, 24–26, 2010 – after one year of his death – naturally the TV specials and media reports about Michael Jackson became more frequent. Most of them are the same repetitions with the same madness about skin and shell – often commented by self-proclaimed experts, who don't even know rudimentarily the life work of Michael, coupled with rumors about murder plots and conspiracy theories, that are even promoted by Michael's family. It is understandable that his family is searching for explanations, because they need consolation for the pain body, which is demanding food due to the loss of their famous brother and for sure will determine their lives for some time to come. But those seeking explanations in the outer world will not find inner peace.

Eckart Tolle has meticulously analyzed the pain body and its function and role in our lives. It relates to a part of our emotional inner life, which fills with pain, if we are hurt, traumatized or shocked. But even when the pain diminishes, it longs automatically from time to time for new food. It is not a joke, most people respecting their ego need the pain to feel alive. Only after the death of the ego does the pain body also die. Then the need to open one's old wounds again and again and to revive past suffering comes to an end.

When pain body and ego have melted away like snow under the sun, then man lives in the Here and Now, where pain and problems no longer have a basis. Then it leaves no more marks, then the memories and the past fade. What stays is...Alas there still was still something!...Not more. The past and the personal story have lost their meaning, and there exists no more a personality. The experience has lost its power and influence on the mind of the one who is freed from everything he has undergone.

As of yet I have not seen any documentary on television which was really dealing with more than superficialities and banalities in Michael's life. Only on MTV Germany did we witness a laudable exception to that, in 2010 – maybe due to pressure of fans, who bombarded MTV with comments because they had slid over Michael Jackson's death in June 2009 with "business as usual." June 26, 2010 was dedicated to Michael and they aired his hits during the entire day.

Then followed the documentary, "Michael Jackson's Human Nature," which at least looked a little bit deeper (www.mtv.news.com)

Teddy Riley, who produced the "Dangerous" album together with Michael, praises Michael's attitudes as a father. Correspondingly he said that the kids were the love of his life. "He reads them a book every day....He's an incredible father....He would never scold them....His time-out is the kids gotta go lay in the bed and stay in the bed...he sent them to the bunks with no TV. They loved their dad,...they loved him so much."

Kenny Ortega felt that Michael Jackson was not only the King of Pop, but also the King of Charity. Michael's work beyond the stage deeply impressed him. "This guy was the hero in every aspect of what I loved." When Michael called, everyone said "Yes." As Kenny was once working at the opening and closing ceremonies of the Olympic games, he got a call from Michael that he needed him, and even then Michael was his priority. "This guy had the biggest heart of anybody and really, really did care about improving the human condition."

Also singer and hiphopper Akon speaks in this MTV contribution about his meeting and cooperation with Michael. He did not expect that Michael would be so "cool." When he arrived in the studio, Michael was sitting with his back towards him in a chair, and he spun around, stood up and said, "Yo, what up, man?...I've been waiting to meet you for so long...thanks for making the time." Akon in turn rather had the nice feeling that Michael took the time for him.

He speaks about a visit to a cinema with Michael's kids where they were undisguised and Michael only went with a hoodie on that hid his face. In the cinema he at first had called him Mike, until he feared that others would recognize him, and then he had chosen another name. But some younger girls nearby had already taken notice. Michael and he had then left the cinema early and realized that Michael's presence had already got around, as outside fans had already come together.

Akon confirms that Michael had much humor, whereas when working in the studio seriousness had always prevailed. Michael Jackson would never be content with the quality of his work, was always working to improve each piece, and would be very rigorous with himself. (MTV 26th of June 2010)

The following comment of a fan, which reached me on June 26, 2010 via email from Chile summarizes everything that fans and everyone who gets involved with his energy feel and experience:

"I have read letters and comments from friends and fans all over the world and they all told me similar stories. They cannot explain what has happened to them, why they love him, but their eyes fill with tears when they try to express these deep emotions. Thousands of tributes, poems, letters and gifts were sent to Holly Terrace, and yet we cannot express in words why we love him and when we try words are not enough. There is another thing in relation to Michael Jackson's effect on the souls of people which cannot be grasped and analyzed.

It is the awakening of a new dimension of LOVE, a simple and direct emotion, which has no need of the mediation of any part of the brain, however elaborate it might be.

"*Awakening*: Michael Jackson's fans can sense an awakening of the soul, in the heart as well as in the mind.

Awakening: Like windows that are opening in the morning to inhale fresh air and sweet soft and warm light, to be one with nature.

Awakening: Like the opening of a window of our heart for new friendships with a smile and humility to be one with the world.

Awakening: Like a renewed view, renewed listening, renewed awakening. We sense that we are reborn. Birth is accompanied by tears. A seed which grows into a plant has to burst to become bigger and more powerful, so that it can show its blossom to the sun. Michael left behind great joy which we never before had experienced. That is the miracle of Michael Jackson, which is living in all of us." Thanks to Inesita.

"It was only through the death of Michael Jackson that I got around to looking really deeply at what had happened there....My life long I have been searching for essential answers; everywhere I searched and found something....But that a pop star could be a Mahatma – as you say - ...that seemed unbelievable. I would never have thought of this, not even in my dreams. I always liked Michael, as I said, I don't have very much....When I saw a picture of him I felt the limitless softness in his eyes. Naturally it was clear to me that the accusations in relation to children against him were bullshit....But after his death a wave of sadness took possession of me which was more powerful than anything I have ever sensed before. It lasted for weeks and I could do nothing except deal with Michael. I am bewildered since the whole dimension of this 'story' became clear for me. Especially the verse of 'Dancing the Dream,' which I found during my intense research, touch me to the core...." (Sandra, Oct. 30, 2009)

An overview about the tributes after Michael's first year of death is not possible due to the large number, and therefore here only follow some examples. In the magazine, "Rolling Stone" (June 2010), Janet Jackson, Stevie Nicks, Stevie Wonder, the Band U2, Brooke Shields, Mark Romanek, Barack Obama, Adam Lambert, Wyclef Jean, John Singleton, Daryl Hall, Patrick Stump, Adam Levine, Randy Jackson, Chris Cornell, Weird Al Yankovic and Glen Ballard honoured Michael (www.michaeljackson.com)

On this official Michael Jackson Site we also find the video, "Musicians pay Tribute to Michael Jackson" (YouTube) where Usher, Miley Cyrus, Jason Mraz, David Foster, Aretha Franklin, Jennifer Lopez, Marc Anthony, Bruno Mars, Estelle and Macy Gray are bestowing honour on him.

Or in Argentina, "Viernes 25 de Junio 18.00 hs, OBELISCO – Buenos Aires – VIGILIA EN honour A MICHAEL JACKSON – Todos los seguidores unidos pedimos justicia por Michael Jackson."

New projects are always arising which pay tribute to Michael. Slowly humanity is recognizing who we had with us and who went much too soon. On 15th August, 2010 Michael was inducted into the Hall of Fame of the National Museum of Dance in Saratoga Springs, New York. In an exposition, "Garden of Remembrance," Michael's career and his contribution to the art of dance shall be appreciated.

56. To Be Continued

Let's look forward to everything to come, to magic and things never seen before, and let's take potluck from all that Michael Jackson initiated by his boundary-transcending, separation-terminating, all-is-possible being.

A press release from 20th April, 2010 announces that the Estate of Michael Jackson and Cirque du Soleil have agreed to create a project together. In autumn 2011 Cirque du Soleil will go on tour with a show which intends to revive the fascination of Michael Jackson concerts for all fans, old and new. And at the end of 2012, a permanent Michael Jackson Cirque du Soleil show will commence in cooperation with MGM Mirage in Las Vegas.

We know that the stone will continue to form ripples once it has been thrown in the water – until eternity. Even in a hundred years we will experience tributes and reviews of the year's events on his death day and birthday. Even a hundred years from now people will do research and publish about Michael Jackson and even a hundred years from now we will witness memorial concerts. Before we arrive at the finish, and following the tour of the Michael Jackson Tribute Portrait consisting of a million fans (= dots) and feel the anticipation as to when, how and where the curtain falls, when how and were Isis is unveiled, when, how and where the action and work of Michael Jackson will be recognized and appreciated as that what it was and is – unreachable, unbeatable, unsurpassed - atita in Sanskrit.

L.O.V.E.

"Silently he serves all and everything, but his service cannot be grasped and conceived by the world, because he acts from non-action, from the eternally unfathomable, from the natural source. The stillness of the still one is so deep that even death does not dare to come close to him." (Mantese, 2009, p. 61)

L.O.V.E.

To little Michael

That Am I
Wishing to mourn
At first shiver
Do you see the leaves there in the wind?
They are many – surely
And one of them
See the clouds over the sky
Life was only borrowed
That Am I.
Created perfectly – masterlike
And one of them
The waves carried by the creek
You don't need to ask for long
That Am I.
The roses and even the plantain
And a flower
I don't you mourn now
Do things which you never regret
That AM I.

Well there you stand
Perhaps you may
But look once more precisely.

But look how beautiful
That Am I.
Watch them and think of me
And a cloud
The butterflies on the meadow
I am so joyful, so as them
That Am I.
May be they remember me?
Because a wave
Flowers blossom in all their glory
And all are made for you
That Am I.
That would be outrageous for me
Because your joy

(Author unknown, found by Eva at the Michael Jackson Memorial in Munich)

L.O.V.E.

Appendix

Michael Jackson Solo Tours:
Bad Tour, 12 Sept. 1987 to 24 Jan. 1989, 123 concerts, 4,4 mil attendees
Dangerous Tour, 27 June 1992 to 11 Nov. 1993, 67 concerts, 3.5 mil attendees
HIStory Tour, 7 Sept. 1996 to 15 Oct. 199, 82 concerts in 58 cities, 4.5 mil attendees in 5 continents and 35 countries

Albums, Singles and Books:
"Off the Wall", 1979, 4 Top Ten Singles, 8 weeks in Billboard's Top10, 84 weeks in Top 100. 5,000,000 albums sold in USA, 3,000,000 worldwide.
"Thriller", 1982, 7 Top 10 Singles, Guinness Book of world record – most sold album in history; 104,000,000 copies sold. 7 American Music Awards, 8 Grammy Awards in 1984
Video **"The Making of Michael Jackson's Thriller,"** 1983, most sold home video of all times, 900,000 copies
We Are The World, 1985, with Lionel Richie – in cooperation with 45 top artists, most sold single in history, 4 Grammy Awards
"Bad", 1987, 1st album in history with 5 Number One Hits on the Billboard's Top 100, 2nd most sold albums in history
Autobiography "Moonwalk" (written by Stephen Davis), 1988, bestseller in USA
Film "Moonwalker" (94 minutes), 1988, No. 1 on Billboard's Video Sales Chart, most sold music home video of all time (replaced "Making of Thriller")
"Dangerous", 1991, 30 million sold; 1st album with 8 (!) top 20 hits in Great Britain
"Dancing the Dream," 1992 – Poems and Reflections
HIStory, Present, Past & Future, Book I, 1995
"Blood on the Dance Floor, HIStory in the Mix", 1997
"Ghosts", 40-minute film with co-producer Stephen King, 1997
"Invincible", 2001, Number 1 in 25 countries
Maxi-CD "On the Line," 2001
What more can I give, 2001, – Charity Single (with Maria Carey, Shakira, Beyonce, Usher, Mya, Celine Dion and others
"This Is It," 2009 (written with Paul Anka 1983)

Cited Books, Films and CDs:
Agassi, Andre: Open, 2009
Baader, Roland: Freiheitsfunken – aphoristische Impfungen, 2008
Bashir, Martin: Living with Michael Jackson, Film 2003
Bergmann, Wolfgang: Computersucht
Bhagavadgita, Gesang des Erhabenen, Freiburg, 6. Aufl. 1994
Borysenko, Joan: Feuer in der Seele, 1995
Byron, Katie: Lieben was ist, 2002
Das unpersönliche Leben, 9. Auflage 1993
Die Bibel, Einheitsübersetzung
Drucker, Al., Hrsg: Verwirklichung des Selbst – Das Wissen vom Absoluten, 1997
Ebmeier, Jochen: Das Phänomen Michael Jackson, 2. erw. Aufl. 1999
Ebony: Michael – in his own words and notes from those who loved him, Special Tribute 2009
English, Fanita: Transaktionsanalyse, 7. Auflage 2003
Fischer, Mary A.: Was Michael Jackson framed? GQ Magazine, October 1994, also available now as paperback, October 2012
Harris, Tomas A.: Ich bin OK – Du bist OK, 1975
Hawkins, David. R: Die Ebenen des Bewusstseins, 1997
Hellinger, Bert: Verdichtet es, 7. Auflage 2008
Hübl, Thomas: Sharing the Presence, Bielefeld 2009
Hughes, Geraldine: Redemption, 2004
Jackson, Michael: Dancing the Dream, Doubleday New York, 1992
Jackson, Michael: Invincible (Lyrics), MIJAC MUSIC 2002
Jackson, Michael: Moonwalk, Goldman, 1992
Jackson, Michael: Rede an der Universität Oxford, 21. März 2001
Jackson, Michael: The Complete, Int. Music Publications, 1997
Jackson, Michael: A Celebration of the Life of Michael Jackson, 1958 – 2009
Jones, Aphrodite: Conspiracy, 2007
Kenyon, Tom: Aufbruch ins höhere Bewusstsein – Die Hathoren-Botschaften, 2009
Kerkeling, Hape: Ich bin dann mal weg, 2007
Krishna, Gopi: Kundalini, 2000
Laotse, Tao te King, Diederichs, 1978
Nimmer, Larry: Michael Jackson – The untold story of Neverland, DVD 2009
Mantese Mario: Im Herzen der Welt, 2006
Mantese, Mario: Das, was du wirklich bist, Hammelburg 2008
Mantese, Mario: Lebenstiefen deiner Seele, Hammelburg 2009
Mecca, Carol: Michael Jackson – American Master, O.J.
Mittermaier, Rosi: Ski-Zirkus, 1976

Patterson, 2009
Preuße, Georg: Mary – Mein Leben in ihrem Schatten, o. J.
Puigchinet, M. Ines: Historia de un Amor Cosmico, Chile 1996
Redfield, James: Die Prophezeiungen von Celestine, 1995
de Saint Exupéry, Antoine: Der kleine Prinz, Düsseldorf 1992
Schürings, Margott: Das Mysterium von Michael Jackson und Sathya Sai Baba, 1999, 2. Auflage 2009
Sheldrake, Rupert: Die Wiedergeburt der Natur, 1990
Silbermond: Krieger des Lichts, CD
T., Anne: Die Gier war grenzenlos, 2009
Tolle, Eckart: Jetzt - Die Kraft der Gegenwart, 2001
Turner, Tina: Beyond, CD 2009
Thriller Live: Souvenir Programme, 2009
Upanishaden – Die Geheimlehre der Inder, 1958 und 1977
Vogel, Joe: Man in the Music – The creative Life and Work of Michael Jackson, 2011
We Are The World, The story behind the Song, 20th Anniversary Special Edition, DVD 2 discs, Paul Brownstein Productions image entertainment
Wilber, Ken: One Taste, 1999

www.ingramcontent.com/pod-product-compliance
Lightning Source LLC
Chambersburg PA
CBHW031727230426
43669CB00007B/274